Also by Peter Jenkins:

A WALK ACROSS AMERICA*
THE WALK WEST *(with Barbara Jenkins)**
THE ROAD UNSEEN *(with Barbara Jenkins)**
THE TENNESSEE SAMPLER *(with friends)*
ACROSS CHINA*

*Published by Fawcett Books

CLOSE FRIENDS

Peter Jenkins

FAWCETT CREST • NEW YORK

This book is dedicated to my mother,
Mary Robie Jenkins,
who taught all of her children many good things.

Contents

1. Night One, Night Two   1
2. "No Warm-blooded Animals"   6
3. "We'd Never Come Home Naked Before"   23
4. Bad Baby   29
5. The Summer Before Woodstock   33
6. The Falconer   44
7. A Birth Announcement   58
8. He's Not Gone From Me   66
9. Summons From a Shaman   76
10. Going to Alaska   80
11. Gerald Roy Riley   84
12. An Angry Bull-necked Policeman   91
13. Grr and Lacy   98
14. The Puppy-Killer   106
15. A Barn Cat Named Tigger   111
16. A Wise Man   118
17. The Skillfully Reckless Pilot   124
18. Cattle Haulers   134
19. The Book-Man   137
20. I Thought She Was Beautiful   150
21. My Shocker   157
22. Night Moves   163
23. Radar, The Macho One   174

24. A Few Thousand Acres to Explore   178
25. Blue-eyed Omi   182
26. Gray Nose   185
27. A Very Particular Lady   191
28. Lie Down Beside Me   199
29. Hunting Machines   210
30. Chicken Wipeout   219
31. The Rival   225
32. Wolf Blood   236
33. Call Lane Thrasher   244
34. "It Should Not Be This Way"   257
35. Double Rainbow   268
    Epilogue: A New Nest   285

Acknowledgments

Writing this book has made me think more than usual about the importance of friends, old friends, real friends, close friends. Many of the human ones are characters in this book and I won't repeat their names here. But I will list some of you who didn't make this book. The following list is in no specific order of significance. M. C. and Margaret Jenkins, Lamar and Honey Alexander, Walt Quinn, Bill and Camille Morris, Jim and Shirley Dobson, Lucinda Dyer, Dale and Kathy Martin, Paul Bogaards, Bob and Bobbie Wolgemuth, Mike and Gail Hyatt, Bess and the late Bill Luther, Buzz and June Morton, Jewell Hooten, Phil Yancey, Ray and Cindy and Tiffany Williams, Mia Matsuoka, Jim and Nita Cathey, Alberta Kinnard, Tommy Kinnard, Barbara Morgan, Bill and Mary Lucy Fuqua, Gary Sisco, Sam and Lucy Kuykendall, John and Patti Thompson, Tom Smith, Harpeth Academy, Cliff and Gayle Gillespie, Mona Martin, Debbie and Larry Davis, Ed and Ran Ying Porter, Zephyr Fite, Dot and Horace Murphy, Bill and Linda Baltzer, Glyn and Toby Smith, Welch Hill, Gary and Jean Wysocki plus Angie and Ben, Bernard Schwartz, Ginger Manley, Rodney and Carol Hopwood, David Howard, Bill and Debbie Koch, Ron and Linda Scott, David Vardaman,

Lou and Ingrid Whittaker, Leo Hicks and family, Fred Smith, Mike Blanton, Dan Harrell, Steve Baker, Crystal and David Andrews, Sr. and Jr., Perry Hall, Mary Elizabeth Lloyd, Gary Barnes, Charles Street, Mimi Wallace, Jim Sickel, George and Jackie Dantin, Garlon and Marie Pemberton, Suzanne, Lulu, and Bailey McAllister, Susan Van Epps and Quinn Van Yowell, and John and Susan Galloway.

I've been publishing books with William Morrow for ten years and during those years I've had the privilege of working with a lot of excellent people there. I appreciate the fine job they've done in publishing my books. A special thanks must go to my editor, the brilliant lady who has edited all my Morrow books, the lady who has had more impact on my writing than anyone, and also a considerable influence on my life as well. Pat Golbitz, you're extraordinary and I love you for all you've done. And special thanks to Jill Hamilton for all her terrific work and for her typing that's far better than any Wyoming Buffalo's. Also, for the productive decade I've been at Morrow I've been especially privileged to work with the following people: THANK YOU, Larry Hughes, Al Marchioni, Sherry Arden, Cheryl Asherman, Lisa Queen, Malcolm Magruder, Adene Corn, and Alan Fuller. Thanks, too, to the other fine people at Morrow I work with: Howard Kaminsky, Jim Landis, Lori Ames, Susan Halligan, Will Schwalbe, Greg Mowery, Joan Amico, Harvey Hoffman, Andy Ambraziejus, Nick Mazzella, Jaye Zimet, Marcia Nass, Lorraine Acevedo, Odetta Davis, and Tanhya Fisher. Also, many thanks to the top-of-the-line Morrow sales staff: Larry Norton, Mark Maxwell, Mark Kohut, Bob Werner, Sue Farr, Tom Rusch, Joan Vogel, Allen Kalman, Mark McDiarmid, Burt Rynders, James Riggs, Lewis Rice, Liz Tzetzo, Mickie Searcy, Kristine Searcy, Kristine Herman, and Jennifer Ward. Without ya'all I'd be up some kind of creek. A special thanks to the man at Morrow on the first floor, Naji Khaleb.

Also, a special thank-you to my longtime paperback publishers at Fawcett/Ballantine: Leona Nevler, Susan Petersen, Clare Ferraro, Stephen Black and the sales force, and everyone else at Fawcett/Ballantine who have helped make my four paperbacks into best sellers.

Extra special thanks to Glenda Baltzer Andrews, my assistant and true friend. We make a fine team and I thank God for that.

For this book some fine photographic, cartographic, and artistic work was done—and much appreciated—by Paul Breeden (illustrator), Robin Hood (cover photographer), Markie Hunsiker and Jim McClelland, Jr. (cartographers), ProPhoto, Chromatics, Bob Wyatt (computer advice), and Murray Lee (photographer).

To get the two Tennessee Walking Horse stallions to China took a monumental effort. Many, many people toiled for many hours and much money was spent to pull it off. Thanks especially to Betty Sain for getting the "horse thing" going and for all her great advice and work. Thanks to the Honorable Governor of Tennessee, Ned McWherter, for believing in the project and allowing the great State of Tennessee to get involved. Special thanks to the Tennessee Department of Agriculture, especially Keith Harrison, Joe Gaines, David Waddell, A. C. Clark, Judy Kenderine, and Michelle Shields. A big thank-you also to the Tennessee Walking Horse Breeders and Exhibitors Association of America, headquartered in Lewisburg, Tennessee, for their generous involvement. Especially, the T.W.H.B.E.A.'s Board of Directors: Steve Beech, Charles Gleghorn, Dr. Dewitt Owen, Val Caruthers, Susan Kent, Sam Yarborough, David Landrum, Bill Harlin, Charles Tisher, Bill Crawford, Buddy Moore, and Andrew Shaw. Also thanks to Walter Bussart and Sharon Brandon. And thanks to Buddy Payne for helping me get Shocker, observing my riding technique, and all he did with the China horse adventure. And thanks again, too, to Steve Beech for lining up the magnificent Prides Generator, owned by Claude and Linda Crowley, for the cover photo. Also thanks to State Representative Tommy Burnett, Harold Twitty, Rick and Rita Ondrik, Dr. Victor Wakefield, Dr. and Mrs. Marvin Powers, the Jack Daniel's Company, Bobby Beech and the National Bridle Shop, and Ambassador Winston Lord and his distinguished wife, Betty Bao Lord.

I always listen to the same few cassettes over and over when I write a book. For this book the music was Amy Grant's "Lead Me On" and Anita Baker's "Giving You the Best That I Got." Thanks, ladies.

I would like to thank certain members of the mass media who have been nice enough to interview me quite a few times over the years. The order of the following list is in no way meant to show any favoritism: Charlie Boone, Roy Leonard, Joan Hamburg, Ed Busch, Warren Pierce, Larry King, Mike Murphy, Ralph Emory, Dave Walker, Lois Hart, John Siegenthaler, Charlie Chase, Randy Barlow, Maggie Kennedy, Meredith MaCrae, Marsha Alvar, Sylvia Sachs, Anne Keefe, Teddy Bart, Peter Rose, Ed Ferenc, Ruth Ann Leach, Fred Griffith, Ira Joe Fisher, Peter Boyles, John Rayburn, Dan Cook, Bruce Cook, Jim Burns, Steve Raible, Susan Hutchinson, David Smith, John Eastman, George Putnam, Rich Buehler, Gary Todd, Dick Wolfsie, Jackie Mitchem, Molly Young, Rod Patterson, Matt Schaeffer, Gary Frazier, Don Heider, Debbie Alan, Harry Chapman, and, last but certainly not least, Jane Pauley.

* * *

More than ever I appreciate my family and their love and support. There is a whole lot of family, with more being added all the time. Thanks to all of you for making my life so much richer. The Jenkins Family: Frederick and Mary Jenkins, Rhoda Jenkins, Betsy Jenkins, Abbi Jenkins, Randy and Winky Rice plus Alex, Jesse, and Tyler; Fred and Coleen Jenkins plus Molly, Sarah, and Derick; Scott and Bonnie Jenkins plus Isaiah and Andrew. The Jorgensen Family: Jerry and Dorothy Jorgensen, Inez Keith, Kevin and Valerie Karikomi plus Matthew, Michael, and David; Mike and LeAnn Turner plus John, Michael and Scott; Eric Jorgensen plus Tammi, Kari, and Rachel; Aaron and Sherri Jorgensen plus Gena, Julie, J.J. and Cory Bo; and Chris Jorgensen. And especially, my beloved Rita, plus Rebekah Jenkins, Jed Jenkins, Luke Jenkins, Aaron Davis, and Brooke Davis.

Author's note: Blue Springs is a fictitious name for a real town in Tennessee.

1

Night One, Night Two

My body was tired, my mind was tired. I lay down on my stomach and looked out our bedroom window into this moonlit expanse which was now the Jenkins farm. Barbara was already asleep, drained from our moving-in-day unpacking of a mountain full of boxes. This was our first night on our new farm. Silhouettes of trees with their arching black branches reached out as if to grab me. I heard sounds of the dairy cows ambling through the darkened pasture. Shouldn't they be lying down sleeping? Shouldn't milk cows be sleeping inside a barn? Which was the milking barn?

It was DARK outside. I'd seen it this dark before, but that was when I was walking across America. This was supposed to be *home*—full-time living. The cows were just beyond the window now, making odd sounds, with no apparent plan to stop. I had noticed that the black-and-white spotted cows seemed to lie in the shade during the heat of the day. Maybe they ate their grass, or whatever they ate, at night.

As I lay in bed, unable to sleep, I thought about cows. What do the cows eat anyway? Do they eat just grass? What about weeds? Are there weeds in the pastures? Surely there are. Do they eat tree leaves? Do you feed them hay all the time? What about regular feed, pellet-type stuff, that looked like dry dog food? Corn? Do they attack people? The are so BIG.

With these kinds of questions going through my fevered head I'd never get to sleep. To cool off I stepped out on the porch, bare-body naked except for my white socks because no one was around to see me. A crashing sound jolted through my body. I leaped inside, then quieted down a second to see if I could locate the sound, and listened to see if it happened again. Could something big have fallen on the tin roof? Was the house falling apart? We'd never owned an old house before. Had termites eaten it in half? No, stupid, it was tested for termites, no termite problem here.

Could the brick chimneys be falling apart? Are the trees . . . ? I opened the front door again and went back out on the porch. A moon as thin as an almond sliver created only the slightest night-light and in the deep blue outside I saw the palest silver shapes.

The whole herd was standing around our Ford pickup and my 650 CC Yamaha motorcycle.

When I sneaked up to the fence, I saw the damage they'd done. They'd knocked down my motorcycle, and one was now rubbing its legs on it. I had no idea what to do. I wasn't planning on going OUT THERE, among those massive animals in the dark. The motorcycle would have to survive till daylight when they'd be gone. I went back in. I lay down again on the clean sheet and figured I'd made a mistake. Fortunately for Barbara, I did not wake her with the news of the cow attack. We had been too adventuresome moving to a farm in Tennessee.

Daylight came to the farm but the cows were still there. Fifteen black-and-white holsteins lay in a circle around the fallen motorcycle and pickup truck. The Plexiglas windshield on the motorcycle was shattered, knocked down by the rubbing, scratching animals. They had rubbed all over the side of the pickup truck, bent a side mirror, and dulled the paint on the driver's door. There were green cow patties semi-dried on the sides of the truck, plopped on the motorcycle, and spread out all over the yard like a field planted with mines. The message from those doe-eyed, completely relaxed cows seemed to be "Welcome to your farm."

After a couple of pieces of peanut-butter-and-jelly toast and some orange juice, I decided it was time to stop looking out the windows of this old farmhouse and tackle the outside.

Our land was all sown down (a farmer's expression for planted) in what local people called permanent pasture. Permanent pasture is similar in concept to permanent lawn except I assumed the cows were the lawnmowers for pastures. Cows as lawnmowers seemed wonderful to me, considering how long it takes to mow a lawn of half an acre, much less 135 acres. I walked over all of it: the pastures, the meadows, the creek and the pond, the woods, the hill-cresting stand of cedars.

I was amped out. Deer, owls, walnut trees, spring-fed ponds by our fence rows, shagbark hickories, forest, acres of hardwoods, scents of crushed cedar branches, pastures sprawling over more area than the entire mass of land under the apartment building I grew up in. I was about to have an attack from owning this place. Would I fall over right in this back field, overdosed by too much to take into my heart? My mind couldn't handle all this responsibility. I wondered if beginning this new life, this farm, was the right thing to do. Could we cope with it all? Would we enjoy it if we could? Was the dream, the wish, the fantasy going to be the best part of what was now a green reality that seemed as big as Rhode Island?

The second night on the farm I didn't know whether to sleep or not to sleep: to stay up reading, watching late night TV (Johnny Carson and beyond). Would it be a night worse than night number one?

There were millions of blades of grass outside the win-

dow of this house, thousands of rocks, weeds, thorn trees.
There were wild animals known as cows. I wasn't sure I
wanted to shut my eyes and watch them all grow out of
control. Maybe they'd choke off the house and I'd be
stranded here. Wouldn't a condo with a backyard twenty
foot by twenty foot be easier?

Johnny Carson was on Channel 4 here on a Nashville
station and since the antenna was wired to the brick
chimney, he came in clear. It was comforting to watch
him; it took away some of my growing fear of the organic
greenland outside.

I would try to lie down for night number two and this
time go to sleep as fast as Barbara. The window was
open, no unusual noises. A seductive breeze begged me
to put a sheet over my body. Then I heard them again.
The cows had come back. I thought of Alfred Hitch-
cock's movie *The Birds*.

I fell deeper into rest when CRACK! A noise.
AWAKE. The smells of outside, farm scents, cool night
air now inside the house. A moment to orient. Was I still
walking across America, living in Louisiana? No, it
sounded like the front porch was falling off the house.

This couldn't be a nightmare, I was awake. I heard a
wet plopping sound. The porch was not falling off. The
cows were on it! THERE WERE COWS ON MY
FRONT PORCH! I flew into the entry hall and turned
the light on and off, on and off, hoping to scare them
away. The two monsters each weighed about half a ton.
The blinking lights only attracted the others; the whole
herd was in the front yard. Damn.

I rushed out and pushed those cows off my porch. I
was too mad to be scared. The trespassers joined their
friends in the yard and all of them ran, their long legs
trotting to the north and then looping east to the back of
the house, by the stone root cellar. I was running in the
dew-coated lawn naked, trying to herd them like a
drunken cattle dog with amnesia. I had no idea how to

herd anything. Being mad was a mistake. Rushing at them in the dark was a mistake. Throwing a fallen limb was a mistake. Being naked was a big mistake.

The black-and-white cows had dispersed to all corners of the yard. I decided to give up and let them spend the night there. I would have a lot of fresh shoveling to do at sunup.

The way I felt now, if I never saw a cow again it would be too soon. I didn't even want one on a belt buckle.

2
"No Warm-blooded Animals"

At Wilber Peck Court, the apartment complex where I lived till I went to college, we were not allowed to have any warm-blooded animals. No cats, no dogs, nothing. My mother was exceptionally honest (we used to think *too* honest). So she would never let us sneak in a warm-blooded pet. Mother *did* let us feed the gray squirrel who lived in a gum tree outside our kitchen window, but the squirrel never came inside the window. At least not often.

Our three-bedroom apartment was part of Wilbur Peck Court, a federal housing project of red brick with three or four separate buildings of about one hundred families. It was one of two federally subsidized apartment complexes in Greenwich, Connecticut. "Federally subsidized" are bad, dirty, *Democratic* words in Greenwich. Of course we kids didn't know any of this till we got older.

The other project in Greenwich was Armstrong Court, also by the interstate. It was next to Chicahominy, and St. Rock's Church, in the biggest Italian neighborhood in town. Greenwich had so few ethnic people, they would probably all have fitted on the fairway of one of the shortest holes on one of the golf courses. Ethnics (Italians,

6

Polish, anyone whose name ended with an *i*, like Lew-indowski) were not encouraged to move in. What few blacks and Asians there were in town lived in one of the projects or resided in servants' quarters on the acred estates of the rich.

Wilbur Peck Court was near the interstate and the rail-road tracks, near one of the few working-class neighbor-hoods in town. The big-money people lived in "back Greenwich."

We Jenkinses (WASPs) were in the minority at Wilbur Peck Court. Our childhood friends were the Lewindow-skis, the Grokowskis (Russian), the Darulas (Czechs), the Bailys (from Trinidad), the Fortes (Italian), the Robin-sons (Jamaicans), the Phillipses (Alabama blacks), and many Irish Catholics: the McMurrays (eight or nine kids), the Purdys (twelve kids), the Murphys (a bunch of blonds).

I know my dad wished we didn't live there, wished he could give us a big house, because he said so all the time. But as a kid I loved Wilbur Peck Court. There was al-ways someone outside to play with. We had a special whistle to call each other. Windows would pop open on the first floor, second floor, or the third floor. When I was a kid, the one thing I didn't like about Wilbur Peck Court was that I couldn't have a dog.

Dr. Cornell's Veterinary Hospital was in Old Greenwich, about six miles from home. He had a "small animal" practice, dogs and cats, and a "large animal practice," the hunters and show horses of the gentry.

Dr. Cornell kept a standing request at the employment office for kennel help. There weren't too many in Green-wich who wanted to shovel dog and cat "dookey." There were plenty who wanted to take care of the cute dogs and cats, but the shoveling was what kept kids from lasting long down in the basement of Dr. Cornell's clinic. I didn't care how much dookey I had to shovel. I wanted to be near those warm-blooded animals.

So I got the job, feeding and cleaning in the cellar. I'd fill spooned-out cans (*never* leave *any* dog food in the tin can) with hot water and pour it into a huge vat of dried dog food. Then I'd mix it all up with my hands. That was gross. The dog-food smell got in my clothes, not to mention the other smells. I used a lot of Lysol. A lot of times I sprayed my shoes with the stuff.

The sick animals at Dr. Cornell's had to be fed special high-protein, medicated food. Sometimes the sick ones would lie in the corners of their cages, sullen and extremely distressed that their masters had left them at the vet's. When I'd place their food inside their cages they acted as though they'd like to bite off my hand. The most ornery dogs were the toy poodles, the miniature poodles, the silkies, and the Yorkies. They did not repress their anger at being sent away. They took it out on me.

The clinic was on the Post Road, U.S. Route 1, one of the oldest roads in the whole U.S.A. It was the main road between Maine and Florida, my father kept telling us. My father knew something about an amazing number of things—there wasn't anything on the face of the earth that he couldn't talk about. There was a Hess gas station across the street backing up to I-95 and a pizza place. It turned out a distant cousin of mine worked there, at least that's what Dad said.

Discovering that my distant cousin ran a pizza place was a miracle. Every day I worked at Dr. Cornell's I went over there for a free pizza. I had to pay only for my cream sodas. My cousin taught me how to make pizza and I'd bake my own, loaded with cheese and meat, and cook it real well done. That was one fine pizza, but what was *beyond* fine was being with all those dogs across the street. Working there was like having my own LIVING book of *Dog Breeds of the World*. If there was a kind of

dog available to human beings, someone in Greenwich
had one, and given enough time, the breed would come
here to be boarded or cured. There were not a lot of
mongrel dogs in this town.

The animal-hospital building was built out of cinder-
block and had glass blocks in the front of the building
and black tile on the floor in the entry area. In the back
was the operating room, with two stainless-steel operating tables. All the scalpels and doctor's tools were kept
in glass jars filled with antiseptic.

Beyond the operating rooms was a metal door with
scratches in the paint about dog-high. That was the entry
to my kingdom. Behind the door was a stairway that went
down into the kennel, where the food and the cough syrup
was stored.

The cages were all down there—big ones for Great
Danes, German shepherds, bull mastiffs, St. Bernards, or
any large dog that came to stay. The cages looked almost
as big as the bathroom in our apartment. There were the
medium-size cages for the Dalmations, the boxers, the
collies, the Dobermans, the cocker spaniels, the black
Labradors, the Irish setters and I guess the most popular
dogs, the yellow Labradors. Some of these yellow Labs
were so big, really fat, that they had to go into the big
cages.

Many in Greenwich thought that yellow Labs looked
wonderful lying on a truly fine Oriental rug. I once heard
a lady say that her Lab looked just like an English still-
life painting when he lay on a particular Persian rug in
the hallway, with its old oak floors and elaborately curved
stairway. The only thing missing, she said, were the two
dead pheasants, but she would never have *that* since she
was opposed to hunting.

The smallest cages held the cats, which made me itch.
They usually were depressed while they stayed with us
and their eyes went dull. Only one of them ever got mean.
His name was Capricorn. Every time I went anywhere

near his cage he reached through the bars with claws out, hoping to draw blood. He strained for every centimeter of reach. One time, trying to make friends, I gave him a small dish of cough syrup, the kind with codeine in it. He was cautious. He ignored it. He sniffed it. He touched his nose to it. He took a small lick. He instantly loved it. The next day when I walked by Capricorn on my feeding rounds, instead of attempting to claw me, he was purring and rubbing his body on the cage, trying hard to get more cough syrup.

Because their legs were too short to make the stairs, I carried the small dogs down. A few times I almost got my ears pierced with holes just the size of a Chihuahua's teeth.

The doctor had always told me to try to get the owners to leave as soon as possible so that they would not hear their animals cry, wail, moan, or howl. Many animals did that when left here and some did it the whole time they were here until they went hoarse or their masters came back to get them.

Into these cages went all kinds of poodles, dachshunds, whippets, Yorkshire terriers, Welsh corgis, a few bull terriers, beagles, all kinds of "cute" little dogs. Sometimes the little puppies came in with strict instructions about when to put their sweaters on and when not to.

After I had worked there a few months, Dr. Cornell asked me to come in on Saturdays. I would basically run the place, take in patients, and be nice and soothing to the nervous owners.

When the dogs and cats came in I filled out a form: I took the owner's name, address, phone number, animal's name, breed, age, and reason for stay. In winter, most dogs and cats came to us because their masters were either going skiing at Stowe or Stratton in Vermont or were headed to the ski area in Telluride, Colorado, or Vail or Aspen, also in Colorado, or to the great powder skiing of Utah. That was our winter rush, which started right before Christmas. The older people came in wearing rumpled khaki pants, white socks, scraped-up Topsiders, dark-blue sweaters, and some kind of button-down shirt. They brought in their bigger dogs when they headed to their winter homes in the Caribbean—St. Thomas, St. Martin. . . . Florida was not quite the WASPs' place in the sun, unless it was Palm Beach. Sometimes they came on the way to the airport, with the animals in the back of the station wagon, which had a Christmas wreath wired to the front hood. One of us usually had to go out and get the pet unless the chauffeur was driving.

There was one lady who had a woman chauffeur. This lady was unusual for Greenwich. She wore leather pants, had a tan all year round, and had no loose skin on her over-fifty-year-old face. She walked like an eighteen-year-old who knew she had a great body and wasn't trying to hide it. I don't think she saw my teenage face watching her. The woman chauffeur usually brought the dog in a white Mercedes.

Her dog was a bull mastiff. Bull mastiffs look like two-thousand-pound Angus bulls, except that Angus bulls don't have sharp teeth. His name was Voltaire and he was a stunning dog. His hair was naturally very short and camel color, like the color of an expensive cashmere sports coat. His neck looked as thick as a hundred-year-old tree. He acted as though he ruled the earth. And he HATED men. Boys. HUMAN males.

The female chauffeur barked out orders like a German commandant:

1. "Feed him three times a day." They brought his own special food.
2. "Do not let him close to any other dog; he'll kill it." He looked like he would like to kill me.
3. "We will be back for him in ten days, exactly."

4. "You must not take him, sir, to his cage. I will do
   it," said the chauffeur-ess.

Anytime Voltaire had to be taken out, Betty, who
worked at Dr. Cornell's veterinary clinic full time, had
to do it. I went upstairs in case he got loose. If Betty
wasn't there Voltaire did not get any fresh air. He didn't
like men, that was the truth. I weighed 170. The dog
weighed 180. I was always glad to see that bull mastiff
leave. I never felt comfortable down in the basement
while he was there. I had this stupid fear that he was
possessed, supernatural. Maybe he could open his cage,
and when I turned around, he'd be leaping at my throat.

It was a Saturday in March. I'd brought in a radio and
had it on really loud. Early in the morning on Saturdays
the clinic was usually very quiet. Once I got everybody
fed, which I did first thing, I'd come into the upstairs
front-entry area and jam the volume dial on that FM station as loud as it would go. I loved it because I was the
only one there, which was never the case in our tiny
apartment. Also the floor was expansive, there was space
to move, another impossible thing at our house. I'd close
the door to the back hallway if there were any dogs or
cats recovering back in the operating room. We had a
few cages upstairs for animals who were critically ill or
just coming out of surgery. It was our intensive-care unit.
Led Zeppelin or the Allman Brothers at number 10 on
the volume knob probably was not optimum recovery
music.

Some Saturday mornings I'd get out on that black li-
noleum floor and dance. I would keep my face toward
the door as I danced my fool heart away, always keeping
a lookout for customers. I definitely did not want to get
caught dancing by myself by a customer, or, nightmare
of nightmares, by Dr. Cornell!

This particular Saturday morning I was dancing to a
Sly and the Family Stone album, and I was doing 360-

degree spins. At the end of a full spin, I looked up to see a station wagon pulling to a stop. It wasn't Dr. Cornell; he was somewhere up on Round Hill Road, sewing up a horse that had hit a wire fence. The car was a yellow Ford Country Squire, with fake wood on the side. I knew that kind because I'd always wished we had one. In all my growing-up years we never had a new car.

The driver had short brown hair frosted with blond streaks. She walked with a bounce, as though she were about to step onto a racquetball court or tennis court. Her face was not the usual "young Greenwich mother" sunny. She looked more like she was painfully hung over, or had just come from a funeral. She did not have a dog or cat with her. Maybe she was here to pick something up.

"Hello, can I help you?" My heart was pumping from all my dancing.

"Yes, um, I . . . never mind, I'll do it," she said.

She went back out the door and stood at the back of the station wagon. The back door was swung open, which I had not noticed before. She bent down slightly so she could see in. I was looking out the front window and I could see nothing in the back of the wagon.

The young woman clapped her hands together as if she was saying, "Come here. . . . Come here." From the expression on her face it looked like she was using that peppy, sweet voice people use to call their animals when the animal does not want to cooperate because it knows what it's in for.

She did this for quite a while. I'd seen a lot of dogs who didn't want to come to the vet's, especially those that knew they would be boarded here for a long time while their people lived somewhere else. There were dogs that totally refused to move, and when they were big and strong, it took more than one person to get them inside. Usually I could get almost any dog to do anything.

I could see nothing through the tinted side windows.

Finally, I did see what looked like a couple of pointed ears, but I wasn't sure.

Then the woman reached inside the station wagon till only her legs stuck out. Almost before she got all the way inside she popped out of there like she'd been shot out of a cannon. Maybe whatever was in there had bitten her.

She then came back inside, holding her head down, her chin almost to her chest. Once a lady had brought in some neighbor's dog that had been hit by a car; the impact had shattered some bones in the back legs, and when she tried to pick it up, it bit her. Maybe whatever was in there had been hit by a car, was lying down, or dead.

Another time, a whippet came in after being attacked by a German shepherd. A whippet is a beautifully graceful, doe-eyed dog that is more or less a half-size greyhound. It had canine teeth holes all over it, was bleeding a lot. The couple that brought it in couldn't bear to carry it; I had to. That time Dr. Cornell saved its life and let me, for the first time, assist him in its surgery.

"You need to go out there and bring Katey in here, please, please," she pleaded.

"Okay. Can you tell me what's wrong with her?" I asked.

"We, I, um, my family and me, we've . . . um . . . she . . . ah . . . she . . . we want to . . . uh . . . put her to sleep." So that explains it. She didn't have the heart to bring it in. I certainly could understand that. I'd seen a few families bring in their old, arthritic, beloved dogs before. The dog was a faithful part of the family. Sometimes they were more than that. They could be a calm center in an angry family. They could be like another child, a brother or sister to the human kids. The people I had helped bring their dogs inside for the last few minutes of life were often devastated. Usually the hair around the dogs' muzzles had long been gray, their reflexes gone. Their ability to climb stairs was no longer there. The tail

wagged but much more slowly; the walks it once took
that were never long enough were now only a few painful
yards. The dog that had licked their kids' baby-fat cheeks,
and walked them to school, watched them learn to ride
their bikes and sometimes seen them off to college were
about to die. It tore the people up, as well it should. I
always tried to do all I could to be compassionate to these
grieving people.

I went down the four or five steps, and looked in the
back of the station wagon. Lying there was no old dog.
No run-over animal. What lay there was a pile of longish
brown-and-cream-colored fur, with big patches of scab
and pus and red, irritated skin. This dog was not old, but
it had the worst case of mange I'd ever seen. I could see
why the lady did not want to touch it.

I crawled into the back and petted the dog, avoiding
the sores. What was her name? Katey. Katey couldn't
even wag her tail or lift her head. Maybe she could tell
she was coming here to go on death row. Surely she
did—she seemed like one of those sensitive dogs, often
females, who cowered away, very upset, if you ever
raised your voice to them.

As I reached for her collar my hand was repelled when
I felt some damp scabs and no collar. I guessed her skin
was too irritated to wear a collar. I don't know what
really set me off, but as I picked Katey up in my arms
and she whimpered, I became weak with sorrow for her.
She definitely was not old. I thought the stupidest, non-
related thought. What if my parents had me put to sleep
because my pimples got really bad? I knew it was ridiculous but still . . . I thought mange was treatable. Maybe
not.

Possibly once it got to this extreme degree of infection
there was no cure. Katey looked as if she could be part
collie, part German shepherd, part Irish setter, part English setter, and part hound. But most of all, she looked
horrible. Every movement was painful for her. All the

special things you can do with your dog—pet it, sit close to it, have it lie in your lap—you could not do with this pathetic animal.

I carried her inside and when I laid her down on the floor, she yelped with pain. She seemed to know exactly why she was here. Perhaps she was suffering so much with this mange that she wanted to die. I drew a deep, slow breath and asked the owner her name, address, phone number, dog's name, and reason for visit or stay.

To the last question she said, "I told you earlier why she's here; I can't say it again."

"Excuse me. I'm sorry." I said. She turned and walked out.

Katey did not get up to follow; she looked up for a second, then let her head flop down on the floor again. She was too weak to walk down the stairs, so I got a towel, wrapped her in it, and carried her downstairs. I put her in our biggest cage, put towels on the metal floor instead of newspapers, which of course I wasn't supposed to do, and tried to think of things I could do to make her last few days comfortable.

I wondered if I poured some of the cough medicine the cat loved into her water bowl it might dull some of her excruciating pain. She pulled herself over to the bowl with her front paws and drank it. I gave her water, and she drank that. Then I ran across the street to the pizza place and bought a few pints of milk for her. She drank them. Why was she so thirsty?

Back in the storage room we had some very expensive canned dog food, supposed to be eaten only by dogs coming out of serious surgery. It had antibiotics added to it and a high percentage of protein as well. I fed Katey some of that. She licked at it, so weak that she couldn't really lift her head up.

Katey's neighbor in the next large cage was a gray Weimaraner, a German breed of hunting dogs filled with hyperactive muscle and bodies that never stopped moving. The family of my ninth-grade girlfriend had a Wei-maraner once for about a week. When it tried to eat down their house, they had to let it go live in a place where it could be outside on a lot of land. Kathy's mother was extremely neat and they had a beautiful home at the end of a long paved lane, set back among some mature hard-woods. Anyway, their Weimaraner was even more in-tense than normal. One night Kathy's mother put him in the laundry room to sleep. Maybe he wouldn't make a mess in there. She put everything up that he might get to. She put a clean little rag rug down for him to lie on.

That rambunctious dog got hungry sometime in the middle of the night, and when he couldn't find anything to eat in the laundry room, he ate right through the wall into the kitchen. When Kathy's dad came down for his morning coffee he saw above the kitchen table what looked like a mounted Weimaraner head on the wall, ex-cept that it was moving. The dog had chewed and bit his way through wallpaper, Sheetrock, and more Sheetrock and wallpaper on the kitchen side. That dog did not stay at the Flanigans' long enough to eat its way into the for-mal dining room.

The Weimaraner in the cage next to Katey was wig-gling and wagging his tail. His eyes were bright. He wanted to play, run, wrestle, eat, fight, walk, swim—anything but be still. Katey, on the other hand, couldn't or wouldn't even stand up. Her fur was flat, dull, covered with peeling white flakes of skin. Her eyes were tor-mented and dimmed by pain and despair.

I found myself thinking that, yes, she probably would be better off "put to sleep," sent to a place where there was no more pain, weakness, infection, and rejection. I guessed her master could not bear to watch her and her condition anymore. Dr. Cornell would come in on Mon-day and I'd tell him what she was here for. Usually he filled a needle with a drug and came downstairs. We called it Euthanasia solution. I would bring the dog out of its cage, stroking it to calm it down, and Dr. Cornell would place the shot in one of the veins in its front leg, and in seconds it would collapse, dead. Sometimes, if it had any premonition that something bad was about to happen, I'd have to put a nylon leash around its neck, and a couple a of times we even had to wrap the leash around its snout to keep it from biting us.

After getting Katey settled in, I went back upstairs to man the reception desk again. The FM, all-album radio station was now playing something by Jethro Tull. I turned it off. For the remainder of the day just a few people came in, and then it was time to go downstairs and feed everybody. Feeding time was the last thing I did before I closed up the hospital and went home. The place was about full; it was a prime time then for people to go on vacations seeking the southern sun.

The moment I opened the upstairs door to head down-stairs, the dogs knew they were going to eat. It was prob-ably the highlight of the day, especially since I was such a gourmet maker of dog food. I always added more canned food than was called for, and I let the dry stuff soak in hot water to make it more tasty. The barking began and just about every one of them barked until they got their portion. The cats, or most of them, began to pace, back and forth, back and forth, rubbing against the fronts of their cages and purring.

First I went to the feed room to get the water running hot. Then I opened can after can of dog and cat food, mixed up the dry food with hot water, and topped it off, like hot fudge on a sundae, with canned food. I always started in the eastern corner of the basement and went around the outside of the basement cages. When I got to Adolph, the Weimaraner, he was pawing the cage door. He was always starving. I was anxious about looking over at Katey. Maybe her body would be flopped over, stretched out and dead. Instead, she held her head up, looking much more attentive.

I went to the stock room and got her some more cough medicine, which had a cherry taste. I took the gallon jar and poured some into her water dish. She almost got up and walked over to it. She drank it all down. Then I gave her some more water, real cold. She liked cold water. I had finished feeding everybody else by then, even the pet raccoon that was staying with us. Then I mixed up what I thought Katey might consider a super-deluxe meal, crunching in expensive dog vitamins, and pouring in some more milk. She did take a few licks, but not much more.

When I got ready to leave and shut down Dr. Cornell's Veterinary Hospital that Saturday, I wondered if Dr. Cornell might come in on Sunday. Sometimes he would, especially if there were any critically ill animals, and then he'd breeze through the basement to see how any dogs or cats that had been spayed were coming along, give any shots that were needed, and so on.

Maybe it would be best if he did come in and give Katey her "death shot." That way I wouldn't have to hold her while he did it or dispose of her skin-and-bones body. No, I wanted to see her again. So, before I left, I took her registration card and hid it in a drawer in the feed room. No one would find it, and Dr. Cornell, if he came in, would assume the card had fallen off the front of the cage and he'd just leave Katey alone.

When I came back Monday after school, I went downstairs first thing and Katey actually wagged her lethargic tail a few times. She looked about the same. Her tail, which should have been bushy and beautiful, had only about a quarter of the hair it should have had. It thumped on the metal floor of her cage. I mixed her up another mega-meal, with enough protein and vitamins to make a hard-breeding St. Bernard stud happy. The sun was in a healing mood that afternoon, so I took her out in a clean run and let her lie in its rays. She walked as if she had crippling arthritis. Katey stayed out in the sun of a Connecticut pre-spring day while all the others just had their turns.

Day by day, Katey got stronger. After ten days she could stand up and walk again. I began taking her into the feed room and giving her the usual whopper of a meal, while I worked on mixing up everybody else's. I'd found some medicated shampoo, stuck back in the storeroom, and I thought maybe that would help her condition. She loved the warm water, the loving rubbing of my hands as I massaged in the hopeful healing of the shampoo.

When Katey was out I was always a bit tense, expecting Dr. Cornell or Betty the manager to come down the stairs and wonder what the dog was doing in the sink. They never realized that Katey had checked in. Her registration card had stayed lost all this time. I figured that if they found out—if the people who used to own her called and asked why they didn't get a bill—if that happened I would pay for all her food and medicine and let them do with her whatever they wanted. I was feeling close to Katey, beginning to feel like she was mine. Even though we couldn't have a dog at WPC I could sort of have one here. She wasn't mine, but I did feel responsible for making her healthy, for keeping her alive. And Katey sure was getting much healthier.

The medicated shampoos really helped her, as did the sun, and the special diet. After a month her fur began to grow back. She'd gained eight pounds (she only weighed thirty-eight pounds when she arrived) and her tail almost never stopped wagging. Afternoons when I worked I let her out of her cage and gave her the run of the place. She became queen of the basement, and many of the other dogs seemed to be jealous. Wherever I went, she was at my side. If I stopped to change an empty water dish, she sat quietly and watched me. If I forgot to give her a special meal or her cough syrup, she'd take me over to the storage room. After a few weeks I had to stop giving her the cherry-flavored cough syrup. I was afraid it might be habit-forming.

After a month, and more treatments of medicated shampoo, healthy fur had grown back all over her body. There were no patchy spots, pus, or scabs—Katey learned how to jump up on the counter and plop down into the sink to get a hot, soothing bath.

After six or seven weeks her hair was shiny and gleaming with luster. Her fur had many shades of cream and tan on her stomach and many shades of brown up the sides of her body, becoming darkest along her backbone. Her tail was now luxurious enough to be wrapped around her face on a below-zero night to keep her cozy and secure. It was also obvious now that she was a mutt. When occasionally another dog would growl at Katey or try to fight, she would not retaliate. She was not a fighter.

Either Dr. Cornell never noticed Katey or he decided not to notice. He was a man who some days said nothing, but that certainly did not mean he was hardhearted or cold. He knew I lived in WPC and he knew there were no pets there. He also knew that I wished I could be a vet, since I sneaked every spare moment to talk to the rushing doctor. About the only time I ever got to actually have a conversation with him was when I assisted him in surgery. At this point in my high-school education I doubted I could ever become a vet. Dr. Cornell said there was a great deal of math and science, and I'd never applied myself in those subjects. Actually I felt more attracted to English and art, but in 1967, a young man was supposed to go in for "male" subjects like math, science, engineering, business. I figured I'd find the thing I wanted to do when I got to college. Still, I wished I didn't need math to be a vet.

One Saturday before the summer holidays, I decided I'd slip Katey outside into the unrestrained sunlight. The winds blew over from Long Island Sound and were tinged with a soft, salty flavor. She hadn't been outside the Vet-

erinary Hospital since she'd been brought in many weeks
ago. Not only was she healed now, but she glowed with
vigor.

Her first steps onto the spongy grass were funny because she acted afraid to place her paws down on it. It
had become almost unnatural to her; she seemed to have
forgotten what grass felt like. She was so used to her
cage and the concrete floor and the sink where she got
her baths that they had become the real world to her. She
pressed her body against my leg, feeling for security.
Then a squirrel sprinted toward a tree and she was transformed into what I figured was her old self. She sprinted
after it.

After her adventure outside in the air and clumps of
green grass, I found an old dog collar and took her across
the street to the pizza place. Katey fell in love with pizza.
She ate almost half of mine as I loaded it with more meat
than usual. The delightful warm scents of pizza running
out of the stainless-steel oven, the bright fluorescent
lights, the red-checkered curtains—Katey loved it all.

3

"We'd Never Come Home Naked Before"

So much did Katey enjoy going out that I decided I would risk bringing Katey home for Saturday and Sunday night. I'd call Mom or Dad and, instead of hitchhiking home as I usually did, ask them to come and get me. Because our apartment was so small—three small bedrooms, six kids (all three of us Jenkins boys in one room, with one dresser), and a bathroom the size of a slightly bigger than average closet—I never had friends over to spend the night. Sometimes, especially in the summer, I'd spend a week at a time at my friend Bob's, on Cornelia Drive in back Greenwich. Their maid's quarters over the garage seemed bigger than our whole apartment. The Elsaessers had formal gardens in back, and huge rhododendron bushes in front, at the end of their long winding driveway.

Comparing my place to theirs, I was ashamed, although I never admitted it to anyone. Really I didn't want friends knowing where I lived, much less coming there. Never, ever, did I bring one of my girlfriends home to the apartment. But Katey wouldn't care how crowded our place was, and my little sisters, Betsy and Abbi, would enjoy her.

When my dad pulled up I was sitting on the front steps

of the clinic and Katey was laying her head in my lap.
Never before had a dog been inside our apartment.

"Whose dog is that, Peter?" Dad wanted to know.

"Oh, it's one I've sort of adopted."

"Adopted? Well, get in, let's go home." I guessed
Dad figured if I'd adopted a dog from a vet it was okay.
If it had been some obviously expensive, valuable purebred, like a yellow Lab or Welsh terrier, then he would
have asked more questions. Dad was the type of man
who respected people's private places. Although a big
six two and powerful, he was an exceedingly sensitive
man.

When we pulled into the parking lot of WPC, Katey
jumped out the window. Her fur glistened in the light of
late afternoon. A bunch from my gang were hanging out
on the front steps—Johnnie and Winston Robinson, Paul
and Floyd Fountain, "G.J." Grokowski, Skippy Waddell, and my brother Freddy. They were either planning
some baseball game or organizing a raid on one of the
other buildings. Five of the guys were black, and Katey
acted as if she'd never met a black person before.

The guys were there, my youngest brother, Freddy,
told me, because "Bones" Johnson, a huge black guy
who lived in our building, was supposed to be coming
through with his motorcycle gang. They weren't Hell's
Angels but they had beautiful motorcycles; there were
about seventy-five in their "riding club." Bones was
married to an Italian woman, and not long ago we saw
Bones almost kill a man in the driveway because he had
scratched Bones's wife's car. He got the guy on the pavement and began punching him viciously. It was terrifying
the way he kept it up. Freddy pulled me over to the side
as Dad went on inside.

"Pete, we've got something planned for later. We're
going pool hopping tonight. Wanna come with us?"

Usually I hung around with "Bobo" and "Crazed,"
Bob and Craig, but they weren't out of their respective

prep schools for the summer yet. Being with my two younger brothers, Freddy and Scott, and their friends was not usually acceptable but, okay, I told Freddy, I'd go.

"What are you going to do with that dog?" he asked.

"She'll just have to come with us," I answered, after thinking about leaving her in our apartment her first time there. I didn't know yet if she could swim, but she wouldn't have to if she didn't want to. She acted like she'd follow me anywhere.

When it got dark, a bunch of us took off walking, up Davis Avenue, past Sammy Visarrio's store, cutting over to Greenwich Avenue, the main shopping street in town. When I was five or six I had stolen a penny bubble gum from Sammy's and Mother took me back there and made me admit to Sammy that I did it. It was incredibly embarrassing.

We were headed to one of the most exclusive streets in Greenwich, guarded by big, gray stone pillars. The area called Deer Park was not far from Greenwich Hospital. There was a little string of mansions on this one street, most of them built of stone, or Tudor-styled. We were headed for Deer Park because in every backyard of every house was a swimming pool. Perfect for "chain pool hopping." You could practically dive from one to the other like a porpoise, except the yards were too big for that.

The plan was that we would take our clothes off—our jeans, Converse sneakers, and T-shirts—and pile them at the end of the chain of pools. Then we'd sneak along the backs of the neon-green backyards, being careful to keep out of range of the floodlights aimed to pierce any shadows. We would sneak from one tree to the next, careful to avoid view. There had been no chance to get any tans this early in June. Our skins were as white as Craig's mother's gleaming Mercedes. The yards had various rock patios with carefully arranged lawn furniture, mostly in white. The flowers and shrubs were set out perfectly;

there were no loose toys or bicycles; no clotheslines, no doghouses, no worn areas in the grass where a volleyball net had been; nothing that wasn't right out of *Town and Country* magazine.

Our commando unit was ready: our only weak link, Katey. We'd all done this before, but this time we could not be sure that our dog could handle the precise maneuvers, the split-second timing demanded if we were to leap in and out of the pools quickly and keep our naked bodies hidden behind trees. We hoped Katey would not begin barking from the excitement of the moment.

Beginning with pool one, we'd jump in and out, go to pool two, and so on, till we got to the last pool. Fortunately, no one had pool lights on, and only two still had backyard lights on. There were no barking dogs. In one house, right as we readied ourselves to dive, the lights went out and only the TV glow shone from a window.

When we came to the last pool, we'd decided that we'd all line up at the diving board for our finale. As each one went off, he'd do a goofy dive or jump, making as big a splash and noise as possible, then leap out. I would go first; Freddy said he'd go last. There were five of us plus Katey.

All of the first four pools went off smoothly. Our unit functioned efficiently; everyone followed commando orders. Katey just stood around and watched. She didn't pull a black Lab move and leap in the pool nor did she start barking. Then, during the last dip at the fifth pool, while Freddy was in midair, all the lights in the last three yards we'd just attacked blasted on. A man in his pajamas came sprinting to the edge of the pool, yelling something. He seemed quite agitated. Maybe he seemed more than quite agitated; it was hard to tell with the kind of people who lived around there.

Freddy, a good athlete and swimmer, changed direction in midair and in one smooth, slick motion hit the water and came out on the opposite side from the barefoot man in the pajamas. We all hit the safety of the woods directly behind us, but our clothes were in the other direction. The man hit Freddy like it was tackle football without pads. Had they already called their private police? The private police in Greenwich surely wouldn't be able to move too fast, and anyway, the man never did get a grip on Freddy's slippery, naked body. The man landed on the ground and Freddy lit out for the dark woods with the rest of us.

Our clothes would never be retrieved; they were donated to the Greenwich Police Department. We all had to slide our way to our homes in the shadows of maple trees and stone walls. One time we spooked a cat in the shadows. Fortunately, we Jenkins brothers could climb into our bedroom window. We were skilled at explaining various situations to our parents when we came home, but we'd never came home naked before. They left me outside with Katey and threw my clothes out the window to me. I walked in as though it had been an ordinary night.

Katey braved her first adventure weekend with me, and everybody loved her. She was so well-mannered and calm. Sunday night she slept in my sisters' room on Winky's bed, although Betsy and Abbi tried hard to coax her into their bunk bed. That was the first time we'd ever had a dog of any kind in our apartment and we'd lived there at least fourteen or fifteen years.

The hours had turned to months since Katey had come to live in the basement of Dr. Cornell's Veterinary Hospital. Her mange, which I'd since learned was caused by parasitic mites, had been completely healed and she had gained about fifteen pounds. She was beautiful. One afternoon right before I left work, one of Dr. Cornell's assistants came down to the basement. Katey lay at my feet as I mixed the buckets filled with food.

"Peter, what are you going to do with Katey? She can't live here forever, you know."

"How did you know about her?" I thought my basement area was a secret cavern, and what went on down
there was unknown to anyone.

"Oh, we all know. We know how much she means to
you, but she's going to have to live somewhere else."

I knew that was it for Katey and me. I had about $3,000
in the bank, which I had saved for college. I wished I
could buy my folks a house. Then Katey'd have a place
to live. Surely they wouldn't now put her to sleep. How
long had they known about her? Did they know how she
got here or did they think I had just brought a stray in
the back door?

"Well, I can't keep her; they don't allow it in our
apartments," I said.

"I have an idea for her," she said. Her white lab coat
was very clean this day. "My husband and I just got a
divorce and my daughter and I need company. We have
a small house out in Danbury. What would you think if
I took Katey home?"

I knew that she would give Katey a real home and that
she'd be loved as long as she lived and there'd never be
any way she'd be abused. I knew Katey would be excellent for them, too. I had known this day was coming,
sometime. I'd just not wanted to think about it. The next
afternoon when I got to work, Katey was gone. The basement of Dr. Cornell's animal hospital was never the
same.

4
Bad Baby

Before I was twelve, I was crazy about fish, and I had a couple of fish tanks, populated first with guppies. I loved it when they had whole bunches of babies. Then, as my income from my paper route and snow shoveling increased, I bought nicer fish: neons, tetras, black mollies, zebra fish, angelfish, catfish. They required a lot more work, were more sensitive to temperature fluctuations in their water, and needed cleaner water since they weren't crazy about big bunches of algae. I had a lot of money invested in that tank for a kid, considering the fish, the plants, the special water filters, the water heater, the Plexiglas top so they wouldn't jump out.

Whenever I could I'd go to the pet shop on lower Greenwich Avenue, across from the movie theater, and see what new kinds of fish they'd got in. One day they had a new kind of fish in stock, called an African sunfish. It was quite a large fish for a twenty gallon fish tank but I didn't think it would bother anyone else, because it sat almost motionless in the tank with the other African sunfish.

My brother Freddy named him Baby. He was beautifully colored in almost-fluorescent shades of orange, turquoise, and purple. I placed him in the tank, still in the

29

water-filled plastic bag I had carried him home in, so that
the water inside the bag could adjust to the tank's temperature. As soon as Baby saw some of the other fish in
the tank, his aura changed from calm, "just let the current carry me," to alert, bordering on frenzied. I guessed
he was just excited to be with fish of other species. It
must get boring always swimming with your own kind.

After supper that night, I let Baby out of the plastic
bag that held him captive. He just floated out into the
tank and seemed so serene. Soon thereafter Dad weaved
his way into our room, said prayers with us, "Now I lay
me down to sleep . . ." and turned out the light. Everything was quiet until the next morning when Freddy shook
me.

"Peter, Peter, wake up. Something happened to your
fish." I leaped up.

Baby was there, but about half my other fish were not.
The biggest angelfish was there, the black mollies, too,
one zebra fish out of six was hiding behind the water
heater, the old ugly catfish was doing his usual patrol of
the bottom of the tank, and that was all. No, there were
two neons, small, thin fish with a green stripe and red
stripe down the side, hovering inside some of my most
luxurious water plants. There were eight or nine fish
missing. Baby seemed at peace.

I had no time to wonder; I had to get dressed for school
and we only had one bathroom for all eight of us, so I
had to get my place in line. When I got home that afternoon from school and my two paper routes, I went immediately past Mother into my room. The only things I
could see in the tank were Baby and the catfish. Something had uprooted half of the plants I'd worked so hard
to get growing. There was a top on the tank so I knew
that none of the fish could have jumped out and landed
behind the steam-supplied room heater.

Something had eaten them all and it had to be that
mini-barracuda, Baby. I was so mad I wanted to flush

that killer down the toilet; maybe one of the alligators down there would eat it. How about Mother's blender? No, that would stink.

Nope, I'd just leave him in there, and punish him by turning off the heater and filter and light. I did that, but not before he ate the catfish, with its knife-sharp bone spurs on its back. I figured Baby would just have to starve. He didn't.

The algae got so deep-green and abundant that after a while you couldn't see through the tank from one side to the other. How could Baby be living so long? All the plants were uprooted and seemingly eaten now. All those fish he'd eaten, all that protein had to have run its course. What was Baby, that killing machine, living on? Nothing could kill him, but he could kill everything, even a small, spiny-backed catfish.

So I decided one day what would become of bad Baby. I would transfer him to a plastic bag filled with water. Even with a net it took me awhile to catch him, since all I could see was an occasional ripple on top of the by now totally green water. When I ran the net through the water, it would clog up with algae, not Baby. I scooped and scooped, dumping the algae out our window, where we often bombed the skunk family. A couple of times the fish tried to jump out of his hideaway with the form of a hooked tarpon.

Finally I corralled him in a corner of the tank and kept the net pressed tight against the glass and brought him out of the once delightful, clean-smelling, sparkling water. I transferred him to the bag and went out the door toward Baby's new home. I climbed the chain-link fence into Millbrook, the private subdivision, walked through some woods, behind some houses, down to the lake. The lake where the big, freshwater eels lurked and the snapping turtles, some bigger than a hubcap, crushed frogs like jelly beans. The lake where largemouth bass, some of them lunkers, ruled and swam much faster than Baby.

Where mean water snakes swallowed anything alive near them. Where sunfish as big as a grown-up's hand were constantly hungry. I opened Baby's bag, and he plopped in. Almost everything that lived in this lake could and would be trying to eat poor Baby. Bye-bye, Baby.

5

The Summer
Before Woodstock

It was the summer before Woodstock. And although Craig and I obviously had no idea what Woodstock would be, we were getting ready for it just the same by having our own training period.

I'm not sure why, exactly, but until this summer (the summer before my senior year in high school), I'd not really partied the way most of my good friends had. It might have been because I was the oldest of the six Jenkins kids and was told that everything I did would set the example for all my brothers and sisters who followed. If I got good grades and aimed for college, so would they. If I did a lot of partying, abused my system, I'd turn into a blob and waste, and so would they.

Maybe it had something to do with going out for the wrestling team, the track team, and soccer. I used to say that I didn't want to hurt my body, or use anything to pollute it. It was all this, certainly. Besides, my father always said that a Jenkins could out-party and out-dance anyone without drink or drugs. I certainly seemed to be proving him right.

Craig McAllister, one of my very best friends, lived in back Greenwich, where the kids lived whose fathers were presidents of something. When Craig came home

from his prep school on vacations we were inseparable.
His nickname was "Crazy." He deserved it. Across his
expansive backyard, over the swimming pool, and down
a narrow trail through the woods was Cornelia Drive,
where "Bobo" lived. Bobo, alias Bob Elsaesser, lived
in a rock home once so large it had to be partially dismantled before the original builders could sell it. It had
a slate roof, rhododendron thickets, a circular drive, for-
mal gardens, and servants' quarters over the garage.

That summer of '68, Bobo and I had decided we'd
make some megabucks cutting people's yards, cleaning
out their garages, washing their station wagons. We put
an ad in the *Greenwich Times*, said we liked to work,
said we'd cut the lawn cheap if they supplied the mower
and gas. I gave the phone number at our place. Our phone
rang constantly.

We made a lot the first month or so, got some not-too-
demanding clients, and went at it hard. We'd take our
shirts off and push those old mowers till we sweated our
hair together. Those yards in back Greenwich are big;
they seemed as large as small states. I'd never cut a yard
before, and had always wanted to. One of my biggest
thrills as a kid was watering my grandfather's plants with
his hose. There was nothing like that to be done at WPC.

On one of those summer nights when you could lie
down in the grass and not move, just gaze, almost hal-
lucinate, into the psychedelic stars and black sky, Crazy
and I decided to hitchhike to Nantucket for a weekend.
Nantucket and Martha's Vineyard are islands off Massachusetts that were old whaling communities. We'd
hitchhike up there, see what we could see, and get into
whatever there was to get into. We'd scout out for babes.
We wanted salt air, hot summer winds, ocean, sand, and
to be on the road, out of our boring hometown.

We packed stuff for the weekend in one small day pack.
In those days everybody could hitchhike. It seemed that
there were hitchhikers on every corner at every stop sign

and at every exit on the interstate. It was great, except
that it was very competitive out there on the roads. Craig
and I thought we had golden thumbs. A lot of it was our
technique.

When we could not get a ride, we would get down on
our hands and knees and pray to the drivers. That often
made them stop, but when it didn't, Crazy would sometimes fall over on the pavement like he'd just collapsed
from heat stroke. That worked a couple of times.

It was a happy New England summer day. Everyone
seemed in a good mood, even the Greenwich cop who
stopped and asked us where were we going and did our
parents know. We told him where we were going and
yes, our folks knew. He said, "Well, you boys have fun,
don't do anything I wouldn't do." He winked at us when
he left.

We got a ride within fifteen minutes, all the way past
Norwalk. The people let us out of their car and we sta-
tioned ourselves on an entrance ramp to I-95. The grass
had been cut a few days before and it was browning
slightly. The wind was dry, I remember distinctly.

Crazy was talking his usual 100 mph, being cynical
about something, talking about their Irish maid, Mary, a
taciturn woman. Craig loved to drive Mary home to her
tiny apartment downtown in his mother's white Mercedes. He'd go 85, 90 mph on narrow roads just to try
to get Mary to say something to him. Crazy was border-
line sadistic.

On our left, off in the short grass, I saw something
move. It could have been a paper bag blowing in the
breeze. Craig kept on talking. I kept trying to figure what
was over there. It seemed to be a bird—too large to be a
robin and too small and brown to be a crow. Wouldn't it
be great if that were a red-tailed hawk landing on a rabbit
or mouse! Hawks, falcons, eagles, all birds of prey, were
a passion of mine. I would have given anything in fifth
or sixth grade if I could have been transported back to

medieval times so that I could be falconer to a castle owner in the English countryside. To have had a stable of hunting birds: goshawks, Cooper's hawks, peregrine falcons, an eagle or two, maybe even a gyrfalcon.

Each bird in my stable would be used in a particular hunting locale. The goshawk hunted the woods, the woods filled with dark-gray shadows and smells of pine needles. Goshawks had short wings for fast bursts of speed and long tails for quick turns and fast, sharply taken angles. The Cooper's hawk was a smaller version of the goshawk and was used for smaller animals, smaller birds.

The peregrine falcon was used out under the open sky, over weaving land covered with wild grasses and marshes, where there were few trees. The peregrine, with the black head and slate-gray feathers, was the speed burner of the birds of prey. It could take out any bird on the wing: fast-flying pigeons; sprinting, spinning, dropping wood ducks; just about anything with feathers. They assaulted the air, used the sky like a giant roller coaster. They dove from above, sometimes at speeds of 200 mph, and knocked their prey out of the sky. I was nuts for birds of prey and for all those years since I'd first learned of them I'd craved one. I read everything I could find on them. It was a bizarre interest for a kid, but I was addicted. I'd drive my folks nuts on vacation trips when I saw one flying, soaring, or perched on a fence post. I'd come unglued, practically jumping out the window of our moving car.

Near Craig and me was a bird of some kind. It was not a starling. It bobbed its head, getting a better look at us. It was about the size of a quail but had a longer, more sleek body. The bobbing of the head to get a better look, to focus more clearly, could it be a sparrow hawk?! Yes. It must be sitting on a mouse. It seemed to be on some kind of small gray lump. It was a sparrow hawk, the smallest member of the falcon family.

I pointed over at it. Craig was quiet.

I began to walk over toward it, as if I'd been imagining this moment for years. Then I began to run. It all happened fast, but the hawk didn't fly off as I'd expected. Maybe it did not want to give up its mouse. I was closing fast, within fifteen feet, when it jumped off the ground, setting its long pointed wings at the right angle for the wind to lift it up into the strong blowing air and up into the sky. Then it would scold me and maybe even dive at me to keep me away from its mouse. But when it lifted up, either the wind was too strong or it had not realized there was a fence near the boundary of the right-of-way. The wind gusted, and the sparrow hawk hit the fence and was momentarily stunned. Actually, it seemed knocked out or dead.

Craig was by now running next to me. At the fence of woven wire lay the small brown falcon. From my years of study I immediately knew it was a female for the males are more vividly colored. She was not dead! Her dark-brown eyes opened and began to blink. Her yellow foot, with sharp, black talons, began to clench and open. She was only dazed. Unbelievable.

I picked her up and held her lightly. It's bad to put human fingers on any bird's body, since the oil on a human's skin messes up the water-shedding oils of their feathers.

"What do we do now, Craig?" I wanted to turn around immediately and head home. "How can we hitchhike with a stunned falcon?"

"What do you want to do, live here on the side of I-95, in Norwalk? I vote for us just heading on to Nantucket," said Craig. "You can hide the hawk in your pants; there's plenty of room." Typical Crazy reaction. I was never sure the guy was serious, no matter what we talked about.

"All right, so let's say we do go on to Nantucket. Let's say someone does stop, with the falcon stuffed down my pants. What happens when she comes back to life

and wants to fly around inside the people's car? What do
we do then, when it freaks the driver out and we crash
into a bridge? I'd rather live in Norwalk.'' By now the
falcon was much more alert, had both eyes open, and
was bobbing her head around, trying to figure out what
kind of monster was holding on to her with both hands.

"If the hawk starts flying around in the car, I'll jump
in the front seat and start driving. A hawk attack couldn't
be any worse than a Petey attack.'' (Petey was Craig's
mother's mean blue parakeet. Craig blamed Petey's
meanness on the maid, Mary.)

I wrapped the falcon in an old gray sweatshirt, un-
zipped the day pack, laid it on its side, and slipped her
into it. Only her head stuck out, as I zipped it up around
her. My outstretched hands rested loosely below her and
above her.

Our golden thumbs were rereleased, and in a few minutes we had a ride. It was a couple of college guys. We
got in the backseat. I didn't say anything; they didn't say
much. They were headed toward the Connecticut–Rhode
Island border, since they worked at a big old hotel in
Watch Hill. We didn't even show them the falcon till
just as we were getting out. They were mildly interested
until they realized she was real.

Our next ride took us right to where we were going,
to Woods Hole, Massachusetts, where we would catch
the ferry to Nantucket. Instead of making people nervous, the falcon made them curious and intrigued. Craig
wondered if she would have the same influence on any
young women we might meet. Craig was always hunting.

The falcon would love the cold ocean winds that blew
in from the Muskeget Channel, although unfortunately
we'd missed the last ferry. We were all three stranded in
Woods Hole for the night. Of course, we could not afford
a motel room; in fact, for some reason we had not brought
much money with us, only about twenty-five dollars. We
hadn't even tried to feed the falcon yet. What would she

eat? We slept in the back of an open post-office truck. The falcon slept in my shoe.

I remembered something I'd read, that if you were training a hawk or falcon, one of the best foods, and the cheapest, was chicken livers and chicken gizzards. So we went to the local grocery. They had no chicken livers or gizzards. When the owner of the neighborhood market, Mr. Kennedy, saw me holding her, he became very inquisitive and gave us some pretty expensive fresh beef liver. We, of course, didn't have a knife, so Mr. Kennedy loaned us one from his meat department. We sat out on the grass by the parking lot, took the falcon out, held on to her, and fed her beef liver. She ate quickly from my hand, or really my finger. I hoped she wouldn't bite down too far and eat part of my index finger. Mr. Kennedy sat with us and watched. Craig played real dumb, faked a foreign accent, his Hungarian one, and asked Mr. Kennedy if he was one of *the* Kennedys, and if so, why he didn't live in Washington in a mansion. Mr. Kennedy ignored Crazy.

Being that beef liver is a real limber meat, we couldn't put the leftovers in our pockets, so we just fed her as much as she'd eat and left the rest with Mr. Kennedy. Mr. Kennedy, no relation to the rich Democrats up the road in Hyannis Port, took out the Polaroid he usually used to take pictures of Pepsi and potato-chip displays, and took a picture of Crazy, me, and the falcon in front of his store. I had by now put some hemp-type string around her legs so that she could be free of the day pack. Falconers usually use leather strips for this and put one on each leg but we had no leather and since she was amazingly calm so far, she wouldn't do herself any harm. She did not like being zipped in that day pack at all. Was she brain-damaged or still stunned? How could she be acting so calmly, adjusting so readily to me feeding her, not fighting the string tether she was on? We decided she must still be stunned. Craig said it wasn't that, it was that I had a hypnotic effect on females of any species.

It didn't take us long to realize that with our falcon we could get a lot of attention. On the ferry ride to Nantucket, all the seagulls tried to attack the falcon by dive-bombing it. Just about everyone wanted to see her, talk about her, tell us how much they loved birds of prey.

"It's *soooo* cute," a tourist said. "Is it some kind of parrot?"

Oh no, a perfect line for Craig to operate from!

"Yep. That's right," Craig said. "It's the rage in Brazil, you know. It's a rare Amazonian, brown, feathered, ah . . . [pause to think up some original line of jive] monkey-eating parrot. That's right. It eats baby monkeys. Of course, in this country you can't feed it baby monkeys, that's too expensive. Little kittens will do."

"Oh, come now, young man. Surely you would not feed that little thing kittens. My God, that's horrible." The tourist's face contorted.

"Well, kittens are pretty hard to find, usually. A lot of times we just let it hunt for itself around our neighborhood." The lady got up from her wooden bench on the ferry and walked away. Before she got out of hearing range, Craig laughed hysterically to be sure she'd hear him. She looked disgusted, a reaction Crazy was an expert at getting. It was out-of-control laughing, another reaction Craig got from me all the time.

Nantucket was absolutely wonderful that weekend. The island must have been a terrific place for all those Yankee whalers to live when they weren't out roaming the oceans. Our jeans and sneakers, socks, all that we had was peppered with sand, as we'd slept on the beach both nights. We stayed one extra day and left Monday morning. The regal little falcon seemed to love the beach as much as everyone else. I don't know exactly why, whether we glowed with sun-drenched health or what, but we got home hitching almost as fast as we would have if we'd had a car, except we didn't have to pay any tolls.

Craig and I parted ways at the I-95 Bruce Park exit. He went north toward back Greenwich. I went south, through the park and home. I ended up walking most of the few miles home; it was always hard getting a ride through there. But it did give me extra time to think about how I was going to get the falcon inside our apartment. I hadn't really thought much about it over the weekend.

I could just go in the front and only door and greet everybody, show them the falcon, and go straight to my room. I could go in the front door, hide her inside the day pack, and hope she didn't squawk or scream or chirp, all sounds she made for different reasons. If someone asked what the sound was, I could say it was just one of the neighbor kids running across our communal porch screaming. Or I could climb over the fence that enclosed the front yard of the apartments, and climb in our window. We left the screen off for easy access, in case we wanted to throw something at the skunks that rummaged for food at night outside our windows. We would try to get the skunk to go around the corner of our building, and then throw things at it so it would spray right under the bedroom window of the Lerners, an old, cranky couple who lived next to us. The people on either side of our apartment, the Lerners and Adlers, were old, retired couples, poor things. Living on either side of the eight Jenkinses was not the way to spend your golden years if you yearned for peace and quiet.

I decided after much deliberation to climb in the window. Mother had had about all she could take with the parakeets, baby robins that fell out of their nests, snapping turtles I brought home and a couple of times threw into bathtubs occupied by my brothers. Salamanders, snakes, fish, mice and more mice, white ones, spotted ones, black ones. In fact, more than once whole tankfuls of mice would get out and escape into our room, where

they could conceivably hide for years. No wonder Mother
didn't love coming into our room. She cleaned our sisters' room a lot more.

Now, inside our room with the falcon, I surveyed the
already crammed quarters. The north end of the room
was taken up with Scott and Freddy's bunk bed, and a
dresser. The dresser was near the window. My bed was
across from the bunk bed and the room was narrow
enough that there was not a lot of extra room to walk
between the beds. There was a desk at the end of my bed
but it was crammed up to the foot of it so that it could
not really be used. It collected three brothers' junk. The
dresser was shared by all of us; we each had one drawer.
It was in the southwest corner of the room, where my
now empty fish tank sat. Absolutely the only place for
the little falcon was right in front of the dresser.

I got a wooden chair, pulled out one of the top drawers
full of junk, and emptied it. I laid the drawer on top of
the chair. I got an old stickball bat and laid it on top of
the drawer to serve as the falcon's perch. Whenever one
of us had to get clothes out of the dresser, the perch
would have to be removed. It was a pain but there was
no other place she could go.

I would immediately have to get some narrow leather
strips, about a third of an inch wide, in order to make
bands, like little belts, that would go around each leg.
Then the bands would be connected to a leather leash
that would be tied to the perch. I certainly hoped the
falcon would be as calm and self-controlled as she had
been so far. I was still not convinced that the falcon had
fully recovered from her crash into the wire fence. It
would be bad if she sunk her talons into Scott's hand as
he reached for his morning underwear.

What really concerned me most was Mother's reaction
when she found that a bird of prey was living in one of
the bedrooms. I could only imagine the scream-scene if
the falcon got loose and flew into my mother's blond hair

when she walked in to tell us it was time to get up for school. Mother stayed out of our room most of the time, but what if an escaped black-and-white mouse ran across my covers as she reached down to shake me awake and the falcon swooped down from the curtain rod and caught it in her talons!

At some point Mother would have to be told about the falcon, but not right now. First I'd have to spring it on my brothers. They came in about an hour later, first Scott, then Freddy. They plopped down on their bunks. Neither of them noticed. There was a lot to look at in our room, where the word "minimalist" could never be used. Nor did they notice until little four-year-old Abbi, our brown-haired, pug-nosed little sister, came in and said, "Look, look, a birdy." The brothers Jenkins thought the hawk was cool. Neither one of them was as into animals as I was and they didn't focus very long on the small falcon. They were hungry.

6
The Falconer

It was time for the training of the falcon to begin. I had the leather thongs around each leg attached to a leather leash. She really was settling down. Now, all the knowledge from all the books I'd read about Arabian falconers and medieval falconers and how they trained their birds was needed. I could not remember much, although I did recall how one began to get these naturally wary birds of prey to "come to the fist."

First, the larger the bird of prey, the thicker the leather glove one needs. Large, mature golden eagles can crush a hand and sink their talons through flesh from one side of the hand to the other, so a very thick leather glove is required. Also, it needs to be long, in case the bird begins moving up your arm. How do you tell an eagle to stop? The red-tailed hawk, a broad-winged *Buteo* with a wide copper-colored tail, has very powerful talons and its feet are about half the size of a golden eagle's. They are much more common, found almost everywhere in the United States. The glove need not be as substantial for them. My falcon, called a kestrel, or sparrow hawk, really didn't require a glove, but I just had to have one, anyway.

All hawks and falcons have different personalities, both

as species and individually. Some take to humans and training more easily than others, and to get one to come to the fist can be either extremely difficult or relatively easy. Also, of course, the age of the bird makes a great deal of difference. The longer the bird has been on its own, the more difficult the adjustment to captivity. Early falconers liked to find nests and take young birds right before they were ready to leave on their own.

The first step in teaching a falcon to come to you is to get it hungry. Then you must put a piece of raw meat, chicken liver or chicken gizzard, on your fist, which is rounded yet not clenched. Very gently then, ease your hand close to the hawk or falcon, let it focus in on the meat, and move the meat as close to the bird as possible. The idea is to get it to stretch its neck out and lean forward to get a piece of the meat in its sharp, curved beak. Its beak can easily tear up any animal it can catch.

I did this for about two weeks. Some days the falcon would refuse even to reach for anything, no matter how long I tempted her, no matter how patient I was. I would end up just laying it on the ground and moving back, and she would pounce on it, sink her talons deep, and eat by tearing small pieces off. By now I had built a perch for her, which was a short and round piece of wooden pole, about four inches wide, with a piece of iron rod stuck in the end. I could put the end of her "leash" around the iron rod and stick it in the ground. I'd leave her perched out there all day long, as long as it wasn't raining.

The first week, she reached over and got her meat twice, the first time on the second day, and again on the seventh day. The second week she did it about half the time. The third week into her training, she began to act interested in me and what I had. She would bob her head in concentration, and a few times she flapped her wings, fanned her wings, almost like a hummingbird's wings in slow motion, as if she were thinking about flying to me, or to the meat. She preferred the chicken gizzards, which was a good thing since they were cheaper.

At the end of the fourth week, she actually hopped to my fist from a few feet away. I got so excited I wanted to start flying myself. I was doing it, I was training my first bird of prey! I could begin to visualize the magnificence of a carefully trained falcon hunting grouse on the Scottish moors, or a desert falcon in pursuit of a long-legged, tawny-colored jackrabbit, the twists of the fleeing rabbit, the brilliant turns of the falcon, the speed cranked up by one trying to keep life, the other trying to take it.

I'd seen these little rulers of the sky in the wild, perched on telephone wires, flying down and scooping up mice. They could also hover like a helicopter over a pasture, then zap, dive on their prey. They were such spectacular flyers. To watch them hugging the wavy ground, chasing after a small bird, was a view of absolute grace and effortlessness.

The fifth week the hawk began jumping to my fist. First the jump required no wing movements; then later in the week she actually flew to my fist. When she began coming to me the full length of her tether, I got a longer one, maybe eight, ten feet long. She flew that distance without hesitation. It may have been only ten feet, but it was like a mile to me. A bird of prey is not like a dog you can pat or hug. It is not like a horse, who has a powerful neck that a pleased rider can pat with energy and excitement to praise a good jump or a long gallop. Hawks don't purr like cats or talk like parakeets. But there was no less a feeling of deep affection and appreciation for the falcon. I just couldn't show it in the usual way. Of course, the way I could really have shown my appreciation would have been to let her go back to the free sky again. The dog and cat and horse could not, really, be freed. The falcon could. But I just couldn't. Not right then, if ever.

On dry sunny days, I would fill a plastic spray bottle with warm water and go out and fill the air over her with a fine mist. The small beads of water would settle on her elegant brown feathers until there were too many, then she'd shake and ruffle all her feathers, puffing up to twice her size. Gradually, after she fluffed up, her feathers would settle back down and she'd look normal again except that she'd just shine in the sun.

My friend Crazy figured that the falcon was at least part his and he should have visitation rights. So every so often during the summer the falcon and I would go up to back Greenwich, to Cedarwood Lane, where there were two stone mansions and the McAllisters' place, which was a custom-built home, circa the 1950s.

It was hard to believe that Cedarwood Lane and WPC were in the same town, they were so different. Mrs. McAllister's home was as clean and neat as a hospital, perhaps even neater, considering there was little human traffic at the McAllisters'. And if there was human traffic, it was not to be humans like me from the wrong side of the tracks.

My clothes did not come from Brooks Brothers, Van Drivers, or Outdoor Traders, and if they did they were bought at the Thrift Shop, a secondhand store run by the Hospital Auxiliary. My father and I joke now that a lot of the kids in Greenwich today would rather wear nothing but what comes from the Thrift Shop, but that is now.

I would definitely not be attending an Ivy League university, like Princeton, Yale, Columbia, Harvard, Brown. My grades, SATs, and bank account could not handle it. My grandfather went to Columbia and my grandmother went to Barnard and my cousin was a brain surgeon, Dad kept telling us, but it didn't help me any. "You must go to college," he started to tell us from the time we knew what it meant. It was true that Craig's folks and Bob's folks were first generation rich, and my family was first

generation poor. Maybe that mix had something to do
with our ability to get along.

So, Craig often had to kind of sneak me into his house,
really into his room mostly, which was originally the
servants' quarters over the two-car garage. Crazy could
never be confused with a servant; I never saw him do
one minute's work in or around his house, unless we had
trashed the place when his folks were away and had to
clean it up before they got home.

If I had to be eased into Craig's house, the falcon definitely did. It was a wild animal! Craig had his *own* room,
which seemed fantastic to me, and there was a couch in
it. I thought the only place one could afford to have a
couch was in the living room. He also had his own TV,
a stereo, some weights for us to lift, and a bunch of
posters.

The first time the falcon and I spent the night at the
McAllisters', there was no place to put the wild bird so
he spent the night in one of Craig's closets, where his
father stored his suits out of season. The suits were dark
and the falcon excreted stuff that was chalk white and ran
down smooth fabric. It was horrible. Later, Crazy had to
pay the cleaning bill, deducted from his allowance.

I'd forgotten to bring the hawk any food, so we had to
feed her some of Mr. McAllister's high-priced, thinly
sliced ham. We even sliced off a chunk of filet mignon
that Mrs. McAllister had under Saran Wrap in the refrig-
erator to eat that night. The falcon never flew into the
main part of the house but she did get a headache later
that night when she flew out of the closet and into Craig's
mirror on his dresser. That Saturday, while the Mc-
Allisters golfed and we swam in the pool, the falcon was
attacked by a swarm of bluejays. She had to get on her
back and bare her talons to fight off the jays. Jays hate
hawks, falcons, and owls.

Mrs. McAllister never invited the falcon back into her
home. That's not to say Craig didn't sneak her in; he

was adept at that. When I got her back home again in the secure, tight confines of our room, she had regressed somewhat. It took her a few days to settle in and get back to her former level of training.

The mornings were when we made the most progress. Maybe it was because she was the hungriest then. Usually she came flying to me with little hesitation. First she would see me, instantly; then she'd focus on my hand and the meat. Then I'd kneel on one knee and the hungry predator would flap to her food. I'd let her eat half a liver, then I'd take her back to her perch and move back a bit farther. She'd come to me and eat a couple more bites. I'd tied another length to her tether, and now it was about fifteen feet long. The only problem was that the thin leather leash was getting heavy; it would weigh down her beautiful flight. I decided that it was time to take the tether off, let her fly free to me. We would do it tomorrow.

The moment was here for the incredible bird to fly unattached. She would either fly away or fly to me. I unsnapped the tether, which was attached by a little metal swivel used for fishing line. I had the meat in my pocket so she'd wait to take off. She bobbed her head incessantly, staring a hole through me as I stepped off about twenty-five feet. Reaching into my pocket and grasping the meat, I slowly brought it up from my side and held it out to her in plain view. She had such excellent eyesight she could see a small grasshopper from the top of a telephone pole. No matter what I did I wanted to be sure not to move too erratically. And oh, how I wished for no interruptions. No "friends" screaming out their windows to me or at me. No old junker car backfiring. No motorcycle gang drive-through. No fights from the couple upstairs. That's why I was doing this early in the morning, when the air still smelled damp and felt a bit like night.

She jumped off her perch and began flying. It took her

a mini-moment to realize that something was different, that the weight of the leather leash was gone. Coming fast, completely under control, she focused on the meat and was at it in a few instants. Her landing on my hand was done with an ease and precision that was wildly exciting to me. The meat was eaten quickly, with gusto, as she relaxed, with her sharp talons gripping tightly, one to the glove, one to the meat. After she ate, I took her back and placed her down on her perch. Should I try it again? I wondered. It was one of those mornings that made you feel confident.

I walked slowly backward, this time maybe forty feet away, and stopped by the hemlock tree outside our kitchen window. Mother was up and gave me that look: "Son, what are you doing now?" She knew something was odd, for me to be up this early. My eyes glanced up at her for a split second and when I looked back, the hungry falcon had already left her perch. She was almost to me when a renegade bluejay dove into our little world, dive-bombing the falcon. She ejected from her straight-line path toward my glove and went up like a jet fighter toward the treetop. Was she gone for good? Would she take on the bluejay? Soon there would be other bluejays, since they loved trouble and flocked to it, those damn pests. The falcon landed in the top of the hemlock tree. There were now two jays, then there were three. I didn't know what to do. I wanted to throw rocks at them, but the falcon was still there and the bluejays were flying, bolting, darting, screeching, diving at her. I might hit her with a rock, not them. Then she'd be gone for sure.

Maybe waving my arms would scare the stupid blue-jays. It didn't at first; but then it did. They inexplicably flew off. Now how would I get her out of that tree? I stood under her with the biggest piece of meat I could find plopped onto my leather glove. She wouldn't budge, although she was definitely focusing on me. For twenty long torturous minutes I stood under her, calling, moving my meat-covered fist to get her to come down. She wouldn't.

So I decided to climb the tree. The branches were not huge, but hemlock branches are strong and bend a lot before they break. As I climbed close to the top of the tree, the trunk got too small for me—I was holding on with one arm. The tree started bending and swaying.

When my outstretched left hand got within two or three feet of her, she almost immediately hopped down one wobbly branch, then bounced onto another to my fist. Her talons gripped into the leather of my glove and as I descended with some speed, her long wings extended and flapped slightly to help her retain her balance.

On the green grass of the ground, I held her on my relaxed right fist and thought about almost losing her. She seemed to have actually grown a bit since I'd caught her on the side of I-95. Maybe she was not fully mature then. Now, a bit over twelve inches long, her undersides were the most diluted shade of rust, intermingled with white. If there were a thousand feathers on her chest, about seventy-five of them were black-tipped, which made a beautiful counterpoint to the creamy colors of her chest. The color on top of her wings and body was a bright cinnamon, the skin on her feet slicker yellow and her talons black.

Although the kestrel is a true falcon, when English settlers came to this country, they named it a sparrow hawk because it resembled the sparrow hawk in Britain. When falconry was high fashion in Great Britain, a person could tell the status of someone by what species of bird was on his fist. The priest had the sparrow hawk and the servant had a kestrel. This bird I was now training, who lived in my room, was actually a kestrel.

I was perplexed about what to do with her now. Should I put her back on her perch and leave her there for a few days or let her fly to me again? If she did fly again right away she might think about going back, high into the top of that tree. Or she might just take off and keep on flying, not even stopping in any trees till she was out of my sight. I realized that the reason I wanted her was not because I wished to own her, control her. It was because I respected her so, I wanted to be with her. I could not get enough of her, watching her fly and land and preen. I had waited so long to be this close to a bird of prey. Just seeing one on a fence post or soaring far above or darting into a small opening between some branches in the forest was not enough.

Instead of risking losing her now, I decided to connect her again to her perch, climb back inside our room, get my stuff ready, and hitchhike up to Misquamacut, Rhode Island. Mom and Dad and the other Jenkins kids had already left for our summer vacation. I'd had to stay behind because of some crucial lawn jobs Bob and I had to get done. One lady's daughter was getting married, and the father of the bride, her husband, had just two months ago left her. There was little money and no one to cut the lawn. She actually broke down crying in front of me in her garage, almost begging me to help her. Dad said it would be OK to help her. He wanted me to take the train, though. I doubted the falcon would make it on a passenger train.

Hitchhiking with the falcon, now that she was much livelier, might get a bit wild, especially when the potential ride saw her. I got a ride fast with four Jehovah's Witnesses from Brooklyn. They said they printed the *Watchtower* and asked me, before they actually saw the falcon, if I wanted to know God's plan for my life. It was as if they were so consumed by their mission that they could see nothing else, but when the falcon flapped her wings when she felt a breeze from an open window, they noticed. They were going to New London, Connecticut, a city with a big sub base, and between Greenwich and New London we did not talk of God again. We did talk though: They asked, and I answered, questions about the falcon.

After the Witnesses I stood out in the sun at the curved entrance to I-95 for a very long time. Waiting and waiting for a ride, thumb out, was when hitching became bad, made me feel like a beggar. Pleading eyes didn't work. Holding the falcon behind my back didn't work. Scowling at the people who passed me had no effect. Either the local people were not too generous or I was losing my touch or people were seeing the falcon too clearly.

Finally a man stopped. He was driving a new car; the interior was gray. I sat in the front seat. The seats were vinyl. Believe it or not, I think I had somehow house/car-trained this beautiful, regal bird of prey. The man giving the ride seemed friendly—he asked me where I was from, where I was going. He asked why I was hitchhiking. However, he seemed to be merely putting up with the falcon; he asked me nothing about it.

He asked me what kind of music I liked. I told him James Taylor, the Doobie Brothers, Curtis Mayfield, the Rolling Stones. I told him that I liked to secretly listen to black gospel music on the preaching station I got out of New York City. I told him I didn't tell my friends about it though. He said he did know who the Rolling Stones were. He also said he liked secrets, too. He asked me if I had a lot of secrets. That took me off guard a little, but I recovered fast and told him, no, I wasn't the type that was into a lot of secrets. One thing I liked about hitchhiking was that you could have interesting conversations with total strangers.

The man drove with his left hand, had dark hair, and was slim. He pushed the button on his radio and out came a rock-and-roll station. He knew which button to push but he knew nothing about rock, if all he'd heard of was the Rolling Stones. He asked me if I had a girlfriend. I told him yes. He asked me her name. Kimberly, I said.

He wanted to know what she looked like. I said she was about five four, had long blond hair, and she was a ballet dancer, even took dance classes in NYC. He asked if I liked her a lot. I said yes.

He told me that he'd never been married. He appeared to be over forty. He said he loved the ballet. I told him I loved to dance to the music of Sly and the Family Stone. He looked puzzled.

I reached out to turn the radio down a bit and noticed he was scratching his leg with his right hand. It hadn't been but a few weeks ago that I'd turned seventeen. Something was weird. A chill, an uneasy vibration jittered around my body. He kept on scratching his leg. He wasn't really scratching it, he was rubbing it. Slowly. He looked over at me, his chin down, his eyes sleepy, half-open.

He asked me if I'd ever thought about being with a man. I said no. (Actually, if I knew anything in 1968 about what a homosexual was, it wasn't much.) The man kept rubbing his leg. I began to think about what I was going to do, just in case he had any ideas about me other than just giving me a ride. If he tried to touch me and I punched him, we'd get in a wreck. I was much bigger and stronger than he was. If he got off the interstate and acted like he would try to take me onto some back road, then I would hit him, but now, going at least 70 mph, I needed to try something else.

"Don't you think this falcon is beautiful?" I asked the thin man.

"What'd you say?" His voice sounded like I was interrupting him.

"I said, don't you think this falcon is beautiful?" I spoke louder, trying to lower my voice.

"Oh, that. Yeah, I do." His voice was agitated.

"Can you believe that this bird is attack-trained? I have trained it to fly into a person's eyes in case anyone ever tries to hurt me. His claws are long enough and curved enough so that they can actually pull someone's eyeball right out. Can you believe that!'' I asked.

"WHAT did you say?" the man asked, now with both hands on the wheel.

"I said, this falcon has been trained to attack people's eyes and face on command. It is a bit odd, I realize, but falconers used to do it all the time in medieval times [lie]. In fact, they used to use eagles to hunt down and kill escaped servants [lie].'' For effect I dropped my fist about six inches, the one the falcon was on, and she extended her pointed wings all the way out to steady herself. He almost ran off the road.

"Would you like to hear what this falcon did last week to a guy who tried to hurt my younger brother?" I asked, feeling that invincible, untouchable cockiness of being seventeen. Now I was not even slightly worried.

"No, no," the man said. He was so slender he looked like you could bend him into a pretzel. He pulled over immediately, said that he'd missed his exit, and told me and the "attack-trained falcon" to get out of his car. He pulled an instant U-turn by a sign that said NO U-TURN.

I was pretty shook up after that, but I made it to Rhode Island without getting any more strange rides. The whole family was down at the beach when I got there. My brothers were body-surfing and instantly challenged me to get out there and see who could catch the longest ride. We could ride the waves right onto the beach if we caught it right. I never told my folks or anyone except Crazy about that ride. The folks probably would have ordered me to stop hitchhiking.

The falcon enjoyed the beaches and our vacation. Everyone did. The second day we were back home at WPC I decided it was time for her to fly to me again. Keep our good progress going. This time she flew instantly to me from about fifty feet. I stepped back farther and farther past the hemlock tree. The exquisite morning sun made deep-golden halos around everything, even the chain-link fence that hemmed us in. I stepped backward even more, past another hemlock, the biggest one, which was right outside our kitchen window. There was a dead tree trunk up by the fence near a retaining wall. She had probably been born in the hole of a hollow, dead tree colored gray by the aging of weather and sun and ice. It could have been an old woodpecker's hole that served as her birthplace, where her mother would have sat for thirty days on four or five eggs, spotted with many shades of brown.

I kept stepping back, like I was walking off the edge of the earth, past the picture window of our living room, and stopped next to the Adlers' picture window. Their curtains were always perfectly adjusted to the same height, with undisturbed and dusted figurines and plants on the windowsills. The falcon bobbed her head, staring a hole in my fist, seemingly waiting for me to stop and push my fist out toward her. I did.

She did not jump quickly off her perch; she sat there and looked, she focused, she gazed. Then she did it. She leaped into her free flight, flapping easily, only about three feet off the ground, in a straight line right at me. I marveled at her talent, her ability to move like that. She had eyes only for me. She was closing in on the finish of her longest flight when . . .

"Pete, what are you doing?" someone yelled from over on the other side of the fence. It was George Grokowski, "Grigger," "G.J.," the kid who lived on the third floor of our building. He hit the fence on the run, planning to climb over it. His big wide foot made a gigantic metallic noise. Within a tiny part of a second I knew that sound could prove hellish to me.

When the zooming falcon heard Grigger, her flight path lurched and she flew by me, circled back and up and flew over four stories up, high up, into a monstrous sugar-gum tree behind me. I wanted to kill Grigger, that goofy dork. He was always saying something at the worst time or doing lame things, and he'd just really screwed things up. He asked me what was I doing. I wouldn't speak to him. My lips were tightened down and crinkled-mad. I finally told him to get away from me, without saying the horrible things about him I was thinking.

I stood under that straight gum tree, bending my neck backward, looking up at her. It was like looking up Jack's beanstalk and the beanstalk went directly into space. The tree did not have any branches on it for about the first seventy-five feet. There would be no climbing to get her. I thought about how people call the fire department to rescue their cats. She was too high up for a hook and ladder. Moving my fist under her accomplished nothing. She was high above the human ground, far above even the top of the three-story apartment building. Certainly the falcon could see the hills to the north and the other free birds flying into the opening of the green tree canopy.

She no longer even looked at me; she seemed to see only the sky, and feel the warmed streams of wind up as high as she was. She flapped her wings a few times, still holding on to the tree, and then she leaped off the branch. She caught one of those warm, undulating streams of summer air and she flew toward the woods and Millbrook. She headed to Millbrook where the mansions were, where there were a lot of trees and small birds to hunt. Over there was even the occasional piece of open grassland and the long green pieces of golf course she could patrol. The falcon was gone. I would not see her again. But every time I saw a hovering or perched sparrow hawk, I thought of her and wondered about her life. Had she mated yet? Did she have a home tree, babies? Did her experience with me teach her valuable lessons or did it hurt her ability to survive?

7

A Birth Announcement

I had never browsed in the card section of a bookstore before. I was not the type to send cards, never had been, but there had never been an occasion like this before to celebrate. It was March of 1972, two and a half years after Woodstock, and I was nearing the end of my junior year at Alfred University. But college and outrageous memories from our days at Woodstock were lower-level stuff compared to the mighty occasion I was celebrating now.

I found a card with a blue and pink bootee on it. I bought a dozen.

I planned to send one of the birth announcements to my folks in Greenwich. They'd be shocked. They weren't ready for grandchildren yet. There were still three kids at home, and three of us Jenkins kids in college, all on scholarships. Scott, my blond brother, three years younger, was now taller than I and had shoulder-length hair that looked like a lion's mane. He was a freshman here at Alfred now. Scott already knew of this grand occasion so he didn't need a card. I'd send one to red-headed Winky, who was in college in Pennsylvania. Craig would need one. He wouldn't believe that he had not known about the big event till now. Bobo would need an announcement; so would some of my more liberated aunts and uncles.

I wrote out the announcements in Art History class while the professor was lecturing about Paul Gaugin. I wrote the date of birth: March 3, 1972; the weight: 6 lbs. 6 oz. I included, of course, the baby's name and the names of his parents.

Fortunately my father, who has an off-the-wall sense of humor, got the mail that day. My mother, for whom the word *gullible* was an understatement, would have come unglued if she'd opened my little card. Mother could take off and rocket into outer space before even hearing the second sentence of the whole story.

The baby's name was Cooper H. M. Jenkins. I got the name Cooper from Cooper's hawk. The initials H. M. stood for Half Malamute. His parents were Karma and the Dark Black Shadow. Karma was purebred Alaskan Malamute and an exquisite animal; gentle, power-packed, marked regally, and possessed of a fantastic temperament. Cooper's father was listed as the "Dark Black Shadow" because when Karma came into her first heat, her master, Larry Sell, a graduate-student potter, put her in a shed. It was, I was told, a stout, weathered-wood shed. Larry lived far out in the upper New York State countryside on a farm. Some strangely powerful animal came to Karma's shed, tore the wooden door off, and mated her. Little Cooper was made that moonless evening. No one was ever to know who that dark black shadow really was, except there was no doubt he was big, strong, and fertile.

I listed Cooper's length at twelve inches. I also inserted a black-and-white picture taken of him when I'd first picked him out at three weeks old. He was lying in the palms of my hands. He looked like a little seal, Cooper did, and when he moved he lurched along like one, too.

When Cooper finally came home, there would be no

specially painted nursery, though there would be a special corner of the kitchen where he would live. A flat box filled with a soft, tattered towel would be his bed. Coming home in March in upper New York State meant it would still be cold, and the third floor of this old home on 51 North Main was the warmest. I bought a loud ticking windup alarm clock and wrapped it in another old towel, and put it in the box. Someone told me that a ticking clock was like a heartbeat, soothing to a just-weaned puppy homesick for his mama's milk and her warm tummy to curl up next to.

While little puppy Cooper paced back and forth upstairs and cried and howled, I lay on my back in bed downstairs. I so wanted to go to sleep because I was exhausted from the excitement of bringing Cooper home. That little stocky puff of fur had no idea how long I'd wanted him, how I'd yearned to have one like him.

But I couldn't sleep. Long after baby Cooper stopped barking and whining and howling for Karma, I ran movies in my mind. I could see the "story" of White Fang, as I'd seen it when I read the book by Jack London ten years ago. As a fifth grader in Mrs. Kooze's class I'd be transported from the red-brick elementary school in Greenwich to the edge of an Indian village near the Yukon River in the interior of Alaska. Other kids were reading of baseball players, teenage romance, and horses, or writing notes to each other. I was gone in Alaska with "my dogs," thoroughly consumed.

I tried lying on my side, my left arm under the coolness of the pillow. That always worked. My eyes were shut but my brain was on. Nothing would turn it off. I had A DOG!!! A half Alaskan Malamute, A Jack London dog! Cooper's whimpering roused me sometime just past dawn. I stubbed my bare feet three or four times making my way upstairs to feed him some Puppy Chow mixed with warm milk. That done I slept a few more hours, until Cooper began making a lot of noise again. He was a very demanding baby.

Before Cooper and I could have any Jack London wilderness-type adventures, there was much teaching to do. Cooper knew little except how to get milk from his mother, how to walk on those short, stocky legs, and how to see. He had to be carried from Larry's old white farmhouse to my '64 navy-blue Chevy Caprice. Then I put him on the ground for a minute when we got home. When his soft little paws hit the late winter snow he didn't like it at all. He seemed to be trying to pick his four paws up, all at once, to get them out of that damp-cold white stuff. He fell over. I scooped him up quickly.

Once on the third floor, I realized Coops would be up here until he learned to go downstairs. These stairs were particularly narrow, especially going up from the second to the third floor. I hadn't had the little wolf long before I also experienced firsthand how needlelike puppy teeth are. I was sitting at the garage-sale-reject table eating granola and drinking Red Zinger tea. I had James Taylor's album on for the umpteenth time. The song was "You've Got a Friend."

I'd poured an extra bunch of raisins on the granola. Then Cooper bit my bare toes with his puppy teeth. It felt as if fifty pins had sunk into my now-pincushion foot. I grabbed up the innocent little brat and told him as firmly as I could, NO. He tried to gnaw on my hand. I put him down on the floor. He went over and started biting down on the chair leg; he sounded like a beaver. What could I give him before he chewed up everything? I was a panicky, first-time parent. What could he chew on?! Bones were too big, too tough for those puppy teeth. Schoolbooks. No, that excuse wouldn't work here. There was a pair of black Converse high tops, with holes in the soles—he could use those if I hadn't thrown them out yet. Great. They were under the old black chair by the front window next to the KLH stereo. I had one of those adjustable gates to keep kids and puppies in a particular room, so I stepped over it, got the old sneaks, and threw them to him. It was love at first bite. They lasted a couple of weeks.

It was like I was his mother and he would have to learn everything he knew from me. . . . Cooper, you can't bite me. . . . You can't chew on other people either, no matter who you find. Cooper, you can't do *that* on the floor. It was radically discouraged except on newspapers. I used *The New York Times*. One Sunday *New York Times* would last a couple of weeks.

Teaching him to walk downstairs held great potential for bone breakage, more for me than for him. Cooper seemed to be born with a kind of a lunging gait, good for pulling sleds but not for navigating down two flights of stairs.

I'd bend over and ease Coops down one stair and try to get him to settle there for a second to get himself under control. Instead he wanted to leap to the next stair, until quickly he would be out of control like a snowball made of fur. It was obvious he had that "leap now, figure out the consequences later" kind of personality.

One of Cooper's first big adventures was riding in my '64 Chevy. He didn't have sturdy balance yet, so every time I'd go around any type of curve, Cooper would fall over. The "blue boat" drove and rode and rocked like a pioneer's wagon. The front seat was so wide across I could fit four people in it, so Cooper began to lie down on the cool vinyl and rest his head in my lap as we cruised. It wouldn't take him long to fall asleep. Whenever he had a hard time getting to sleep, I'd load him into the Chevy turned cradle and take him for a ride.

When Coops entered his adolescent growth spurt, his paws looked even more oversized than ever. By the time he was four months old his paws were larger than those of some grown dogs. They were coated with golden-tan fur.

His legs looked too long for his slim and narrow body, and now if a passenger was in the front seat when Cooper wanted to lie down, he had to leap into the backseat. There he sprawled out, his backbone resting up against the back support of the seat, his long legs hanging over so far that his paws would just about touch the front seat.

Cooper also began to put his front paws on the dashboard as we drove, to improve his view. Or he'd hang his head and—as he became more confident—his front paws out the passenger window. Once I had to swerve out of the way of a streaking cat at such a sharp angle that if I'd not reached over and grabbed his back legs he would have slid out the window onto the lawn I had to swing into. Reaching for my little growing boy seemed to be pure instinct.

Cooper Half Malamute had strong instincts to hunt. Out back, behind the gravel driveway where the African grad students barbecued their goats, was a small creek. It was here where Cooper first learned to "hunt" and swim.

The Malamute breed was created by an Inuit Indian tribe from Alaska called the Malemutes. The Alaskan Malamute is considered the oldest Arctic sled dog. Many, many, many generations before the Russians "discovered" Alaska it was called "Alakshak" or Alyeska," which meant "vast country." The land is so unfathomably huge and so often frozen that short, two-legged humans cannot travel over it easily. Over many years the Malemute tribe developed a special breed of dogs by choosing the best of the litter, those pups who had the instinct and power to meet the unusual demands of Arctic life. The Malemute needed a powerfully built dog with a deep chest and compact, strong body to pull runnerless sleds full of fresh-killed meat. The dog could not be too short in its back, but not too long to be paired in a team.

To keep the Arctic dog alive when the whiteout blizzards attacked, it had to have two coats of fur: one an undercoat of incredibly warm, impenetrable, wooly fur from one to two inches thick, and the other a guard coat, long enough to protect the undercoat. The guard fur would help to shed snowflakes; it could grow icicles in frigid rains, keeping the underfur dry and warm. The depth of both coats also helped to shield the dog's sensitive skin from tormenting bites of the pervasive mosquitos.

The Malemutes bred an incredible animal. Like the people, the dogs displayed great humor and an indomitable spirit. Never were the Malemute tribes mentioned without their dogs being spoken of too.

An early miner who went to explore Alaska soon after it became a possession of the United States wrote that he found a small band of Malemutes with their dog teams. They were carrying mail from Point Barrow down the wild coast. The explorer described the Malemute as industrious, skilled in hunting and fishing, people who made perfect sleds and had dogs of beauty and endurance. Their dogs, he said, had traveled hundreds of miles and yet were still affectionate and tireless.

Cooper seemed incapable of exhaustion. At night when he curled up he only appeared to be resting, and now that he'd learned to hunt crawfish in the water, he wanted to do nothing else. I'd turn over rocks for him and he'd put his nose underneath, his eyes remaining above the water while he chased down the crusty-shelled crawfish. They looked like tiny lobsters and bit like them. Once Cooper lifted his nose with a pinkfish crawfish clinging to it. Cooper ran in circles, outraged at the turn of events, trying to swat the bites off his tender anatomy. The next time I took Cooper to the creek he approached his prey as warily as a polar bear hunting a seal. He was learning.

I remember the first time Cooper actually killed something. I'd lifted up a rock in the creek for him to see what was underneath. After the water cleared again, we saw two huge old crawfish and Coops started pawing at them. They clawed back with their pincers. Right away the biggest crawfish got hold of Cooper's paw, but he shook it off. A look I'd never seen before came over his face, over his wide smile and confident eyes. It was the look of a killer, the surfacing of an instinct stored in his genes and passed down to him from thousands of Alaskan ancestors. Cooper didn't care how bloodied he got—he was going to hurt that crawfish.

He slapped at it with his big right paw as it tried to get away. He followed it into the creek. He didn't feel the ice-cold water—he seemed to be trying to step *on* it. Then I heard a yelp as Cooper ran out onto the bank. The crawfish had him by one of his toes. It must have hurt a lot because Cooper's yelps were becoming short howls.

Then Cooper bent his head and bit down and crunched that sharp-clawed crawfish to death, all the while emitting a strange noise, a series of passionate yelps. I would come to learn that those were his kill-making cries. I'd never heard a dog make those sounds before.

8

He's Not Gone From Me

From the very beginning Cooper loved the water and went in it all the time. Often, I'd come home from class and whistle for him if he wasn't on the front porch. In a couple of minutes he'd come running out from the trees, his wet fur covered with dripping green algae. He'd been lounging in the creek, lying in a pool he even cleared of a few rocks himself.

He would be smiling as always. "Peter, what do you want to do now?" he seemed to say. I'd motion to him to come with me, down a hill, past a bank, and over to a delivery dock where there was a big hose, and I'd wash all the creek slime off him. Once Cooper, fresh from the creek, tracked me into an art class, walked right up to the naked young woman who was our model, lay down on her feet—and became part of the drawing. He moved even less than she did. He may have been wet, but he sure knew he was handsome.

One of my profs, a carefully trim, unmarried man, had a polar bear–like white dog, as tall as a St. Bernard. The prof liked to talk about his dog's Tibetan breed, Kuvasz, and its unexcelled guarding instinct. The prof's dog was powerfully impressive, even scary. It was more stream-lined than a St. Bernard, faster, much faster, and instead of having the mean, killer, guardian instinct bred out (as is the case with the St. Bernard), it was purposely bred into the Kuvasz.

Seven or eight centuries ago, these Kuvasz dogs were the companions of rulers, kings, and princes. In fact, only royalty was allowed to own a Kuvasz. The Kuvasz breed reached the zenith of its royal popularity in Hungary in the late 1400s, when a justly paranoid king could trust no one, not even in his personal household. There were too many ambitious noblemen about with assassination on their minds. What guarded the monarch from these ruthless contenders were his giant white dogs who would and did tear the king's enemies to bloody pieces of flesh and hair and bone.

Every time I was around that dog, I felt that he wanted to hurt me. He unnerved me. I felt that he might suddenly decide I was a threat to Dan. Dan led him around campus, all 110 pounds of him, on a short leash. Sometimes they looked like an ad from *Esquire*. Dan and his white dog were a handsome pair. I saw a lot of nice-looking co-eds stopping Dan to talk about his big white Kuvasz.

Dan brought his Kuvasz to the Art School party and I brought Cooper. Cooper, being only eight months old, was close to his full height but hadn't even come close to filling out fully yet. He was a puppy in a dog's body. He was a touch goofy at times, falling over his excited self, sometimes seeming all legs and hair and moving tail.

Spring had finally come to upper New York State and the day of the party was exquisite.

The expansive yard sloped down to the pond and I'd forgotten momentarily about Cooper until I saw him trotting across the green. Cooper was beginning to feel his maleness. There was even a hint of a strut to his gait and a slight change to the way he held his neck.

The mask around his face had more definition now; it was such a gentle color of yellowish tan and was so beautifully contrasted by the wedge shape of his massive head and the sable-brown fur on top of it. His ears were held higher and his thick plume of a tail was beginning to curl more. I had been worried about that tail of his since he was a few months old. A pure Malamute tail should have curled back so as to rest in about the middle of his back. Cooper's tail was just now occasionally heading far enough that way to touch his broad back. With the fullness of the fur around his neck, I could see why a Malamute would be such a formidable foe in an all-out fight, fang to fang, going for a grip on the underside of the throat. His fur, both the undercoat and guard hairs, was almost impenetrable. I'd seen young Coops go through tangles of pricker bushes and not even notice the flesh-ripping thorns.

A young couple in love walked into my picture of Cooper strutting across the lawn. They were walking alone at the edge of the pond, holding hands. Then something happened that I'd dreaded, that I'd prayed would never happen to Cooper, especially not before he reached maturity. A blue of white streaked through the air and hit Cooper so hard it knocked him down, and he went rolling over and over toward the pond. Dan's Kuvasz had just attacked Cooper for absolutely no reason except that Cooper was a male, a dog, and in his "territory."

Cooper was totally shocked, stunned, and the only thing I could think of was that he might get killed by this potentially dangerous white dog. Dan's dog must have outweighed Cooper by fifty to sixty pounds. Before Cooper even stopped rolling, the Kuvasz ran to him and pinned him to the ground between his long legs. He seemed as big as a small pony. I was the first one there, as Dan's dog put his furious head down and went for Cooper's innocent throat. Somehow Cooper must have pushed up with his huge front paws and skidded back out of the way of the dog's teeth.

Cooper and I wrestled all the time and I would try to

pin him down on his back. When I did that, all his Alaskan survival instinct came exploding through his normal fun-loving, carefree personality, and he showed amazing power, even occasionally enough to push me away from him. He had a great, natural sense of balance and he knew exactly where he was at any particular second when he was off his feet. But when we wrestled he was fighting with his best friend. This white dog might be his killer.

The noise the Kuvasz made, the deep-throated growl, the angry bark, was frightening. No one made a move toward them but me and Dan. The white dog lunged again toward Cooper's exposed underside.

I didn't know what to do. I'd never had to break up anything like this before, never wanted to, had never seen anything like it. My mind ran way past its speed limit. I was thinking ten, twenty things, all jumbled together. There was no one to call for help, no cold water to throw, no big sticks, baseball bats, no one to risk their hands getting punctured or worse. There was no time to waste either. Now the white dog, crazed-mad by Cooper's lack of submission, had a hold on his neck. I could only hope his grip was mostly hair.

There was nothing else to do but rear back and kick that Kuvasz in the ribs, just as hard as my right leg could muscle my foot. I was good with my feet, having played soccer through high school, and I powered my foot like I was kicking a penalty kick. He lifted his head up only long enough to look at me as if he was wondering whether to leave Cooper and attack me. He had Cooper pinned beneath his four legs and chest. Right then Dan arrived and had anger in his voice. He commanded the Kuvasz: "Stop that." His dog kept Cooper pinned, but started wagging his tail. The dog's expression was like, "Do you want me to kill it right now or what?" "Why did that other man kick me? You want me to get him too?"

Dan grabbed the white dog by the collar and pulled him off Cooper. The dog's whole body stayed stiff, in case Cooper tried to go after him while Dan held him in check. I didn't know what to do now. Could Dan hold his dog if I bent down to attend to badly shaken Cooper? I would need to feel closely for any puncture wounds, broken bones, spurting blood. Dan was a fit, strong man, and angry now at his dog's actions. He wouldn't release his grip.

Coops was quivering and terribly frightened, too anxious to get up. I knelt on one knee, petting him, stroking his soft fur on his forehead, comforting him. Dan dragged his potent animal over to his car and locked him in there. It was guaranteed no one would ever steal Dan's car! I took Cooper over to the Chevy. He normally loved sleeping in the backseat of the car, but now he cried, whined not to be left in there. After what he'd just experienced, being attacked by a Kuvasz, I couldn't leave him right away. I sat with him in the front seat and he put his big, unscarred head in my lap and inched his bear-sized paws under my thighs. I turned the radio on and I listened to some tunes and stroked him till he fell asleep.

The unprovoked attack by the tall white dog would not be Cooper's last fight but it probably was the last one he would ever lose. Cooper's mammoth size normally stopped any sane dog's show of aggression, but there were always the stray toy poodles or "lap" dogs who thought they were tigers.

The first time one of those lapdogs attacked Cooper was during an alumni weekend. An older lady and her even older sister came with their Pomeranians. They carried their babies in their arms as they walked rather spryly along the street.

Cooper was lying in the front yard looking like a statue of a lion, his powerful paws and legs out in front of him. When the elderly alumnae got near our front yard, their lapdogs spotted Cooper. The white one leaped to the ground like a paratrooper jumping out of a fighter plane and the other followed right behind. They ran over to

Cooper and attacked him like two infuriated mice attempting to kill a rhino.

Fortunately for the little Pomeranians, I was right there as they showered Cooper with shrill, earsplitting barks. They bared their teeth, danced around him, and acted vicious. Cooper jumped up with that killer look in his eyes, until I yelled, "NO, Cooper, NO."

From that command on, Cooper stood with all four paws firmly planted on the ground, his head held high, as the little fur balls pummeled him from all sides. Only once, when the tan one bit down and hung on to his left front leg, did Cooper defend himself by swatting it away with his right front paw. The elderly ladies could only stand on the sidewalk and watch.

I walked over to the site of the attempted massacre and grabbed the devilish little dogs one at a time, and gave them back to their grateful owners. The ladies thanked me a lot. Cooper could have crunched them as easily as a crawfish. I was very proud of him.

The only time I ever got hurt in one of Cooper's fights was at a party in a local graveyard. It was Halloween night. The graveyard was dappled with blue shadows and spots of moonlight making their way through the pine branches. Everyone tried to be careful of the stones and grave sites. Someone had started a fire where the graves ended and the woods began. Around the fire were about twenty people, as well as a Siberian husky.

Most of the humans around the fire were sitting or kneeling in a circle. I forget what we were all doing, listening for ghosts perhaps, or spirits, or whatever might come around. Our imaginations were flying high. Circling out there somewhere at the edge of the darkness was Cooper.

Into our peaceful space came raging, wild sounds. The noise, however, was not from evil spirits but Cooper and the Siberian. They were in a hellish fight, spinning in a fury of muscle, fur, and white teeth.

They were moving too fast for us to see which dog was winning until Cooper flipped the Siberian onto his back, knocking the breath out of him. Cooper had the Siberian by the throat. I must reach them or that dog was dead. As I bent down to grab Cooper around the neck, he let go of the dog and half spun around to go at me without realizing who I was. The Siberian leaped to his feet and went at Cooper.

I had to stop them. Their passion to get each other was at a white heat. I reached in to grab Cooper again. He was truly out of control. I tried to latch on to the hair on the back of his neck but the dogs shifted position and one of them bit down on my hand. It felt crushed. Had they hit a vein? I didn't see any spurting blood, but it was dark. I really wanted to walk away but I knew that if I did, one of them would not be alive when it was all over. I reached into the whirling ball of fur and flesh and teeth and claws and rage and again tried to get hold of crazed Cooper. This time I got hold of the scruff of his neck, heaved back, and when the Siberian sprang for his throat or me as we retreated, I timed a perfect kick to its chest and sent it sprawling. I don't know where its owner was; maybe he was one of those creeping around in the shadows of night. When I got Cooper calmed down I saw he was fine; I was the only one bleeding. A canine tooth had gone almost completely through my hand, between my thumb and index finger.

As Cooper continued maturing, he became king of the dogs at our university. He was a kind ruler, never fighting nor punishing unless another dog began the battle first. Then, if the dog was of a competitive size, it might as well forfeit the fight, for Cooper was never beaten, either at Alfred University or walking across America. One time in a North Carolina cornfield he whipped up on five or six hound dogs.

But his invincibility was not the reason I loved him so much. I loved him because he was always there for me.

There was never a time of rejection between Cooper and me. There was never the moment when his mood was not ready to respond to mine. If I stroked his head he thanked me; if I did not, he didn't wonder if I still loved him. He knew I did. I loved Cooper like I'd never loved any living thing before him.

It was not a relationship based just on my moods, whims, and wishes. Often, if I was consumed in some sculpture I was working on or too limp from having walked thirty-five miles of Pennsylvania hill country loaded down with a sixty-five-pound backpack, Coops would push his soft cream-colored snout into my free hand. His nose felt like cold, damp dirt. He'd keep shoving his head in there till he got me to touch him the way he wanted to be touched, right then. He liked to have me scratch the narrow space between his dark eyes. He loved for me to flatten my hand and rub his wide beautiful head till he would lay his head down on the ground between his two strong paws.

Cooper didn't care if I was poor or rich. He only cared that I had time for him, time to do something together. He absolutely loved sleeping with me in my little gold-colored mountain tent while an Appalachian whiteout bent our shelter under piles of snow. When he stretched out next to me, he wasn't much shorter than I was. He didn't need a sleeping bag (mine was rated at 10 below zero) and in fact he could have quite comfortably slept outside in the snow, but he *wanted* to be next to me. He'd always make sure his muscular, fur-covered body was curled, curved, flattened up against mine.

We did so much in the mere two and a half years we were together. We went to college together, we walked from upper New York State to Tennessee together. I spent my early twenties with him, years of volcanic rumblings. I've wondered, at times, if something is wrong with me. How can I feel so close to a dog like Cooper, and sometimes be so indifferent, burning and burned out with humans?

I've heard it said that deep love for humans takes much work, and that's the reason certain people will cop out and find it easier to give love to animals. At this moment in my life I don't care what people say. I just know one thing: My friendship with Cooper was a deep and committed love that both of us cherished. I've messed up plenty with people, but I never messed up with Cooper. Cooper's death under those truck tires in Tennessee was a sudden knife in my happy life. Watching the life leave his loved body on that dirt road was a killing, permanent wound.

When I think of Cooper now, sixteen long years later, I know it is unlikely the old boy would still be alive. He'd be eighteen and a half years old. It's hard to say if his living would have changed the last sixteen years of my life, but I think, yes, probably so. If he'd been with me we might have traveled different roads. But that doesn't matter. I do know he'd be at home on this Tennessee farm I love so much, the place I came to when I stopped wandering and began to take hold.

He'd love the mellow green of the wavy pastures, and fencerows filled with trees that shade the calves and horses. He'd lie in the spring-fed creek in the hot days of summer. He'd chase down woodchucks till he tired of catching them; he'd explore my hay-filled barns and chase Tigger, the barn cat who never comes to the house except for food on poor hunting days.

Back in upper New York State, Cooper and I would go long-distance running, up hills, down hills, through woods and fields, till we came to a spring-fed pond. The pond would often be deep and clear and just cool enough on our hot skin to soothe us. The ponds here on the farm in Tennessee get very hot in the summer, with a lot of algae and mud on the bottom. Cooper would miss his cool ponds. Otherwise he would love it here even if he was eighteen and an old dog. But he died before he was three. He may be dead, buried in the ground not far from here, but he's not gone from me. He never will be.

9
Summons From
a Shaman

Jerry knows things because the spirits tell him. Dealing with spirits is as normal and everyday for the Athabaskans as hunting. Jerry's family has had strong spirits in them for as long as anyone can remember. From Jerry's family came many shamans. Jerry believes that spirits hold the records of the past, that history can be understood by understanding the spirits. They are always there. "You just understand," Jerry told me. He explained that it was inborn; it was a "knowing," the way an animal senses danger or prey. "Animals just know," Jerry said. "People can just know, too."

I was here because Jerry wrote me, a stranger. I was living on the edge of a duckweed-coated swamp in Louisiana. Everything was green: green duckweed, green water lilies, green tree snakes, green chameleons, green water, black-green alligator heads. The swamp was south of the Bogue Chitto River, and flowed into Lake Pontchartrain. Jerry Riley's letter said he had read my first book, *A Walk Across America*, and that he "liked the book and really liked Cooper, half Alaskan Malamute." He said he could tell I had "the gift of merging with animal spirits." He said he knew I could get animals to do what I wanted. He said he could, too.

Jerry didn't tell me then that he was one of the world's best dog mushers. I found out later that he'd won the Iditarod, a dogsled race of more than one thousand miles from Anchorage to Nome, across some of the most brutal, dog-killing, man-breaking land on earth. He'd also, twice, come in second. There is no other race like it in the world.

Riley, as his wife, Margie, calls him, wrote me in the simple, strong words he always speaks. He told me he was sad I had lost Cooper. He said that if I'd ever come to Alaska, he would give me a puppy. He knew nothing would ever take Cooper's place. Jerry was right. Until then I had not been able to get another dog; not any kind of animal. It had been almost ten years since Cooper was run over by a truck near Summertown, Tennessee. The bond that Cooper and I had together, all the precious time we spent out on the road traveling and surviving, would never happen again. Jerry said he knew the kind of dog I needed.

It wasn't the first letter I'd gotten from people who'd read my book. One lady from Virginia sent me a photo of herself with her two beagles and wanted to send me one. Another letter came from a young family in upper New York State. They raised Australian shepherds, a gray, white, and black spotted dog, as tough as the Australian outback. They said they had a dairy farm near Syracuse and these dogs were great cow dogs and good with kids. They sent Polaroids of the most recent litter, taken in the old milking parlor.

People, none of whom I'd ever met, wrote me, telling me they cried too when Cooper died and offering me Welsh corgis, German shepherds, toy poodles, Rottweilers, cocker spaniels, Alaskan Malamutes, mutts, and even cats. One fifth-grade girl from South Dakota said she'd send me a white mouse.

Then there was the southern man who offered me Treein' Walker hounds. I remember his letter; in fact I saved it. His name was Billy John Ragsdale. He'd written me on the stationery of the Caterpillar bulldozer dealer where he worked as a diesel mechanic. Billy John explained, "I done figured you liked Dixie from that book you wrote." He said, "A Malamute like Cooper couldn't take the heat below the Mason/Dixon line," but a Treein' Walker hound was a perfect dog for me.

Billy John said that there was "nothin' in this here world as sweet-sounding as a couple hounds runnin' a 'coon up an' down the hollows, lopin' long ridge lines and crossin' creeks." He said he especially loved it on full moon nights. His handwriting looked as if his hands and fingers were too big and thick to hold a pen. Billy John said "hounds liked laying around in the shade or liked to crawl up under your house and hollow them out a round place in the dirt, and sleep till dark. Then them hounds could run all night. Some people try to say they're lazy dogs, that's just cause they never seen 'em run all night." He said since he couldn't lie in the shade all day, but had to work on dozers, "it was rough on a man working all day and chasin' hounds all night." He said he wanted me to have a pup from his favorite bitch. Her name was Thicket, because she could find her way through rhododendron thickets, no matter how thick, "real easy like."

I wrote Billy John back and told him thanks so much, but I wasn't ready for a new dog yet. Also I told him I was moving the family out of Louisiana, to middle Tennessee. We'd been thinking about moving to a farm in the Tennessee hills where they certainly knew all about hounds. I said I'd heard that the hill and hollow people of Tennessee *invented* hound dogs.

I wrote back just about everybody who offered to give me a dog or a cat or a white mouse, those fine people who shared with me the sorrow of Cooper's death. But, it was Jerry's letter that finally changed my mind, that gave me heart to try again, to get me another dog. I'm sure part of my decision was because Jerry offered me an Alaskan dog, but another part was because he was a native Alaskan, and they were people who lived with dogs, whose survival depended upon dogs. In many ways Cooper and I were like that, depending upon each other for our lives.

After reading Jerry's letter, I felt as though someone in the center of Alaska had a rope around me and they were pulling me up there.

10
Going To Alaska

I boarded a jet for Alaska. I wasn't worried about getting there, it was getting back with all the Alaskan huskies that concerned me. I don't like being held up in baggage-checking lines; therefore I try to carry everything on the plane with me. I could only imagine what I'd have to go through to fly the six huskies from the deep interior of Alaska to the lower 48. Yes, an airline official said, they could be transported with the proper papers, shots, and carrying cages. For now, all I had to do was get on the jet in Nashville and make sure I got the appropriate connections through Seattle, through Anchorage, to Fairbanks. There I'd rent a car and make my way to the small village of Nenana, north of Mount McKinley.

Everything I needed for the departure I could carry on the plane. I'd have clothes, cameras, and a tape recorder. The airline rules say that carry-on luggage is supposed to fit in the overhead storage compartment above your seat or underneath your seat. There have been times when this has been an extreme challenge for me, for instance, when I went to Mount Everest and traveled around China and Inner Mongolia for almost two months.

The place I was traveling to is not easily accessible, but I could drive there, a wild bush-plane ride was not

my only choice. I would soon find out that flying airplanes inside Alaska has little or nothing to do with flying in the Outside, which is what Alaskans call the rest of the world. In Alaska the plane is the best form of transport, used to get to places that cannot be reached by road. In fact, a great many places in Alaska have no roads to them. When you arrive, there are roads that will take you around town, but you cannot drive away.

The capital of Alaska, Juneau, has no road entry; you must approach it from the west by boat or plane for there are impassable mountains to the east. Even dogsleds cannot cross those high barriers. So planes are it. You often see planes and their assorted parts—wings, engines, propellers—resting in backyards. Alaskans can land their planes just about anywhere. They set down on glaciers to rescue stranded mountain climbers, and I've seen them land on a rocky stream bed or a convenient road. Basically these pilot-maniacs will land anywhere and pick up anything.

I knew some prospectors who were mining a gold site near Mount McKinley, over Sable Pass and up Moose Creek. They were in two different camps, maybe ten miles apart. Their only companions were caribou and ornery grizzlies. One of the camps needed to borrow some sugar, so two of the folks got in their plane and flew over to the other camp. There was no one in sight, so to get attention they flew low and dropped a few sticks of dynamite. The dynamite got their neighbors' attention all right, and when they rushed out from their cookshack, the plane made another low pass and dropped an empty plastic Pepsi bottle with a note inside: "We need sugar."

Talking to Alaska from my farm in Tennessee wasn't quite like dropping notes from a plane, but it was different. Sometimes the Rileys sounded as though they were on Mars and sometimes next door. I tried to visualize this little village I was going to visit. No place could be as wild as I imagined the interior of Alaska to be. The first time I called Jerry Riley, his wife said he was off in Bristol Bay salmon fishing. The next time he was up at the North Slope working in the oil fields as a carpenter. The third time she said he'd gone to a potlatch.

I visualized their home: It was a stout, squat log cabin, and the spaces between the logs were chinked with mud. There were two small windows; the roof was primitive, thatched with spruce branches. The cabin was always surrounded by snow, with many sled dogs lying outside, curled up, looking like balls of fur. Since Jerry was a native Alaskan that meant he was an Eskimo, which meant that polar bears were prowling just outside the beams of light cast from the cabin windows.

Jerry told me to come see him "after the salmon were no longer in river."

Right before I made my plane reservations, he said to

me, "Would be good to come before first snow. Before I begin running the dogs hard. Before snowshoe rabbit turn white. When snowshoe rabbit start to turn white, means snow not far off."

Jerry Riley is an Athabaskan Indian; his people inhabited Alaska long before any white man had ever seen it, before the thirteen colonies down in the Outside were ever dreamed of.

Jerry told me that his people came over land and ice, when the Bering Strait was probably still part of the landmass that is now Russia. Jerry says he knows his people descend from the nomadic Mongolian warriors who blew across the lands, any lands of Asia and Europe. The bigger the mountain, the longer the battle, the harder the Mongols came. They were not sailors, Jerry says, so water usually stopped them. They were nomads, they hated farming, they despised rooted settlements.

Jerry has heard of carbon-dating and knows that white scientists need proof. But he says he doesn't need scientists to tell him how his people came to be in Alaska. The knowledge is in our blood, says Jerry. That's proof enough for him. He says that the Mongolian heritage is why the Athabaskans do not like to be settled to this day.

11

Gerald Roy Riley

As Jerry requested, I got to the Riley house after the salmon had almost finished swimming in the Nenana River by his village. The main fish run was over, the time when Jerry's people reap their harvest.

Alaska was not what I expected. It had its disappointments. I didn't expect to see an airport like the Fairbanks International Airport. It looked like Anywhere, USA. I'd hoped there was somewhere that was too remote for a McDonald's. But there was one in Fairbanks and it didn't even have a moose in the children's playground. There were Ford dealers like Anywhere, USA. But then all this was in Fairbanks, one of Alaska's largest cities. Alaska doesn't really become the Alaska I had in mind until you get "out there." Then there is no place like it. Jerry lives in the out-there part of Alaska, although Nenana is alongside Alaska's major road, the railroad passes through it, and it's on a river.

Jerry's house wasn't exactly what I expected either. It was smallish, I figured that, but it definitely wasn't made of logs, chinked with moss or mud. It was shaped like a ranch house and had white siding. Margie even coaxed multicolored flowers to grow around it. The house had very few windows. Windows lose a lot of heat, something no one can afford to do in the interior of Alaska. Their place had a brown tin roof and out of that came a stovepipe from their all-important wood stove. Jerry *had* lived in trapline cabins, like the ones I imagined, when he was fourteen. Then he and his father ran a trapline, catching lynx, marten, mink, and an occasional wolf. Few people could survive weeks of 50 below zero in a cabin like that. Some of Jerry's neighbors actually sprayed foam, six to eight inches deep, on top of their roofs to keep out the cold.

Next to Jerry's house there was a long low structure made of spruce logs. Leaning up against it were a couple of doors from old pickup trucks. Lying near them were an old steering wheel, a wheelbarrow, and a well-used lawn mower. That surprised me. I didn't expect people in Alaska to have to cut grass. Inside the log building were a lot of dry dog food, a couple of chainsaws, a caribou hide, a wolverine hide, and a couple of moose racks just lying in a pile. A snowmobile sat partially taken apart. The next-door neighbor's yard was filled with spare airplane parts.

The Riley home was warm and cozy and always open to anyone, drunk or sober, Indian or white. Often trappers would use Jerry's phone when they were in Nenana selling furs or buying supplies. Jerry's house was furnished much like his neighbor's—plain but comfortable, except for a lot of dog-racing trophies, including his prize for winning the Iditarod. Home for Jerry was not elegant wood paneling or a dishwasher or a big-screen TV or a library. These things didn't really mean that much to Jerry. Home was where his wife and son were and that was important. But I believe that he only really felt at home outside with his dogs, or running down a wounded bear, or emptying nets full of king salmon.

Jerry says, ''When salmon run, when moose rut, when geese and pike come to Minto Flats, when lynx move over snow with thick fur, that time when my people must be busy, like they say in Iowa, make hay while sun shines.'' (Margie Riley, a non-Indian, is originally from Iowa.)

The strong salmon with the red flesh and the tired ones whose muscle was already turning gray had been plentiful that year, ''filled the natives' fish wheels and nets,'' Jerry told me. When I arrived many salmon were still drying in wood-pole racks on the banks of the river. They were food for the dogs in the coming winter when it could slam into 50 below for weeks. Many salmon were also hanging in smokehouses. The people smoked the good salmon with red flesh for themselves.

Arriving when I did meant that Jerry had already been salmon fishing down in Bristol Bay, where the salmon run so profusely that it is sometimes like scooping up silver nuggets. Jerry spread his nets near Egegik Bay, ''sometimes closer to Kvichak Bay,'' where the red-meat salmon are funneled into a tight place.

''When salmon come, people move from Minto Flats to river, usually to the fish camp. Most native families have a fish camp, tent, drying poles, smokehouse and stay most of summer. Many years ago when salmon came, they fill river, so thick they stretched from bank to bank, their fins pushing out of the water. No more.''

Jerry kept his dogs in the woods. We followed a well-worn trail to his dog yard. There they were, his Alaskan huskies, some who'd won the Iditarod. Each dog was chained to its own tree. They looked leaner and smaller than I'd imagined. None of them looked anything like any dog I had seen before. None were even close to the size of a Malamute.

Some dogs just sat regally on their haunches. Some dogs paced, jerked their eyes side to side and up and down and didn't want to look anything in the eye.

''Them dogs are super-charged, bred to race,'' said Jerry.

Gerald Roy Riley   87

The sun could not pierce through the dense cover of the spruce branches overhead, and this spot of wilderness was nicely shielded from the howling Arctic winds that would soon come. Jerry did not want any puppies to be born after October because they would be too small to withstand the 75 below zero that could come before the end of the deep freeze and the long darkness. Most of Jerry's females burrowed in the soft black-brown earth to have their litters. The burrow served as protection from the summer mosquitoes and bloodsucking flies that loved the tender flesh of a newborn puppy. The narrow, curved burrow also protected the little huskies from crawling away from their mother's protection before they learned which of Jerry's dogs were puppy killers.

Jerry walked over to the edge of his woods full of dogs, and picked up the chain that was attached to a slinky female. He gently knelt next to her, one of his knees resting on the ground, scratched bare by the mother's nervous patrolling.

"Pete, she's good mother, real good. She's got much blood in her from my father's dogs. She got best trait of Indian dog. Not crazy inbred. Just right." There was a cracking sound overhead and we looked up to see a gray deep-woods owl leave its daytime perch.

"You go over to that burrow," Jerry ordered. "She make extra big wide burrow. Reach in."

"Reach in? Why?" I wasn't sure I wanted to invade this dog's burrow, even though Jerry had a firm grip on her collar.

"Just go ahead, I've got her."

I slipped my feet into her circle and knelt down. My right arm fit easily into the damp hole, until my forward progress stopped. I felt something warm. I pulled out seven pups and ended up holding a light-tan one with a white mask and blue eyes.

"Pete, that's your pup. I want you take him home to Tennessee. He will be your dog, now."

I didn't know what to say to Jerry. I'd held my feelings locked away for so long, since Cooper was killed, that I just knelt there and held the small Alaskan husky. Jerry said he chose this litter for a number of reasons and one of them was because they were the kind of Indian dog whose hair could be short in hot weather. Jerry's name was *Gerald Roy Riley*, so I decided to name my new dog **G.R.R.** . . . Grr. Jerry acted slightly embarrassed when I told him I'd named my dog after him.

We left little Grr to stay with his mother until I left Alaska. While the other six pups in this litter ran around in a minipack, scrounging bits of food, turning over other dogs' dishes, and fighting over a rag, Jerry noticed that Grr usually stayed off to himself. Jerry said, "Unusual for pup. He's a male pup, could be an extremely strong leader. Leaders have to stay off to themselves many times."

The next day, after Jerry fed the wood stove and made us a breakfast of real butter on thick crackers, smoked salmon, and coffee, we got in his pickup and crossed the river bridge and went north toward Fairbanks. A few miles out of town, we pulled onto a gravel road and took it all the way to the riverbank.

The Ketzlers, whose salmon camp was on the banks of the Tanana River, were mostly Athabaskan, and like many, their fish camp is their summer home. They live there as long as salmon are in the waters.

The camp had a roughhewn log cabin with moose antlers nailed to it. There were a few outboard boat engines lying around, and there were fish-drying racks built out of straight willow poles, lashed and nailed together close to the riverbank. Behind the cabin and farther away from the river was a beautiful birch grove. That's where the Ketzlers kept their dogs. They didn't have as many as Jerry because they didn't race; they used their dogs to run traplines, and for occasional hunting.

They were very quiet people with soft voices. Listening to them took a lot of concentration because they half whispered/half sang their words. They didn't say anything to me, and only one of the Ketzlers, the youngest son, would even look at me. There were three sons, all in their twenties, and a mother, a father, and an older woman, maybe a grandmother. It was a sunny, warming day.

Jerry and I got in an aluminum flat-bottomed boat and pushed off into the river current. There was nothing between here and the mouth of the Yukon River but small Indian villages. From the Ketzlers' fish camp on the Tanana to where the river flung itself into the Yukon was only about seventy-five miles. It was almost six hundred river miles to the ocean.

We came to a sandbar island. There were no trees or bushes growing there; however, there was something moving across the top of the gravelly surface. They were the Ketzlers' puppies.

The puppies all massed together when they heard the boat. Jerry had explained to me that one reason the Ketzlers kept the pups on the island was that when they drove the boat around the island, the puppies would naturally give chase. When they began running, the Ketzlers would be able to tell which of the pups were the fastest and had the best endurance and the most competitive spirit.

It was also a great way to wean pups. Pups don't normally want to be weaned and will keep nursing until the mother's milk runs out. At this age, eight to twelve weeks, the pups were too small to chain so the Ketzlers brought them to this island. They would not dare to swim the river, even when they heard their mother howl at night. There were no predators on the island, so the pups were safe.

The Ketzlers had one pet dog, a very well-built extra-large Siberian husky. The dog had obviously had the pull and wild energy bred out of him—he was just "a big ol'

puppy dog, grew up to be so friendly like a living rug.''
He was a classic picture dog, the kind so many think all
Alaskans have. If he were hooked to a sled he would
probably lie down and cry, Jerry told me. But he was
beautiful.

This Siberian Husky picture dog had been bred to a
wild-eyed, slinky black Indian dog. Three of the pups
looked just like him. My daughter, Rebekah, wanted a
female, and there was one. My friends from west Texas,
the Pools, wanted a male. There were two. I picked the
most handsome one. Both these dogs would be pets, although I had hopes of turning Rebekah's into a Tennessee farm dog.

12

An Angry
Bull-necked Policeman

I stood on a concrete sidewalk, something rare in Alaska, right in front of the automatic sliding doors, frozen with indecision. What do I do now? There were three huge containers. And inside them were six squirming puppies. At that moment they all began to howl like a large litter of baby wolves out on the tundra.

They would have to go down in the hold with all the other luggage. Maybe there was a special compartment in the belly of the big silver jet that would carry them all home. Did it have enough oxygen? Luggage doesn't breath, but these fluffy, yelping things do. Did their compartment have heating or cooling? They would get nothing to eat, but considering airplane food that was no loss.

The flight from Fairbanks floated down to the runway into Sea-Tac, Seattle and Tacoma's airport. Light-gray fog greeted me as I made four trips with my rented metal cart to get all the puppy carriers onto the street-side pickup area outside baggage claim. All the baby huskies seemed healthy. They stunned the airport crowds as they howled. They didn't sound like dogs—it was wild.

The puppies howled and howled and then they started to whimper. Skip, my long-time friend, put on a cassette tape of Aretha Franklin and the pups settled down to

Aretha, laying their pointed noses on their paws. Two of
the dog carriers just fit in the backseat and one I held on
my lap.

By the time we got on Interstate 5 headed north, I had
squeezed the seat back far enough so that I could breathe,
and move my left arm. I pushed the buttons on the radio
and hit a country station. First the white female husky
with the blue eyes began to howl. The rest soon followed. Their howls sang out over Interstate 5. And we
still had forty miles to go! I turned off the country music.
The huskies stopped howling.

When we opened the windows to get some fresh non-
puppy-scented air, the wind noise made them howl again.

Skip and I looked at each other, closed the windows, turned off the radio, did not breathe through our
noses. We turned on the Aretha tape again and drove fast
to Mukilteo.

We drove by the massive hangers of the Boeing plant
and passed Skip's place, a big old house with twenty-
seven apple trees in the yard. I didn't say anything for
fear the calmed puppies would begin to howl again. When
we went down the hill headed for the Sound and Mukilteo Speedway, I asked Skip where we were going.

"I guess I didn't tell you. I've moved to an apartment."

An apartment! What were we going to do with six
puppies in an apartment? "Tell me you're kidding,"I
begged Skip.

Before he could answer we took a left into the Saratoga
Apartments. Parked outside were a majority of foreign
cars, a lot of them two-seaters. Skip mumbled something
about no children allowed. Could "no pets" be far behind?

"Where are we going to keep them, Skip?" I asked
when I saw his new apartment hung with Navajo rugs
and signed and numbered Joe Seme prints. There was
newly installed beige carpeting and the foyer was very

nicely tiled. Skip's new, several-thousand-dollar stereo system with speakers as tall as a bear cub dominated the living room. What puppies could do to those expensive stereo speakers, the rugs, the silk pillows on the sofa, and the down comforters on the two beds upstairs was terrible to imagine. No way could they be loose inside this "adults only" apartment.

We had a fast conference. The *only* place we could put them was on the small, wooden back porch, off the dining area, about six foot by six foot. It was an elevated deck built especially for the young yuppie owners, so that they could store their ten-speed bikes outside, have a few plants, and grill some steaks with their Ste. Michelle wine. The porch/deck was suspended over the common backyard. It was made of redwood, and had sufficient space between the slats to allow for drainage. I'm sure the architect never thought of the drainage these puppies would produce. There was no way, we decided, we could keep them in their plastic carriers any longer. They were going nuts being so confined.

When we released the pups, right away the one with floppy ears squirmed through the slats and fell to the ground. Fortunately she was too limber to be hurt.

"OK, what do we do now, Skip?"

"There's a hardware store down the street. How about you go down there and get some chicken wire. I'll stay here and keep them happy."

I left Skip there in the midst of the crawling, squirming, clawing pack of puppies. By the time I returned Skip had scratches all over his arms and I knew exactly what he was thinking. One, these things were only mildly related to dogs, and two, what a mess these things will make!

We got the chicken wire secured and put the litter out on the deck. The white one with the drooping ear tried and almost succeeded in climbing out of the enclosure. Grr just sat in the corner of the porch and watched the

rest of the hyperactive pack. He stayed out of it. I took
him inside and held him, trying to imagine what his life
on my Tennessee farm would be like. How would he
relate to cows? Would he hate the strangling heat of August? Would he be able to stay around the farm or would
he be off like a roaming wolf? Would our relationship be
anything like the one I had with Cooper? Now there were
so many people and things in my life that needed me,
demanded of me, and sustained me, I doubted I would
ever again have a relationship with any dog that was so
exclusive, so dependent on each other, as mine and
Cooper's. What would Grr do when I went to the office?

I looked at the others to see if they were still as ener-
gized as before. Skip's pup had coloring almost exactly
like a gray wolf, with a dark-gray stripe down his back
and around his eyes. Skip already had a name for him,
Gombu, after a Sherpa and a Himalayan climber.

To celebrate the puppies' safe arrival, and to eat up my
payment of smoked salmon from Murray, Skip's cousin
(who was going to name his white puppy Snowball), Skip
planned a party at the Saratoga Apartments. Many people
showed up that night. Word of the smoked king salmon
and the Indian-dog puppies drew a lot of Skip's friends.
As guests began to arrive, the puppies lined up in front
of the glass door, each one sitting alert, their shoulders
touching, their breaths fogging the window in front of
them.

Some of the guests ventured out to see the pups close
up and pet them, but most preferred not to be clawed and
leaped upon by twelve front paws that had just stepped
in whatever. The party kicked in, the dancing started,
and soon Skip's place was standing room only. The puppies had severe trouble settling down on this first night
away from Alaska. They cried, howled, and barked during the entire festivities.

They weren't hungry—they'd been fed—so I put an old

towel out on the porch for them to lie down on. I remembered back to 1972 when I'd gotten Cooper and he'd whined and cried all night. Then I'd tried a loud-ticking alarm clock wrapped in a towel. It sure did work for baby Cooper.

But Skip didn't have a windup alarm clock, only a digital one. No ticking. Anyway, it would have had to have a mighty loud tick to calm so many unhappy huskies. Were they shocked by this strange world they now found themselves in? I knew the occasional touch of my palm did nothing compared to their mothers' nipples and nuzzles. The smells of fallen spruce needles and water-laden bogs had been traded for apartment-complex scents; the sounds of a flowing river for Jimi Hendrix tapes. No wonder they were all howling the lonesome blues.

The party turned up in volume and so did the howling of the puppies. One of Skip's guests went out on the porch and howled with the pups. As night turned to late night, the puppies' insecurities increased. They never lost their voices and they howled and barked and whimpered till none of us were still standing. Nothing I tried to do for them made a bit of difference.

Grr, on the other hand, continued to be the exception, as he sat in the corner of the porch and watched. Finally he just lay down and went to sleep. Was he stupid or smart? I wondered. Before I turned off my lights I gave them some warm milk, which made them more awake than ever.

The next thing I knew I was wakened from a comalike sleep. I thought I heard something. Had I been asleep for ten minutes or ten hours? I heard something again. And again. And again. It sounded like huge rubber balls hitting the roof. No, the sound was below me. Inside the apartment. No, it was the puppies. No. Someone was knocking on the door. "I'm not going to answer," I decided. But Skip wasn't going to answer either. Even a wrecking ball couldn't wake him.

I got up and went down the stairs. By now someone was beating on the door. I peeked out the curtained side-lights and saw the rotating blue light of a police car. I didn't want to open that door. I opened the door. The northwestern light was blinding.

"What in the hell took you so long to answer this damn door!" spit an angry, bullnecked policeman.

"I was asleep."

"Well, you better damn wake up 'cause you're goin' to jail."

"Jail?!"

"You own those puppies, don't you?"

"Well, sort of. I'm in charge of five of them, Officer." Skip could get arrested too! I could use company in jail.

"Well, let me make this real simple, buddy." The policeman sounded like I was a mass murderer. "I've had *complaints* on those dogs; they look like damn baby wolves, all right. . . . The person in the next-door apartment, she's a doctor. Those things kept her awake all night and she's got surgery to do in a few hours. How would you feel if she hurt someone, buddy?

"I'll tell you this," he continued as a few beads of sweat appeared on his forehead. "You get those puppies out of here in no more than thirty minutes or I'll put you and them in jail." The policeman was giving us both an out. He didn't want those baby wolves in his jail, either.

"Yes, sir, I'll take care of them."

"I'll be back in twenty-nine minutes," he growled as he turned to leave.

I woke Skip, which wasn't easy, but he jolted up when I told him the Mukilteo police had just left and we and the puppies were about to go to jail.

After I jump-started Skip's head with that piece of information, he said, "We'll load 'em up and take 'em over to the JanSport factory in Everett." We'd have to squeeze them all in Skip's two-seater Fiat Spider! "Give me some aspirin,'' I said to Skip. We had about fourteen minutes before the cop came back.

With five minutes to go, we got the Fiat top down, the pups in their carriers. The puppies needed a bath, and that back porch they'd spent eighteen hours on needed to be hacked off with an ax and burned. If the sleepless doctor could smell, the puppies would have their revenge.

We had to creep along so that no bumps or fast curves would sling the pups into the road. ''God, don't let a cop see us now,'' I prayed. When we got to the JanSport factory, Skip realized that finding a place for the puppies would not be so easy. We let them out in the loading-dock area, empty except for a forklift. The puppies collapsed around it in five balls of fur. Either they were too tired to move anymore, or they thought the forklift was their mother.

I filled three bowls with Puppy Chow and three with water and Skip and I left them in the shipping and receiving room. We checked on them later that afternoon and then in the morning. Unfortunately for some of the JanSport employees, we got to the puppies after they did. None of them had any idea whose pups they were and what they were doing there. It was obvious what they had *done*. They had eaten so much Puppy Chow and produced such an incredible number of mushy piles and yellow puddles that there would be no freight handling until someone cleaned it all up. The janitor was ecstatic to find out Skip and I were responsible for them. He was seriously contemplating quitting as opposed to cleaning up the mess. Unfortunately for Skip, the puppies and I were about to miss our flight to Tennessee, so we had to leave immediately for the airport.

13

Grr and Lacy

The first big adjustment Grr and Lacy had to make was to Tennessee food. Lacy was the name given Rebekah's puppy. How could they possibly have to eat this dried, hard "junk" I was trying to feed them? They'd grown up on salmon meat fresh from the Tanana River. Their stew had been boiled in a smoke-blackened pot, a mixture of salmon heads, backbones, guts, skin, and meat. Added to this gourmet mix were wild herbs and a small sprinkling of dried dog food. The whole thing was simmered over a fire of split, dried aspen wood, sometimes all day.

Now that they were Tennessee "dawgs," they'd have to get used to some bagged, dry dog food. They both hated it. They'd sniff it from a distance of about four or five inches. They almost curled their noses. They acted as though it would burn off little white hairs on the sides of their snouts. Lacy, a real prissy little pup, wouldn't even smell the stuff the first few days I offered it.

I tried to explain: This was not discount-store, no-name, dried dog food, I told them. This was high-quality stuff. But high-quality here in the Outside could not compare with fresh salmon. So I tried warming milk and pouring it in with the food. Mr. Luther gave me a discount on some milk that was a day or so past its expiration date. At first, only Grr would venture over and all he'd do was lick up the milk just as long as it was not touching the hated dried dog food. Lacy seemed prepared to starve to death.

Raising my voice to Lacy, ordering her to eat, definitely did not work. If I sternly but quietly ordered her to come to me as I knelt next to the hated bowl of lower-48 dog food, she would cower and slink away. The first time I raised my voice above the decibel level of the gentle sounds of an Alaskan river and made a demand on her, she went into the doghouse and would not come out. She stayed in there for the rest of the day, until I finally had to lift the entire doghouse, a heavy-duty thing framed with rough-cut oak, and take her in my arms.

The first time I put Lacy down, she trotted right back into their doghouse again. I reached in, and she let out a little husky, puppy grow. I gently lifted her up in my right hand and carried her, as she straddled my forearm, her left front and rear legs on one side of my arm and the right ones on the other. This time I set her down and petted her in the warming early sun while Grr sat back on his haunches, ready to go wherever I would lead him. He had an Oriental kind of spirit about him. He sat there like a stone-carved Buddha.

I walked the puppies behind the barn, where, when I got around to buying cattle, I would herd them and sort them and do whatever you're supposed to do to cattle. The front of the barn faced west, the hayloft and back opened to the east. The barn was covered with sheet-tin roofing material that people around here used instead of rough-cut oak-boarding siding. The sides were painted a rusty red.

The barn had a central hall and in the hall was a water valve and a big metal watering tank. Grr crawled under a stall door to investigate while Lacy stayed right close to me. I opened the stall door to see Grr about to crawl down a hole in the corner. It was obviously an animal's burrow; I smelled the scent of a nonagitated skunk mingled with the hot smells of hay, dry wood, and the cedar poles that supported the barn, with damp earth where the faucet dripped slowly, and the almost-sweet smell of long-dried-up cow patties. All of it, combined and mixed together by the hot June winds, made an earth-perfume that was delicious to the pups and me.

Grr backed out of the hole, which was surrounded by soft, flaky dirt. He stumbled and fell back into the hole, this time falling in even farther. He must have straightened his long puppy legs and big paws out to break his descent; instead, they improved the straight lines of his trajectory and he fell in far enough to get stuck. His wide sand-colored back paws kicked and the Alaskan husky howled and screamed with fear, the sound of a baby daredevil I would probably hear again before he grew up.

Grr's daring made cautious Lacy nervous. Lacy already reminded me of Rebekah. Grr would jump off a step, not looking to see if there was a next one. Lacy would not go to the next lower step until she reached out and over and felt it with her very own paw. Lacy was exactly like Rebekah was when she learned to go down stairs or do anything new.

Once through the barn I led the pups around some vicious thistle plants. I doubted they had these pricker monsters in Alaska. In front of the barn we cut to our right, over some light-gray limestone, to a place where the springwater had cut deep into flat rock long before the pioneer settlers crossed the Smokies. The spring was here even before the Indians, who had used the ridge in the middle of the farm as a trail while seeking buffalo and elk. The hunting grounds, now part of the state of Tennessee, were so full of game, so filled with moss-coated springs that no tribe ever "owned" this place. The Cherokees came here all the way from east of the Smokies. The Creeks and Chickasaws came out of the

South, from what is now Alabama. Tribes came from north and west, too, and they all took meat and fur and drank from the springs of this abundant land.

The trench into which the springwater flowed was eighteen inches wide and two feet deep. Not difficult to bridge, except for leaping mice and baby Grr. He didn't wait for me to get there and lift him safely across. Grr jumped, but Grr didn't know how to jump yet. He was lucky to step over a fallen maple-tree branch without tripping. So he blurped into the crevasse, a mini-Grand Canyon. He also didn't know what the word *swim* meant yet. Lacy did—she grew up on an island—but she was a "right-thinking kind of pup," as Jerry would say, not to dare to try to swim to shore from that island.

Grr was completely submerged; then his head came up covered with algae and duckweed.

"Cooper, you crazy thing," I found myself calling to him.

But Grr had elements of wild-animal blood burning in him that Cooper did not. Puppy Cooper seemed more domesticated. Was it the wolf in Grr? Jerry told me stories of how his people, the Athabaskan Indians, related to the wolf. Sometimes it was necessary to get new blood into their village dogs so they could lessen the devastating effects of inbreeding. Living in a small, wildly isolated village in the Alaskan interior, usually on the Yukon or some other body of water, they were reachable by boat only after the thaw. Otherwise these small Indian villages could be reached only by plane—when the weather was good enough to fly. It was an easy place for dogs to inbreed. As it was, also, for the people.

So Jerry's villagers would take a female in heat and tie her out at the edge of the wilderness. Usually a young man, already trained in hunting and shooting, would hide in the spruce trees near the bitch. He waited for a wolf to catch the scent of the she-dog and come to her and mate her. This would give them the fresh, strong blood they needed for their dogs. The young hunter was there to keep the wolf from killing the she-dog after it bred her, which the wolf would often try to do. If the mating took, then the villagers could keep a few of the better half-wolf pups, a couple of males and a couple of females, to breed back to their full-dog mates. By "better" Jerry meant those pups who showed the least wolf, the least wildness. So there was no doubt in Jerry's mind that Grr had more than one genetic strain of wolf blood in him, although the percentage of wolf blood, he felt, would have been under an eighth.

In the space of half an hour Grr had gotten stuck in a skunk burrow in the barn and had fallen into the mini-cavern and become an unintentional water baby. Now he was backed into a tree, sitting like a fat bear on his haunches. Lacy followed me across the flat rock and over to the fence that separated our farm from the Mortons'.

I called for Grr; he did not seem to be coming. He was looking down at the base of the tree, barking. Lacy did not run over to investigate; she sat in the pasture next to me. A loud sound, like a high-pitched, high-speed grinding of metal on metal, came from over where Grr was. Sssshhhh. It sounded something like a burst gas pipe. What could he have gotten into now? I rounded the tree to find what looked like a boa constrictor, curled up, its tail vibrating rapidly and hitting up against some dry leaves. It appeared to be at least six feet long, by far the biggest snake I'd seen in years. It was yellow-brown above, with a row of large, rectangular dark blotches down its back and sides. It was no escaped boa, but it was big enough to try to eat Grr.

It was wound in a tight circle and as wild Grr would lunge at it, it would strike viciously at him. I'd never seen a snake like it before. Nor had I seen one any more aggressive. This snake was as aggressive as a cottonmouth.

The big yellow and brown snake struck again at Grr

and hit the side of his head, a glancing blow just under the eye. Grr should have run away, but he didn't. The snake made him angry. He attacked. I didn't know that Grr knew what attack was. He didn't. Once Grr got to the snake he didn't know what to do next. He was supposed to bite it. And kill it.

The snake, surely not a rattler, extended his body straight out to strike and hit Grr. It knocked him over, stunned him. In a blur the snake, as wide as my forearm, was on top of Grr and began to wrap around him, just as I'd seen boas do in nature films. If dogs can scream, Grr was doing just that.

I looked frantically for a stick, a club, a branch, anything to save Grr. There was a fallen branch from a thorn tree lying next to the boundary fence. I grabbed it. Some thorns pierced my hand. The snake was tightening down on Grr. There was no way to whip it with the thorn-laden stick, Grr's body was in the way. The snake was totally consumed with its business of crushing the life out of the cream-colored puppy it so easily wrapped around.

Rapidly, I circled the snake. The only thing I could do was grab the end of his vibrating tail and pick them both up and shake, hoping the snake would, could loosen its death grip.

When I grabbed the muscular snake it opened its eyes and hissed loudly. It also unraveled the front section of its body, about the first foot, so it could strike at my leg. I held it out far enough so that it would have to unravel further. The snake was much heavier than I would have imagined. This close it looked as thick as my forearm. It loosened its hold on Grr, who was genuinely terrified, trembling and emitting a gagging sound.

As it looked at me, rearing its ugly head back in the striking position, it moved its forked tongue in and out, undulating up and down. This hypersensitive tongue gave it information about my smell, maybe told it I was a human. A snake this large and this old obviously had been living around here for a long time and knew to avoid people. Most local folks grabbed the closest hoe and chopped a snake's head off as soon as they saw it, especially if it was this big. As it momentarily watched me, Grr regained his breath and growled the lowest-pitched growl I'd heard him make so far. Then Grr did the unthinkable, although until now he seemed nearing the expert level as a doer of the unthinkable. Grr, the blue-eyed puppy, opened his mouth and bit that snake with all his needlelike teeth.

The startled snake recoiled, confused by the bite and from where it came. This was no ordinary young pup the snake had in the middle of its coiled, scaly body. It was an Alaskan husky, whose bloodlines traced back to wild wolves and semi-tamed Indian dogs. During the snake's momentary confusion I shook it like I'd shake a gym towel rolled into a rattail, and it went limp, uncoiled, and I dropped it on the ground.

Grr fell on top of it, but before I could kick at the reptile, it darted out from under the clawing, yipping, scrambling husky and slipped through the fence between my farm and the Mortons'. It disappeared under an old tractor axle and the bed of a discarded pickup truck.

I reached down to pick up Grr to check for injuries—and he was gone. Did he roll, unconscious, down into the spring where it bubbled out of the ground? Was he dead? No. That maniac was charging the snake! Grr flung himself at the fence, except his body was a bit wider than the snake's, which mean that Grr was stuck, halfway in, halfway out. He squirmed back out and stood at the fence barking.

Lacy sat in the cool shade of the biggest oak tree on the farm and watched and learned. Before Grr could do anything else I scooped him into my arms and we'd doubled back to the doghouse. Our little walk ended before we'd gone one hundred yards. If Grr got into this much trouble before he was six months old, before we'd gone

one hundred yards, and while strolling through the serene pastures of a thoroughly tamed Tennessee farm, I couldn't even imagine what he might have done as a mature dog in Alaska.

As I put Grr back on the grass by his doghouse in the yard, behind the smokehouse and woodpile, I thought of the Bible verse "Train up a child in the way he should go: and when he is old, he will not depart from it." I'd better do as those old Indian women did and teach Grr the way he should be before he grew up. I would have to teach him right from wrong, here on our farm.

Later that evening I called Bud Mitchum to ask him about the snake. Bud, patient and thoughtful as ever, possibly the largest property owner in the area and a long-time bachelor, said he was about sure it was a bull snake. He said, "Bull snakes, they're good to have around, they eat large quantities of mice and rats." He also said they could be over eight feet long. I'd asked Bud so many stupid questions since I'd been on the farm and I realized he'd never asked me one question about anything. Politics. Where I was from. My age. Nothing. Before I hung up I said, "Bud, if you ever want to write a book, I'd be glad to help you." Bud said, "All right." So far he's never asked me about writing a book or anything else.

14
The Puppy-Killer

Grr had the memory of millions of campfires in his genes. The only animal that could be kept and trained to help the Athabaskan people was the dog. From the time they were pups the Alaskan husky dogs were taught not to steal food. Every morsel of food was more precious than gold way back then. The dogs would not touch the drying, smoking salmon, the sun-curing moose meat, the caribou, the fat bear meat. They would eat what they were given and do their work. Mostly, that meant they had to haul meat (moose, caribou, bear) on runnerless bark, wood, or skin sleds.

Some were taught to run till they found the moose, then once found, hold it till the hunter could make the kill. In fall, when it froze, the old Indian dogs would be released to "teach the young, brave dogs how to get the moose, run good on ice, keep moose occupied."

Grr's mother's name is Unanza (pronounced U-NAN-za). Her name means "white woman" in the Indian language, and she is mostly white with glacier-blue eyes. Indian-dog mushers don't like white dogs, especially white dogs with blue eyes. Occasionally, they will keep one, but often those pups are hit on the head and thrown into the silt-laden rivers to wash away. For a puppy to grow up to be a dog in the Alaskan interior is no easy thing. The dog must show promise, must have that certain temperament, toughness, and bright-eyed intelligence. It must show a heart to pull and to work. Exhaustion should not come easily. It must obey. It would be helpful if it were *not* a killer, but have a killer's "strong spirit," Jerry said.

Grr's mother, Unanza, was not only white, she was also a killer, a puppy killer. She killed, she crushed them with her deep, gouging teeth. Any puppy other than her own who roamed within the circle of dirt where she lived had little chance of surviving. Her circle of dirt was defined by the chain that held her to the spruce tree in the woods where Jerry kept his dogs. She would not, however, kill her own pups and she birthed some superior Indian dogs. Unanza was an excellent long-distance sled dog, exceptionally fast, one of the last to tire. She would die before giving up in the harness. So Unanza lived, even though she was white, blue-eyed, and a puppy killer. Jerry said she was "inbred."

Unanza looked insane, too. The way she looked at me from the shadows of the spruce woods with those blue eyes, her neck bent, her lip shaking, made me glad I was here with Jerry. It was as if she would love to remove my stomach with her canine teeth. Unanza had been bred according to a secret native practice, discovered accidentally in the isolated villages. It had to do with inbreeding, the mixing of genes of the same blood. Everyone had always heard that it was very bad to do this, but then sometimes, Jerry's people noticed, a super-dog would be birthed from a certain kind of inbreeding. That exact pairing Jerry knew, but would not tell me. It was one of the few secrets his people had kept from the white dog mushers.

Grr, my little cream-colored puppy, had a bit of inbred blood from Unanza but it was diluted by his sire's blood.

Grr so far did not appear to have any of the supranatural qualities of inbreeding nor did he seem to have any of the damage. He did, however, have all the hunting instincts befitting the wolf blood boiling in his little body.

Jerry thought that Grr would take after his father, Friendly, and Friendly had no inbred blood at all. Friendly was the opposite of Unanza. She slunk, sulked, hid behind any tree, her glacier-blue eyes burning, darting with paranoid-fire. Friendly's tail always flapped back and forth. His tail even moved his back hips, he wagged it so enthusiastically. He loved everybody, man and dog. Ten puppies could crawl all over him, bite on his collar, eat his food, run under him, pull on his flaglike tail with their puppy teeth, and he would just grin. He was the kind of dog who looked as if he was grinning. Unanza's tail did not wag—it pointed straight down and quivered with the desire to bite, lunge, cringe. Her ears were often flattened to her skull. Jerry knew Unanza's pups needed "good blood" from Friendly to balance her clashing, jittering bad genes.

Would Grr turn out like Unanza or Friendly? Only his growing up here on the farm would tell for sure. I hoped I would be able to train him so that he would not have to be chained all the time.

Jerry won the Iditarod in 1976. Grr came from Iditarod-winning sled dogs. Unanza's mother, White Eyes, ran in the swing position on Jerry's team (which is right behind the leader) or ran wheel (right in front of the sled). White Eyes was standoffish, kind of like Unanza, but didn't show any of her daughter's inbred crazy, wild, high-strung temperament. White Eyes never "went down" from the exhaustion of the brutal demands of the Iditarod, never quit. She'd limp on two legs to the finish line if she had to. Besides this, she was smart and 100 percent Alaskan husky. "Smart for husky," Jerry told me. He always said that a straight husky was not a real smart dog. Jerry felt that to get extraordinary intelligence in a sled dog you've got to cross the Alaskan husky with another, more brain-developed, breed. Often used are Irish setters, Belgian sheepdogs, greyhounds, Labs, German shepherds, Australian sheepdogs, and Greenland dogs. Jerry liked the non-Arctic breeds for intelligence. He said most pure huskies were "strong, faithful, extra tough, had good, dense fur, but they were dumb." Jerry didn't really mean dumb, exactly, just thick-headed, too stubborn, dense. "Their brain like a piece of river rock," Jerry said, affectionately. "Alaskan husky good dog for native to run trapline with, good to haul home much moose meat, many fish, but not so good for race.

Unanza's sire was what Jerry called an Aurora husky, which had gone wild from the village. Aurora huskies were a breed developed by Gareth Wright, who was half-Athabaskan, half-English. He had bred hounds to huskies and produced what Jerry called "speed dogs." These dogs had the huskies' ability to survive the 45 below zero weather, and the capacity to run in the snow and on ice. They had the huskies' pulling power and steady, non-hyped-up personalities, yet that was combined with the hound's long legs for speed and a fanatical desire to run and run and run. Instead of using the hound's speed to chase a bear or mountain lion or raccoon, it would be used to run races. In addition, the hound's big chest cavity would give more room for a big, hard-pumping heart and large, expansive lungs.

Grr's granddaddy, the gone-wild Aurora husky, a red-colored, blue-eyed dog, was not meant to breed White Eyes. Jerry was, however, excited with the outcome, since he kept much of that litter, including, of course, Unanza. Jerry said he knew Unanza would be standoffish like White Eyes, but there was no way to tell she'd be a puppy killer. She was a "super-dog," he said, when she was put into her harness and hooked to the team. She was, however, too high-strung to be a leader. But she'd pull her heart out for you. Unanza loved the open trail.

How would little puppy Grr adjust to being a Tennessee farm dog? The hound in him would, I hoped, give him a short coat of hair for the sweltering summers. I hoped, too, that Grr's hound blood would give him a hound's natural inclination to lie under a shade tree. His husky blood would give him that easygoing personality, so the kids could crawl on him, pull his tail, and hug his neck. Jerry said Grr definitely had some of the old Indian-dog, wolf blood showing in his long face, stiff, long legs, and peppering of gray hairs.

But with luck not too many of the bad traits of the hound, husky, and wolf would shape Grr's personality. Hounds like to run after animals, be gone all night. And there was no way to tell what influence a small flow of wolf blood would have in a dog like Grr. I wasn't sure if I wanted to think about it too much. It was fine that Cooper had had the "one man only, forever" temperament. But Grr would need to get along with everyone in the family; it would not be good if he was a jealous, possessive dog.

After our thrilling short walk it appeared that life with Grr could easily be one of constant adventure. Teaching him how to be a dog free to run over our farm and those of our neighbors could prove to be a difficult chore. On the other hand, maybe he would learn easily, and remember what he learned. And maybe Lacy's careful, contemplative personality would help balance Grr's need to leap over the edge. I would see, and he would see.

15

A Barn Cat
Named Tigger

I liked bobcats, mountain lions, black panthers, lions, ocelots, and leopards. I like tigers, jaguars, cheetahs, and lynx. I'm crazy about lynx. And I'm wild about the cat of the Himalayan mists, the snow leopard.

Unfortunately, I don't like house cats, the kind that live with humans. It doesn't matter what they are—Siamese, Persian, Manx, alley cat, black cat, white cat, calico, striped, long-haired, short-haired. I can't stand house cats because I am painfully allergic to them. For this reason I've never wanted them anywhere near me. No rubbing on my leg, no purring near me. I can't even walk into a house where cats live.

Get me near a cat and the home they live in, and my arms break out in red welts. I begin scratching myself and scratching myself. I can't stop. It's a torture. What adds to my torture is that some cats also shed something besides their hair, something called dander.

Dander sends me into orbit, a fiend clawing at my skin now crawling with what feels like thousands of tiny, scampering little bugs. When a cat-hair and cat-dander attack strikes, my eyes water and go bloodshot as though they were full of sand. My nose swells, runs, and turns

as red as W. C. Fields's. My scalp twitches and I want
to scratch off patches of my skin.

If I stay too long in a living room where a cat has the
absolute run of the place, I feel like someone turned my
pants inside out and sprinkled itching powder, ground
thistle leaves, thorns, and horsehair into them, and made
me wear them on a 95-degree, humid August afternoon.
At times I almost hated cats, but our mother taught us
never to hate anything. Hate is bad. She said hate will
eat you up. (In some ways she was like the Buddhists I
met in the Himalayas. She wouldn't even let us step on
an ant.)

Ever since my folks moved from WPC to their very
first home the year I went off to college, they've had cats.
Blond Betsy and brunette Abbi, my youngest sisters, love
cats, and when I go home for a visit, Mother has to keep
their cat outside for a week or so before I get there. The
poor feline baby stays in the basement or climbs up on
the windowsills of the kitchen and purrs and meows and
begs to come in. That calico cat is an expert at sneaking
inside the front door. Mother even keeps a cat-free room
just for me. I suppose I'll always be allergic to the cat.
As much as I envied my sisters' ability to let their cats
sleep with them, even use the cat for a pillow, I could
not get close to one, really like one, until Tigger came
to live on the farm.

A widow and her daughters who lived up the road gave
us Tigger. He was a tiger-striped puffball of a kitten with
long, fine fur, the worst kind as far as my allergic reac-
tions were concerned.

Tigger found out right away that he was going to have
to live outside. That meant he would have to get along
with the dogs—not a natural behavior pattern—and the
first few minutes after little Tigger was dropped off at the
farm, Lacy chased him up into a tree. He climbed up
high into one of the rock maples and stayed there till the
next morning.

Tigger got on my good side because he really enjoyed the barns. In fact, Tigger was thrilled to have a farmful of barns to rule. A barn had to be a lot better than a house, surely. In a barn, especially a hay barn, food scampered around all the time.

Whenever Tigger heard me climbing up the ladder into the hayloft he always materialized like a shadow spirit. Otherwise I rarely saw him.

As I'd lift up a fifty-, sixty-, sometimes Seventy-pound-square bale, Tigger would position himself directly between my legs, his sinew-tight body pressed down low, and if a couple of mice dashed out, the chase began.

One time the fleeing mouse, a mouse who seemed to have been chased before, came right at Tigger. Smart move. It kept him from moving, getting any speed built up. Tigger held out a claw-exposed paw, ready to swat the gray fur bullet as if the mouse was a hockey puck and Tigger the goalie. He caught the very edge of the mouse's rump with one claw, his longest, and the mouse flipped around and around. The scratched rodent landed to my side, then tried to run up the side of a stack of bales eight feet tall. Tigger leaped above it and swiped at the mouse. He missed.

Then the mouse sprinted across the loft, now mostly empty, since I'd already fed two thirds of the stash up here. It was late February; winter would soon be over. Some loose, stemmy hay lay on the floor. The escaping mouse dove into it. Tigger skidded to a halt, sliding across the slippery, dry hay. If he had not sunk his claws into the side wall he would have flown out of the opened upstairs door.

Tigger was aggravated now. His bushy, beautiful tail was twitching rapidly. He began to swipe at the loose hay, trying to flush that mouse out of his hiding place. The hay flew, dust rose, Tigger emitted a low, gritty, killing howl. Then the frightened mouse flew out of the hay, ran straight to the open door and leaped, plunged, to the ground a story below. Mighty hunter Tigger did not follow. There would be another mouse soon enough.

The only time Tigger comes around my house is in the winter when he's been unable to catch anything. He first comes to the side door, facing north, closest to the big, white-doored barn. Then if there's no answer he walks around to the laundry-room door, howling to get attention. Occasionally, when snow is deeper than Tigger's legs are long, even he will not come out of a warm barn. So I wade out there with some cat food and leftovers. Sometimes I buy him fried chicken livers at Luther's in town.

His fur is the kind that gets so deep, luxurious, and warm in the winter that you wouldn't know he was the same cat when he sheds. And when he does shed, I have no idea where all that hair goes, probably into birds' nests and mouse nests and nests of whatever kind of animal locates it. I've never seen even one of his hairs, never seen one on any furniture, clothes, nowhere. His fur grows out wide on the side of his face in winter, and so too on his body and tail. He looks as wide as a badger. And he moves like a wild animal around adults. Any fast movement, any slight noise, and he leaps away. Tigger never really fully relaxes around me, or any adult. He acts like a low-slung, ground-hugging wild cat who's been wild for years. Tigger occasionally is drawn to the human places: the homes, the easy food. But not often. He prefers the life where he's in control.

Although Tigger has little to do with adults, no purring, petting, or being held, when it comes to the three Jenkins kids, he's like a lump of melting Silly Putty. When redheaded Luke was three and wanted to pick him up, he'd grab Tigger by whichever body part was closest to his powerful small hands. Luke would get aggravated because Tigger wasn't as light as his stuffed brown bear but that cat would be as nice as he could be to "Lukey."

Tigger was all muscle and strength, and resistance and movement, not an easy kind of cat to pick up. So three-year-old Luke would attempt another good grip on Tigger, pulling him this way and that. Tigger endured it all, without ever showing a claw.

Tigger really liked Jed, and would follow him around anywhere, even up a spring-fed creek, through water and mud. It was funny to watch Jed rampage through the mud in his wet oversized sneakers and Tigger prissily, ever so daintily, put down his fine little paws as he followed.

All the kids had to do when they wanted Tigger was to call him. He seemed to possess an extraordinary ability to hear their low-volume voices even if they were at one side of the farm and he was at the other. He'd answer immediately. I could call him all night if I had a leftover chunk of chicken breast to feed him and I'd get nothing, no reply. He moved like an easy wind, which you didn't see or feel till it touched you.

For Tigger to move from the south side of the farm to the north side he passed through a total of six buildings before he got to the leaning barn with the white door. These places were his kingdom.

His hunting trails from building to building took him in an order like this: He would walk out the central hall of the red barn, through a fenced-in corral. He'd then go through a wide metal gate, then ease to the north through a corner of the middle pasture, the one that butted up against my stallion Shocker's pasture. This corner of fertile grass slopes down to another small stream of springwater, which runs over flat gray rock. The grass is especially green and fertilized in this area because there are some nice shade trees, which means the cattle congregate under them in summer. When cattle favor a particular area they leave the ground enriched with heavy concentrations of their droppings. At first I was a bit grossed out by cattle crap everywhere in the pastures until I learned how many nutrients it gives back to the soil.

The great thing about cattle is that they eat the grass to live, which takes from the soil, but after they've used the food they give it back to the soil again, which then grows another crop. A cow is an ecology system all its own.

So if Tigger was slinking his way through here in summer, he'd have to slip by some of my possibly high-strung, overprotective mama cows, then leap the stream. There he'd go by a dead tree, too wide to cut up for firewood. In twenty or thirty feet, he'd go through a fence and pass under some small elms, a couple of young oaks, and a few thorny osage orange trees.

He'd then walk over some exceedingly fertile pasture, fertile because this is where Jess Morton's dairy herd used to graze waiting to be milked. Tigger now would be heading toward the silo, where Jess Morton, the man from whom I bought this part of my farm, kept his silage. Silage is ground corn, cornstalks, and corn husks, all of which is blown into the silo, to be fed later to the cattle.

Tigger would turn a hard right toward the east and go twenty-five, thirty feet to an old granary building, once used as a hay barn. After it began to weather and fall apart, it was retired to just plain storage. There certainly was excellent mouse hunting here. Next to it was the one-hole outhouse.

Not more than seven or eight paces farther north Tigger would come to the longest building on the place, a one-story milking barn. It was quite thin and rectangular, running east to west. The two west rooms, built out of concrete blocks, were where Jess used to have all his milking equipment, stainless-steel milk tanks and medicines. Next to it was a large milking parlor that I now used to store round bales of hay. The bales weighed over a thousand pounds each, and it took a big tractor to lift them. I also stored the hand-hewn beams we saved after we tore down the smokehouse that sat in the backyard.

This place was surely one of Tigger's main grocery stops. I was not sure, though, which building he lived in and slept in most. Nor did I know where he did most of his prowling and hunting.

When he left the long barn he could stop in a calf shed next to it, but he wouldn't find much food there. The pump house might have a few field mice, maybe a couple of shrews, but the real bonanza on this farm was the last barn, all the way up against the northside fence.

Tigger was this farm's cat and he thrived here, and we have learned how to be sort-of-detached friends, even if I *am* allergic to him.

16
A Wise Man

I learned something new just about every time Mr. George spoke. The rangy, soft-voiced farmer/carpenter had been restoring our farmhouse for a couple of years and I was fascinated by his knowledge. He could talk about virgin poplar and how to lay it so it made a subtly colored floor, or tell me what field I should use as my hay next season. He'd comment on things far and wide— a black sky in the west and the nature of women. He gave me good advice on how to deal with malicious neighbors as he cut a piece of fine molding. I was a new farmer just learning the ropes and made every dumb mistake in the book, but Mr. George always stopped me before they got too serious. I came to depend on Mr. George; he'd never done anything to surprise me—until the day he took off his glasses.

His eyes startled me. I'd been around Mr. George now for years and I'd not seen his naked eyes before. They hid behind his gold-rimmed glasses, which were usually covered with a fine layer of sawdust. This day he'd been sanding some old chestnut trim and the sawdust was especially thick. He took his glasses off and cleaned them with a white handkerchief. He looked like a different man without them.

Suddenly the wise farmer I knew disappeared and I was staring at the face of a visionary. Mr. George's eyes seemed endlessly deep, as though they understood all life. Those eyes would notice the birth of a snow-covered daffodil and reflect the pain of another man's bad time. They could look at a piece of raw wood and see the finished beauty it would become. They could reassemble a dismantled antique wardrobe in a glance. They would record the first seductive warmth of spring and not be fooled by it. They'd know not to plant a crop too early and have it freeze. Mr. George's eyes were not controlling, or eagerly searching. They were accepting, they *knew*.

He caught me staring at him. He put his glasses back on. I was a bit nervous about my obvious surprise, so I joked and said, "Mr. George, you know a lot of farmers have a tan just on the lower half of their faces because their baseball cap covers up the top half. You don't have a tan on your forehead or behind your glasses." He nodded and said at least he didn't wear shorts like I did when he farmed.

Robert George was the kind of person I wanted to be around. I asked him about almost everything. A time or two I had wanted to ask him for personal advice but I was shy. He told me he used to go to the barn with his son, Enoch, and they'd talk heart to heart, man to man. I got the impression that when someone talked with Mr. George it would never be for anyone else's ears but his. Mr. George knew how to shield people's tender hearts from exposure. I always called him Mr. George because I respected him so.

We could not have come from more different backgrounds. Mr. George had no idea who The Doobie Brothers were, or what a doobie was. I had no idea what a come-along or ball joints were. He didn't know who Tone Lōc was, nor did he want to go to Tibet. I had no idea how to rebuild a carburetor to get rid of broom sage. We did seem to agree on the main things about life: love,

God, death, work, honesty, lies, family, rain, animals, peace, war, money, and children. He just knew a lot more about all of it than I did. He could make it become so clear. There were no fogs or hazes to block his views.

After the eight hours of carpentry he did for me, he went home and worked another five hours farming. Mr. George made a hay field sound like a tropical paradise. He loved hay fields. His were places where the grass grew up to your thighs, meadows knee-deep in red clover, blue-green orchard grass, and hop clover with its small yellow flowers. To hear him talk, always softly, hay cut and baled just right and put in a dry barn was as perfect as anything on God's earth. Mr. George enjoyed getting in the middle of his hay field, right behind his white house with its two-story white columns. He'd stand there and watch the wind blow the hay.

The Georges' house sat beside a creek near the end of a valley a few farms before the road curved like a limp rope and headed into the hills to Theta. This home was where Mrs. George was born and raised, where Mr. George used to come a-courtin' Mrs. George right in the front parlor. Mr. and Mrs. George raised most of their food, including some fine, non-fence-jumping cattle up on the sloping, green hills behind their house. Often when I saw their house and farm and barns and cows and hills all lying there behind Knob Creek, I thought of a Grandma Moses painting.

Now that their two children, a daughter and son, were grown and married, the Georges filled their house with things they'd bought at country auctions. They collected antique American furniture, mostly oak, and refinished and restored it. They rebuilt old pieces, and rooms in their house were like a museum, except it was *their* museum.

It wasn't just Mr. George's eyes that were extraordinary, his hands were too. I'd seen him pound a nail and the next moment pick up baby Jed and hold him gently and rub his little baby-bald head. His hands seemed to have such thick calluses that I sometimes wondered if there was any feeling in them, yet there was probably ten times more feeling in them than in mine. On a winter evening his talented hands would put back together an antique rocking chair. Next day they'd dig a jutting rock out of a field.

One morning I was struggling with my stallion who refused to enter the barn where I could tie him up and brush out his mane. Shocker had something else in mind and didn't care what I wanted. He wouldn't budge. As usual, Mr. George was not far away, ready to step in when it was certain that the book-man was getting nowhere. He came over and took a tough-willed hold of Shocker's lead rope. He pulled the rope hard, hard enough to pull Shocker's head way down. Then he led him easily inside the barn. I'd been trying to get that horse in the barn for ten minutes.

It always surprised me when I saw Mr. George act with rough power, because he almost never did. I never heard him speak that way. I guessed the only reason he would raise his voice would be if someone was about to get run over by a train.

"I been a-studyin' you, son," Mr. George said after taking control of Shocker. "In the spring of the year you'll always notice a stallion will be more disagreeable. The life in him is gettin' stronger, rising up, boilin' sometimes, especially if there's a mare nearby. That stallion won't be good for nothin' less you let him know you are the man in charge."

Later that day, he explained to me that it was best to live life being easy with things. By easy he meant gentle but I doubted I'd ever hear that word from him. He did say, though, that you always needed to reserve the moment to strike strong, bold, decisive. Sometimes, not very often, he said, it took a powerful, forceful action to go

back to being easy again. He said that was especially true
with animals and people.

Mr. George often spoke about how he'd "study a
thing," if he didn't know something. He prided himself
on being able to study something until he had it figured
out. He explained he would lie in bed at night and go
over in his mind again and again some problem that was
perplexing him. One time we couldn't figure out how to
join a new part of our house, made out of oak beams,
with the 1880s original part. He'd never worked on a
house that had twelve-inch-square beams in it before. He
studied on that one about a week till he figured it out.
Another time we couldn't decide how to make one of the
old bedrooms into two rooms with a hall in it. Every time
I thought about the problem, it seemed like trying to read
Chinese. Mr. George, "he studied about it" and worked
it out.

I learned so much at Mr. George's side. A few times
it occurred to me that maybe Mr. George wondered if I
needed to go to the barn with him, like his son, Enoch,
used to do.

There were problems that I had. What would I do with
the rest of my life? How would I support my family?
Could I possibly ever understand all there was to do to
take care of a farm and all these animals? Would the
cloudy confusion I felt about my relationship with Barbara ever become clear? To some of the outside world
we seemed to have the perfect marriage, yet there was
something wrong. I could not understand what it was.
Would we ever learn how to be close to each other?
Would we make it? What was wrong with us? I especially wanted to talk with Mr. George about Barbara and
me. Yet I was too embarrassed, too proud, too shy to
bring it up. Was he waiting for me to ask to go to the
barn and talk?

I never did ask him and I often found myself wishing
he would just take control and TELL me we were going

to the barn. But control was not how Mr. George operated. For him, it was "best to live life easy with things" and maybe he knew there were times I had to find my own way.

17

The Skillfully
Reckless Pilot

The helicopter looked like a little bubble with a spinning blade and runners. It leaped into the hot South Texas sky. *No one* should fly a copter like this pilot was doing! Was the copter heading to a disintegrating end—an explosion of flames, metal, and burned human flesh, or could the pilot pull out? The main problem with the coming death of this wild and crazy, high-tech cowboy/helicopter pilot was that I was sitting next to the maniac. If he died, so did I. I thought of telling him to go back and let me out, but he'd already begun the roundup and they couldn't turn back till they'd herded all the cattle on the range.

We were flying over South Texas rangeland, rarely traveled except by scorpions, wetbacks, roadrunners, diamondback rattlers, and some of the wildest, orneriest, meanest, toughest cattle any cowboy's ever worked. A lot of them had horns that would gladly impale you and your horse if you got near.

We were doing a once-a-year roundup near George West, Texas, not far from the King Ranch. It was the helicopter's job to flush out all the ''wild-ass'' cattle in this two-thousand acre ''pasture.'' The pasture, bigger by far than most people's farms or ranches, looked more like a grown-over brush patch, with a few ponds, open marshy places, and some scrub oak on the river edge. There was no simple way to round up these Santa Gertrudis cattle on horseback, even with famously tough Texas cowboys. The range was too brushy, there were too many places for the wild cattle to hide.

Every time we got to an especially impenetrable mass of brush, nearly twelve feet tall, the rowdy pilot would hover just over the top, so close to the leaves that the runners of the helicopter almost skimmed them. Sometimes he'd even brush the top of a tree or thicket to flush a particularly stubborn creature out. A few times a solitary red bull would refuse to budge, lunging his sword-like horn in our direction. The pilot simply pulled down on his baseball cap that read HALLIBURTON OIL WELL SERVICES, breathed deep, and tried again.

The whole idea of using a helicopter to round up cattle was one that worked in this part of South Texas because the ranches were stretched so massively over the barren landscape. Some ranches ran more than 300,000 acres (640 acres equal a section and a section is a square mile of land). Many ranches around here have more acres than entire cities. It's a different sort of grazing land from the green, tree-dotted pastures of Tennessee.

A thick native brush covered the flat South Texas land. It was hard to kill or burn out. If it was bulldozed, which cost big bucks, it just grew back. The brush provided some shade for the cattle and some wild prairie grasses. The spreading, thorn-coated cactus grew everywhere out there. During periods of grass-wilting drought local ranchers had to send Mexican hands, often illegal aliens, roaming across their land with gas-fired, hand-held burners. They would burn the thorns off the cactus so the skinny cattle had a bit of something to eat. This piece of La Campana Ranch we were flying over was about one hundred miles northwest of Laredo, Texas, which is on the Rio Grande River and the Mexican border.

The helicopter moved the cattle like a cutting horse,

beginning at the back fence line of the rectangular field. The copter flew back and forth, back and forth, as close to the ground as it could get without crashing. We aimed low and a small group of five cows trotted out from under a canopy of live oaks.

We darted back to the other side corner of the back fence line and spooked maybe another twenty, twenty-five head. No horse could easily work cattle in this tangled mass of cactus, thicket, coyote trails, and rattlesnake dens. The cattle, mostly Santa Gertrudis, the first cattle breed created in the U.S.A., were a brick-red color and ran with the long-legged, bounding gait of water buffalo. The land reminded me of aerial views of the African plains I'd seen except it was not as open.

Now the herd of agitated cattle was nearing fifty head. The skillfully reckless pilot saw two mighty red bulls under a low mesquite tree by the edge of a shallow pond, bordered by belly-high marsh grass. He dived at the bulls. They refused to even flinch. We got close enough to see their eyes. One flicked his tail as though he were slapping at flies. Perhaps he thought we were a huge one.

Next the airborne herder got right above the mesquite tree. He clenched his teeth, tensing the muscles in his neck. His right hand held the black stick that controlled the copter's movements. The copter slowly went down, till some leaves blew off the tree and the dust almost obscured our view of the dim-brained bulls. These two bulls acted as if they'd gladly take on the copter.

"They ain't gonna stay under that mesquite. I'll tear the tree down first," he said loud enough for me to hear. Maybe he was giving me notice to get out now, or hold on. My knuckles were white, my fingers bruising.

Tear the tree down! How do I jump out of this helicopter? When will we be low enough to get out? How do you tear a tree down with a copter? The pilot didn't look like a vindictive, self-destructive madman. He wore pressed khakis, an orange-plaid western shirt, thin leather

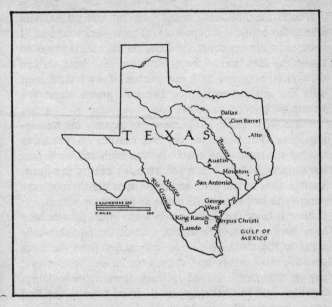

belt, dust-dulled, brown Tony Lama cowboy boots, and a baseball cap. He looked as normal as a hardware-store owner. Maybe he was just kidding.

Then he began to circle the tree about three or four feet above the ground. The wind and flying debris from the spinning blades were terrible. Apparently they made one of the bulls angry, and it charged the copter.

"Watch out," I said out loud. LOUD. The grim-eyed pilot backed up and drew the bull farther away from the tree. The enraged bull was furious. He charged again. Again, the pilot backed up. Maybe this guy was just plain good at this job? He'd said he'd been doing this for five years. He'd lived that long! I calmed down a bit. When he'd enticed the bull out about fifty yards, he darted straight up and came down behind the bull and touched its back with the rungs of the landing gear. WHAT!

* * *

Could the bull kick, butt, jump up and hit us, and knock the copter's balance off? The dust-coated bull (I could now almost count the hairs on his back!) began to run in the direction of the other cattle. The herd walked slowly, circling around a few bushes. They flicked their tails like anxious cattle do. The bull joined them. We swung back to get the other one.

When we returned to the mesquite tree and the remaining Santa Gertrudis bull, the bull ran out from the tree toward the river. The copter revved high and burst past the running bull, cut him off, stopped him in the open, went at him, turned him, and drove him right through the pond. The bull cooled off while swimming across it.

Now both of the copter pilots were in the flow as they sped back and forth from one side of the two thousand acres to the other. We were just inches from the trees and thickets, ponds and open grasslands. Stray cows, calves, and bulls moved quickly toward the mooing, bawling, and ever-growing herd. Even coyotes sprinted away from the helicopters' roar.

The herd now was over one hundred head. The pilot amazed me with his quick sprints, fast curves, backups, and dives from the sky. He kept these wild cattle in a tight herd, something they were not used to. He darted from one side of a tall-grassy area to another to bring back a panicked mother cow trying to get her slow-moving calf out of the path of thundering hoofs. It seemed we moved at speeds over 80 mph. Whatever, it was a lot faster than any horse.

As we neared the end of this two-thousand-acre "piece," I could see five or six pickup trucks, a set of cattle-working pens, and a semitrailer truck pulling an empty cattle-hauling rig. We were going to get all those crazed, drooling, sweating, angry, almost stampeding cattle to funnel into one, fourteen-foot-wide open gate! Getting cattle like this to move through open land was one thing; cornering them, as we were about to do, was something else again.

Tom Martin, a tall intellectual man in his forties, who owned this ranch with his father, stood up on top of a sorting chute made of tubular steel, now rusted, and shielded his face from the blowing dust. He was about six feet four inches tall and had the loose-limbed gait of a basketball player. He was hoping, especially since it was expensive to hire two helicopters and pilots ($200 an hour), that the first pass through to the corrals would do it. The herd had a year to forget how much it despised being driven through brush, ponds, briars, and dust, but after this run most of them remembered again.

Right before we got to the fence line that led to the corrals, the pilot circled the strung-out herd, rapidly compacting them into an easier working group. He had to move fast and efficiently and not let any rogues break loose.

"There's a few rank bulls and a couple of rawboned cows in this bunch who will break away. A few of them damn crazy-acting bulls had got away from me for two, three years in a row. Mr. Martin never even seen some of these cattle before."

Now the pilot was so close to the ground we were eyeball to eyeball with some of the tallest cows. Their horns looked sharp enough to pierce the bubble that shielded our cockpit. The pilot hovered in one place, blocking their escape. They were held in to the rear and to the sides by barbed-wire fence, and to the front by a loud helicopter. They could go in only one direction and that was toward the open pens.

It was a face-off. The helicopter did not move. The cattle would not move. The pilot gently maneuvered us to the herd's left. A few cattle began to run along the fence line, toward the pens. Then they all began moving, while the copter moved slowly enough to stay a bit behind the end of the herd. As the herd vacated the corner,

a single, crumpled brick-red calf lay in the trampled dirt.
It had been killed—either kicked, stepped on, or suffo-
cated.

The pilot shouted. "I hope the mother cows left most
of their calves hid somewheres before they moved on."
There were not many small calves, other than the dead
one.

Tom Martin would sort out the cattle to be sold and
the cattle that would be kept. He could look at a cow
and, in two or three seconds, tell if it was nursing or had
a calf, and probably come pretty close to telling how old
that calf might be by the amount of flesh showing in the
cow's upper hips, around her backbone and around her
ribs. The older a calf got (they are usually weaned at
about eight months), the bigger it got, and the more of a
drain it was on its mother. Tom was looking to sell
weaned calves (yearlings), old bulls, broke-down-wore-
out cows, young bulls that might have escaped previous
roundups, and anything that was lamed or had birth de-
fects. There would be only a few lame or defective cattle
for they would not survive in this harsh land.

The whole herd went into the pens. A Mexican cowboy, a full-time ranch hand at La Campana, ran quickly
to shut the metal gate behind them. Everyone on the
ground, including Wally Hebert, the colleague who'd
driven there with me, gave the pilot a victorious hand
signal. I was astounded at what I'd just witnessed. That
pilot was brilliant: He maneuvered that little copter like
a hyperactive surgeon making rushed but perfect cuts
during a difficult procedure.

We landed, and it was good to be on firm ground. The
pilot winched his copter onto a trailer pulled by a new
blue and silver Ford pickup and went to another ranch to
perform another feat of helicopter wizardry.

Now the people on the ground had to work these frantic
cattle. The sun-dried Texans, all Mexicans except for

Tom and his eighty-year-old dad, didn't even ask us to help. They did, seeing the agitated enthusiasm in my eyes and the overconfident ignorance in my manner, ask me to stand well out of the way. Wally Hebert was more analytical than I and less likely to dive into the action. His every survival instinct told him to keep away. The thick-bodied cowboy, Macario Martinez, mentioned to us that there were cattle in this herd that would gladly kill you. He seemed to enjoy this knowledge.

First the men drove about a third of the cattle into a separate small pen. Every few moments a horned mother cow would get separated from her confused calf, and if a cowboy was in between them she'd attempt to gore him. These Santa Gertrudis cattle were much taller than other, more popular cattle breeds, most of which originated in the U.K. The Hereford (brown with white faces), and Angus (all black), the Shorthorn (red and white mottled), all were short-legged and slower, much more domesticated and thicker-bodied. If a Santa Gertrudis gored one of these Mexican cattlemen right through the heart, it would not be the first time. I didn't think cattle could make me so fearful. I'd never thought of them before as so quick, so wild, so aggressive, so out of control with the desire to get away.

I remember how Mr. George had warned me. Mr. George would never fool with this type of cattle. He thought I was nuts to drive over two thousand miles from Tennessee to Texas and back home to pick up some cattle that would just tear down my fences and my barns, breed my neighbor's cattle (which can make neighbors enemies), attack the kids, the family, the local dogs. Mr. George joked that no coyote, of which we have plenty in Tennessee, would ever kill and eat any calves of these crazy cattle. These South Texas cattle would kill the coyote. I believed it. But until I got right up next to these powerful, wild animals, I would not have dreamed that a supposedly domestic cow would attack things just for the fun of it.

Tom was sitting on the top of the metal bars that supported a chute. Each cow, calf, and bull had to squeeze through this as Tom decided whether to keep them, sell them, or send them back to the neighbor's ranch where they belonged.

If they were to be kept, they were directed into one corral. If they were to be sold, they were sorted into another corral. Tom grew up on this 16,000-acre ranch, a second-generation Martin, and he was lightning quick in his decisions.

I stood out of the way of the pros as they worked their herd. It was noisy, with the cowboys shouting in Spanish, with the bawling of the captured cattle. Then behind me, I heard something. It was a completely different sound, a meek, not a strong, cry. I looked out into the haze and saw a small calf walking as though it had just crossed a desert and was about to flop over dead. The deep-red calf looked starved, its hair was jagged, unruly, its hip protruded. Something was very wrong with it.

I climbed on the sorting chute and pointed it out to Tom. He squinted into the heat and said it looked like an orphan. He called to Macario, asked him to go over and rope it. While Macario's rope was circling over the calf's head, Tom asked me if I would take it home. He said there was no telling what had happened—probably its mother was bitten by a diamondback or died of old age. Anyway, he thought the mother might have been dead about a month. He thought the calf was about three months old but stunted from the lack of mother's milk, and about dead. Tom said another week and this calf would have been wild hog, vulture, or coyote food, whichever found it first. He said it might not live till we got home, but if I'd give it some extra care if might make it.

Marcario roped it easily and pulled it to our cattle

trailer. There Macario's flashy nineteen-year-old son, Mike, had to lift it inside. Mike and I pushed the half-limp calf all the way to the front compartment that could be closed off with a gate, so that it would not get trampled by the others we would put inside there, too.

We loaded up four red heifers and a young bull calf. The freshly weaned bull was bony and threw its head back and forth. It jerked its head spastically, its eyes wide open. Tom said the young bull held his head high, often a sign of too high spirits. He might settle down, Tom said softly, he might not. We headed home to deep green and comparatively gentle Tennessee.

18
Cattle Haulers

Before moving to the farm, the biggest animal I'd ever been responsible for was Cooper, a hundred-pound dog. My largest vehicle was a medium-duty Ford pickup. When I'd got the pickup in 1982, I thought it was huge. So far this past week of March 1983, Wally and I had driven a heavy-duty white pickup, hauling a long cattle trailer, over two thousand miles. Our whole rig was almost as long as a semitrailer truck. I'd borrowed the outfit from Pete Allen, who lived near me, and worked a lawyer's farm for him. Pete also had his own rodeo rink where he held an annual rodeo. Pete taught calf roping, bronc riding, and team roping and raised rodeo stock. His hair was dark and thinning and his face was wide. He was a big-hearted, strong-bodied man.

Pete, unlike Mr. George, thought it was a good idea to bring in some fresh ''Gurt'' blood, from Texas. The Santa Gertrudis breed originated on the county-sized King Ranch. The founders of the King Ranch had crossed the Milking Shorthorn (a hardy English breed that gave much milk and had good, thick muscle) with Brahman cattle. Brahmans, from India and Africa, are bizarre-looking cattle, with humps like camels, long ears that droop straight down, heat-tolerant skin, and the ability to eat almost any plant. They also have a great resistance to insects and disease. Pete told me that Gurts would be good to crossbreed to Hereford or Angus, "real good, boy." I'd planned to take full advantage of the hybrid vigor that occurred when two distinct breeds were mated to each other and produced a superior offspring.

Now that Wally and I had survived our adventure in getting here, I had Texas-sized enthusiasm about making it back to Tennessee with no trouble. We'd so far learned there were no fast turns when you haul a cattle trailer. Also, there was no backing up, at least for me. There was no parking in a normal parking place; in fact, there was basically no place to park, the rig was so long. And backing up, well, we were almost stranded for life in the parking lot of a McDonald's in Corsicana, Texas. We'd been driving so long we were numb in our brains and our bottoms.

Before I could think, out of hunger or in need of caffeine, I was in McDonald's drive-in lane. The window for ordering, with a speaker and microphone, was around the corner behind the building. But I could not get around the corner! When I attempted to back up, I turned the wheel the wrong way and the cattle trailer jackknifed. It formed a 90-degree angle to the truck. I pulled forward and got too far from the little McDonald's speaker that was blurting out in an East Texas accent, "May I take ya oda p-leeze." It kept calling and calling. "Ya oda p-leeze."

The more I tried to back up, the farther away I got from the speaker and the more idiotic the stupid truck acted as I tried to maneuver it. Pete had warned me not to try anything like this. In fact, he warned me not to go through any cities, except on an interstate, just to avoid situations that required skill in this sort of driving.

I turned the wheel one way, then the other, but the trailer went in the wrong direction no matter what I did. I seemed incapable of turning it in the right direction.

Wally and I were stranded in a McDonald's parking lot
north of Mexia, Texas, and south of Gun Barrel City.
The well-trained McDonald's worker kept repeating her
well-rehearsed line. Finally, as I was about to give up,
and go in and ask someone to call the police, or see if
any of the local good old boys could drive one of these
blamed things, I did something right and pulled forward
enough to straighten out. Then we pulled out on the street
and parked along a curb.

We walked across the parking lot and I decided I'd not
tell the local folks it was us out back, the kindergarten
cattle haulers from Tennessee, who couldn't even back
up. I'm sure we looked like the book-men we really were.

Wally and I pulled into my farm just before dawn. We
let the Santa Gertrudis cattle out into the corral right behind the barn. That young, high-headed bull stepped to
the ground and started running. He didn't stop when he
hit the back fence; he smashed it down. I would not be
able to catch him again for almost three years.

19

The Book-Man

"The book-man" was the nickname given me by my dairy-farmer neighbor, Jess Morton. One skin-cracking, dry August afternoon I was attempting to do something I'd heard Mr. George talk about. I was picking up bales of hay by myself and loading them on my hay wagon to take to the barn. Nobody, including me, wants to haul hay by themselves (it is one of the rankest, toughest jobs on the farm) but when a black-gray cloud loaded with rain is lying low and coming toward you just above the trees, there is no time to wait for help. If rain falls on freshly baled hay it can be totally ruined.

It was late afternoon and about 90 degrees. I hooked up my hay wagon, with its flat bed, to my little Massey Ferguson 135 tractor. I'd bought it from Jim Baker, a local Blue Springs boy made good, who owned the John Deere tractor dealership in the big town (pop. 30,000) ten miles south. He bought, sold, and traded new and used tractors, and mine was a 1972 model that had been used on a dairy farm. The rims were rusted pretty badly, the fire-engine-red paint faded to dull rust-red, and the seat cushion and the front tires worn, but it was what I could afford. Also, it was not too big that I felt I couldn't handle it.

Mr. George told me that if I put my tractor in low range, first gear, it would creep along at about average walking speed. If I stayed close and kept it pointed down the rows of just-baled hay, I could walk alongside it, throwing the bales up on the hay wagon. Normally, hauling hay is a three- or four-man job: one to drive the tractor, one or two to throw bales up on the wagon, and one to stack the bales. But it worked, sort of. At first I'd throw the bales too far and they'd fall off the other side. Then I'd oversteer the tractor and it would run into bales. Sometimes I'd go too fast and wear myself out so that I had no strength left by the time I got to the two hundredth or three hundredth fifty-to-sixty-pound bale. Doing this kind of work made me realize why Mr. George never moved too fast, never got too hyper. He moved at the same speed in the beginning of a tough physical job as he did at the end. In the beginning it seemed a bit slow but at the end it looked pretty fast.

In the middle of the third row, after the tractor had stalled from going too slow, run over a couple of bales, jammed a bale sideways underneath the short front wheels, run away from me after I released the clutch and it was in high range, I had a feeling someone was watching me. I looked up to see Jess Morton and black Jess, his farmhand, leaning on our fence watching me. Surely they'd been laughing.

I turned off the tractor, and walked over to the two Jesses with an embarrassed stride.

"You men have any suggestions about how to do this hay hauling?" I asked.

"How about sticking to book writing, Mr. Book-Man," Jess Morton said, with no hint of humor. He slyly peeked over at black Jess and they both smiled big enough to let me know they weren't making "hateful fun" of me.

"That's not a bad idea, Jess. How about you guys? I

Baby Cooper lies in my hands when he was four weeks old, the day I picked him from the rest of his litter mates. *(Photograph by Lynn Underhill)*

Grr, an Alaskan husky, shows his varied bloodlines — part wolf, part Indian dog, and part Aurora husky. The Alaskan husky is not a registered breed. It is just the best, the fastest long-distance sled dogs in the world.

Jerry Riley begins conditioning his dog team in the fall, by hooking them up to an old Honda Civic car frame.

Jerry and Margie stand on either side of their son, Guy, ten, as they take a break from building their log cabin just sixty miles from Mount McKinley.

Grr and Lacy, playing "steal the stick," one of their favorite games at home on the farm. This was shortly before they became hunting machines.

Puppy Lacy, one of Clara Ketzler's sons, and Lacy's father, a Siberian husky.

Grr's father, Friendly, a long-legged Alaskan husky.

Typical brush-, cactus-, and mesquite-covered cattle country of South Texas.

Sorting the Martins' Santa Gertrudis cattle after rounding them up with helicopters. Macario and Mike push them through on horseback, while Tom sorts, on top of the working chute.

T. J. Martin, eighty-seven, was the Patrón (Bossman) of La Campana till the day he died, in 1985. Here he scrutinizes the ranch's cattle while they're sorted. His son, Tom, told me, "My father was one of the last live-and-breathe, old-time Texas cattlemen. He could think like a cow. . . . Through Dad's silence I knew if I was workin' the cattle right." The elder Martin, one of nine children, was never given a name; everyone just called him Bud. So when he went to school and noticed everyone else had a first name he named himself Thomas Jefferson Martin.

Tom Martin, son of T. J. Martin, has run La Campana since his dad's death in 1985. Here, on top of his favorite bay mare, he points to the dust raised by the herd coming to the corrals.

Mike Martinez, Macario's son, born and raised on La Campana, ropes the orphan calf Tom Martin gave me.

Five years later the orphaned bull calf, Cinnamon, has grown up and is now my herd sire.

My Shocker takes his last run on the Jenkins farm before leaving for Inner Mongolia.

One of Shocker's few bad habits was running the cattle. At least I broke him from trying to bite and stomp 'em to death.

Mary Lou Morton on one of Jess's favorite horses they owned in the forties. The photo was taken in what is now my backyard. *(Photograph by Lola Farrell)*

Mary Louise Morton, a very particular lady, and her pampered Muffin at the horse show.

Unanza, Grr's mother, shows signs of Alaskan natives' secret method of sled-dog inbreeding. The name Unanza is the Athabaskan word for "white woman."

Clara Ketzler, an Athabaskan native from Nenana, Alaska, holds baby Lacy.

Jerry Riley, an Athabaskan and winner of the famed Iditarod sled-dog race, with puppy Grr right before giving him to me to take back to my farm in Tennessee.

Headwaters of Teklanika River near Mount McKinley. This river, filled with glacier melt-off, provides much water to Jerry Riley's home village hunting and fishing grounds in the Minto Flats. "Headwaters of Teklanika, place of many grizzly," Jerry told me.

Grr and other puppies from his litter investigate a nearly empty bucket of salmon.

Flying with a helicopter cowboy/pilot as we round up wild Santa Gertrudis cattle for La Campana Ranch in South Texas. I would take some of these young cattle home with me.

The 2,000-acre "pasture" that we fly above is a maze of thickets, cactus, diamondback rattlers and mesquite trees. Sometimes it's best to herd the cattle through open water.

Macario Martinez oversees a group of La Campana's cattle as they head back, after being sorted, to the thickets and wilds of South Texas, just north of the King Ranch.

Texas ranch hand cools off with many large iced teas after brutally hot day of working cattle.

Wearing Dad's boots, Jed, five, sits with CoCo, his Welsh corgi. On top of a round bale of hay is one of their favorite places on the farm. Round bales weigh over a thousand pounds each and are fed one a day to our cow herd in the dead-cold of winter.

A low-slung, Middle Tennessee barn on a crisp fall afternoon.

Cattle and horse people "smile big" when they have an overflowing hay barn heading into the winter.

I like to take the long way around when I'm going to my hay-cutter's house, so that I can go down this narrow road.

Cooper, my beloved friend, is not gone from me, nor will he ever be.

Early morning fog rolls into the pastures from the creek as cattle graze.

UFO, the Brahman bull, owned jointly by my farm and the Kuykendalls, stands in the walnut grove surveying all his cows.

Lane Thrasher and Gray, "hot after" crazed No-Name.

Miss Glenda deciding whether to attack me now or when I get closer. She was Jed's cow. He named her after my secretary, Glenda Andrews. Fortunately, the human Miss Glenda is not anywhere near as ornery as her now-departed namesake.

Lane Thrasher's horse, Gray. They work as a team when they rope local farmers' wild cattle.

Jess Morton atop his favorite horse, Snip, during the 1940s. "He was the meanest one I ever had. He tried to be an outlaw." *(Photograph by Mary Lou Morton)*

Jess and Mary Lou stand in front of their 1956 Buick Century, the one they had when their antebellum home burned down. *(Photograph by Nancy Cleveland)*

I'm standing next to a not-yet-full-grown PJ Snap, a Polled Hereford and my first bull. *(Photograph by Murray Lee)*

The incredible night in 1966 when Shakers Shocker (my stallion's sire) and Betty Sain won the World Championship for Tennessee Walking Horses. Betty, referred to as "that girl," was the first woman to win. The crowd was so ecstatic they charged onto the field, and many were crying like the woman at right.

Shocker's Walking Horse genes will greatly improve the bloodline of Mongol horses. Mongolian officials in charge of him now plan to breed Shocker to about 250 mares per year.

Looking back toward Beijing, from atop a barren, dusty mountain pass on our trip to Inner Mongolia with the stallions.

Dr. Marvin Powers, an Illinois country doctor and donator of Clouds Independence (the second stallion) to Mongolia. Dr. Powers, wearing his Red Chinese Army cap, stands with Mu Ge Bur, a young Mongolian who was assigned to care for both stallions for as long as they live.

A neighbor's young hogs root in the snow in search of some corn cobs lying on top of a harvested field.

A portrait of a typical Mongolian mare, short and stout, not much bigger than a pony. It is to these that our stallions will be bred.

The chilled beauty of dark winter silhouettes surrounded by a rare covering of snow a few miles west of the Jenkins farm.

A Tennessee tin-roofed barn in the middle of a Tennessee spring.

Grr and Lacy spent a lot of time in the spring-fed creek on the front of our farm.

Luke, three, strokes Tigger, the barn cat.

Shocker, my stallion, nuzzles
Rebekah, eight, in the shade
of a thorn tree.

When Shocker got this revved up, Mr. George would say that "the life was
rising in him."

Hippo, the Beefmaster cow, nurses her half-Hereford calf, sired by P.J.

Mr. Robert George: restorationist, mechanic, carpenter, cattleman, and close friend.

The Zen-like October beauty of this seldom-seen Chinese countryside. We had to truck two Tennessee Walking Horse stallions from Beijing to Inner Mongolia through these arid lands. A peasant plows with oxen in the distance.

Chinese use donkeys to haul straw from just-harvested wheat fields to their homes to provide bedding for animals and people alike.

The Inner Mongolian village I stayed in during my first visit across China. Mongolian clouds wash over the grasslands.

As we presented the two stallions, Shockers Buck and Clouds Independence, to the Ta Hao model farm in Inner Mongolia, four Mongolians in ceremonial dress toasted us with drink and song.

A gifted Mongol horseman who someday wishes to ride the descendants of our donated American stallions.

A double rainbow welcomes us back to the dry, golden grasslands of Inner Mongolia.

The winds wail as a typical herd of smallish Mongolian horses runs free. It is our dream that someday a part-Tennessee Walking Horse stallion will be running with them and passing on his great heritage.

There are many places I like to go to be alone, but my favorite is in the hayloft of the leaning barn. *(Photograph by Robin Hood)*

mean ya'all do this for me. Show me how it's done by experts.''

"Oh, no, sir. We's got to get back to farmin' on this side of the fence," black Jess said as they turned to walk up toward Jess Morton's silo and low-slung dairy barn.

Jess Morton, sixty-five, had been looking down the hill at me and my sometimes fractured attempts at farming since we came here. The first week or two after we'd settled in, Mary Lou, his lovely, stylish wife, came by the house one cool summer afternoon with some of her famous mini–chess pies. They tasted delightful, a combination of custard pie and pecan pie without the pecans. Mary Lou would never go out in public without her hair done, and as she stepped out of her late-model Cadillac Eldorado, every hair was in place. Jess and Mary Lou had been married forty-five years.

"Pe-ta," Mary Lou said the first afternoon we met. "You know the last man who owned this farm was not a good neighbor. Jess, my husband, has lived on that farm across that fence all his life and only three other families have owned this before ya'all. The Odils and Boatrights, they always had a gate over there, behind your smokehouse. A gate in a line fence can make a good neighbor."

The next day I hired a man and we put in a gate in the line fence. We put it right where there had always been one when the Odils and Boatrights before us owned this farm, between the pond behind the Mortons' house and the loafing barn, where Jess's cows waited to be milked. Putting in gates and fences was just one of the many farm things I didn't know about. From the time of Mary Lou's first chess pie, from the time Jess called me Book-Man, I've been close friends with the Mortons. And ever since Mary Lou's first suggestion about a gate, I've always done what she asked of me. She just has that effect on me.

Jess saw my first cattle delivered to the farm. It was a

vivid green day and late in the afternoon the lowering sun backlit all the blades of grass, the elm leaves, and the poplar-tree trunks. The light made the creek water look like polished brass. I'd bought ten Hereford steers (castrated bull calves) from a place called Rattle and Snap, one of the original antebellum plantations in our county. It was named Rattle and Snap, storytellers say, because the whole plantation was won in a gambling game, like dice, called "rattle and snap."

Jess told me next time he saw me at the Farmers Co-op in town, where everybody bought their seed, fertilizer, work gloves, horse feed, and other farm sundries, that those brown-and-white steers I bought sure looked fat. "Must have been getting extra feed, in a creep feeder. They'll lose that weight just eating pasture grass. Lose you some money, yes, sir. That rich man that owned them, he's in the purebred business, needs to keep his cars shined up." Jess was right, they lost that grain-fed fat on my grass, but J.B. was right in advising me to start out with steers. I wouldn't have the problems with them I'd have with cows and bulls. I sold them at the stockyard later in the fall—they'd gained weight by then—but most important, I did not have any big traumas with them. None died, none got sick, none got their heads stuck between two trees, none had birthing problems.

J. B. Shepherd had been county agent here for about as long as anyone could remember and he was not what I imagined. He was not a tobacco-spitting, country-talking redneck. He was a soft-spoken, college-educated, wise man who took me under his wing to teach me how to raise cattle, among other things. The second or third time I met J.B., then in his late fifties, he said he'd rather teach someone like me, because I was a blank slate and knew basically nothing.

J.B. advised me that I soon might be ready to try some young cows. He could find me ten, twelve "black baldies," half-Hereford, half-Angus. They'd have black bodies with white, curly-haired faces. He said it would be wise to get them already bred; that way I could learn all about pregnant cows and calves. There was much more to owning ten bred cows than I ever imagined. Jess told me more than once I'd really gotten myself into a mess this time. He said I had more than I could handle.

J.B. told me what to look for when a cow was about to give birth. He said that they would act restless, begin staying off by themselves instead of with the rest of the herd. He said they would swell and become loose and red in the vagina and secrete a clear, jellylike substance. If this was their first calf they'd have to be watched closely because they wouldn't trust their instincts yet and they would do foolish, dangerous things and often lose their calves. The more he told me the more I felt like I needed to be a gynecologist.

He told me horror stories of first-calf heifers (a cow that hasn't had a calf yet) getting so nervous that instead of lying down and having contractions and having the calf, they'd get up every other contraction and have the calf standing up in the middle of a creek. Or they'd get mired in some chest-deep mud, or tangled in rusted barbed wire. J.B. said he'd seen small cows bred to a bull with too big head and shoulders. Then the calf would get stuck in the birth canal and you'd have to hook a chain to the calf's legs and pull it out of the poor cow with a pickup truck. The calf would be dead, and the cow might be paralyzed, or die. J.B. said that once the calf gets its head out of the birth canal, it comes out with its front feet and nose first, and that if it's not all the way out of the mother very quickly, it suffocates and dies. That's when it has to be delivered by you, J.B. said. Sometimes there is not enough time or money to call a vet. I wondered what I was doing getting into all this. I was nuts, that's what. What was a book-man doing here?

It must have been that J.B. could tell I was over-whelmed by all the things I had to know, especially now

that I had ten young, black, white-faced cows about to
have babies. It wasn't like the anxiety of waiting for my
own children; at least with them I knew they had Sam
Kuykendall, the best obstetrician around. In many ways,
I was more nervous about the cows because I was responsible if something went wrong and I had no idea
what to do. I thought of stories I'd heard of police and
cab drivers delivering babies. J.B. told me I needed to
order a plastic-covered three-ring notebook titled *Tennessee Beef Cow-Calf Handbook*, put out by the University of Tennessee. It was three hundred pages of
information, stuff I didn't know. This book made me feel
worse.

The first section was titled "Breeding, Selection and
Reproduction." I opened up to a chapter called "Coping
with Calving Difficulties," by Duane Miksch, Extension
Veterinarian, University of Kentucky. Before I finished
the first paragraph I was ready to call J.B. and tell him
to come get the cows and sell them to someone else. It
said: "Causes of calving difficulty may be separated into
two categories. 1.) Contributing causes can be identified
before the process of giving birth begins. 2.) Immediate
causes are those that can only be recognized after a cow
is in labor. At that point calving difficulty cannot be pre-
vented: only the severity can be minimized. However,
the incidence of calving difficulty can be reduced by
management decisions based *on understanding the contributing causes.*" (HELP.)

There was more. It got worse. "Cattlemen should de-
velop a competence and confidence in determining when
to intervene, in aiding deliveries, and in assessing the
need for professional assistance. A cow should be ex-
amined if she has labored two or three hours without
progress or if the calf has not been born within two hours
after appearance of a waterbag. Overzealous intervention
before the cervix is fully dilated may result in severe
injury to the cow as well as the calf." *All* this informa-

tion was overzealous intervention for my brain. I couldn't read any more. The pictures I looked at were bad enough.

They showed four pictures of a calf in different presentations for birth: the right way (the normal anterior presentation) and three bad ways (breech, anterior presentation with deviation of head, and posterior presentation). Then there was a picture of tools for assisting problem deliveries. There were obstetrical chains and detachable handles, a fetal extractor and antiseptic lubricant.

It seemed like I needed to go to vet school. I had no time—my ten cows were due to start calving any day now, maybe now!

When I left for work the next morning (I had my office in a trailer behind Luther's Grocery Store) I was halfway down the gravel driveway before I saw her. There was a big black body lying on my left. Her head faced the creek, the rising sun shone on her rear end. She had a mighty, body-bending contraction, and her rear legs lifted off the ground.

How long had she been there? Was the calf alive? Certainly. I saw only some small black hooves sticking out, so far. No more yet. That seemed OK. I guessed everything was fine, just the beginning of heavy labor. I'd come back in a few hours. So far, being a cow obstetrician was all right. I felt quite confident. I didn't dare feel anything else.

When I came back she was still lying down on her side, all four legs out at her side, her head on the ground. Great, maybe I'd see the very end of this birth, the first I'd ever witnessed. I got out of my truck and walked around to see the calf. It had made not one quarter inch of progress. Something is BAD WRONG. Not my first birth on the farm! Is the calf stuck? Does this black-and-white cow not know what to do, how to push?

As I walked up to her to see what was happening, she got up and walked down closer to the creek. She walked

like she'd inhaled a five-hundred-pound boulder. I left
and went back to the trailer before she lay back down.
I'd see what the book said. I read the following:

Normal stages of giving birth are as follows:
First Stage begins with uterine contractions, includes
dilation of cervix and ends with entry of fetus into the
birth canal. Restlessness and isolation from the herd
may be the only observable signs during this stage.
[OK we've come this far.] Heifers are generally more
restless than older cows. She did not appear super restless, but then I did not know how to compare her actions. I'd never owned an older cow.] They may appear
colicky [whatever that meant], lying down and getting
up frequently or kicking at their abdomen. The first
water bag may appear toward the end of first stage. [I
had not seen any water bag, had no idea what to look
for.] Stage one continues for two to six hours, or
sometimes longer in heifers. [That bit of info was a
relief. Giving birth takes longer for a heifer.]
The Second Stage includes passage of the fetus through
the birth canal. During this phase the cow actively
participates in the delivery.
Fetal membranes appear and rupture ahead of the fetus, providing lubrication for its passage. [This must
be happening or had already happened. I saw no sign
of any membranes having ruptured.] Pressure exerted
in the cow's pelvis successively by the head, shoulders
and hips of the fetus intensify abdominal contractions.
Mature cows are normally in this second stage less
than two hours. Heifers may normally require three or
four hours. [All right—I felt a bit better. I'd wait one
more hour and come back.]

When I came back she'd moved again, this time into a
little gully next to my southern line fence, in the shade
of my neighbor's little barn. The grass was most luxuri-

ant by the fencerows because shade trees grew there, and the cattle often stood under them, enriching the soil with their droppings and providing food for the clumpy grass. At least the cow had the presence of mind to get out of the zapping heat. I just had an odd feeling that this birth was going to end up a bad experience.

The two little black hooves were now out about four inches farther and during one especially long contraction I saw what looked like the pinkish-purple wet nose. After the contraction was over, what looked like the nose disappeared inside her. She was a short-legged cow with smooth, dense hair. What should I do? I felt so dumb. Should I wait longer, call a vet, call J.B.? I did not want to wait any longer, but then I did not want to react too soon. Perhaps she could have the calf normally. My first calf! I was a pacing, shaky-nerved, first-time cow-man book-man. When Rebekah and Jed were born, all I had to do was stand there, boiling with excitement and anticipation. Somebody *else* was the obstetrician!

I couldn't wait any longer. I'd called J.B. last time I was at the trailer and he was away and wouldn't be back till morning. Young Dr. Porter, the closest vet, was out operating on a horse that got tangled in barbed wire and wouldn't return to the clinic for at least three hours. But Glyn Smith, the Church of Christ pastor, had said if there was anything he could ever do to be a good neighbor, don't hesitate to call. He lived just across the creek. Maybe he could come take a look.

I walked across the creek, climbed the fence between us and his backyard and knocked on his door. Preacher Smith answered.

I told him what was going on and he said he'd change into his work clothes and meet me over by the young cow. Glyn had grown up on his family's farm just across a few ridges west of here. He knew about such things as problem births. I did not yet know if this was one or not.

Glyn was over in less than fifteen minutes. He was a

small, wiry man who moved quickly. He was rolling up his sleeves as he got to the rear of the laboring cow. He looked over the situation, saw that the hooves and end sections of the calf's legs were dried out. He said they shouldn't be—it was a sign things were taking too long. Preacher Smith asked me how long this had been going on. I told him at least since early this morning. He rolled up his sleeves even farther. It was obvious his arms and hands knew what to do with a birthing cow.

He knelt on the grass, slightly brittle from a shortage of rain, and stuck his right arm up inside the cow's birth canal, till I could not see his elbow. The neighbor man worked fast like he was an emergency-room doctor and his patient had stopped breathing. Glyn moved his arm around inside her, in a half circle, assessing whether the calf's head was lined up correctly. Was it breech? He said no. Was it coming out the way it was supposed to? The Preacher Man said yes, but the calf was too large, its shoulders and chest too big around for this small cow. It must have been bred to a bull who was too big.

"Do you have any baling twine?" Glyn asked me. His language and movements indicated there was no time to waste.

I got some from the back of the pickup and Glyn looped it around both hooves.

"I'm going to pull now, see if we can get this calf out of there, you understand?"

"Yes, sir."

First he pulled; he pulled so strongly that he moved the back end of the cow. Preacher Smith asked me to hold on to her front legs. She was so exhausted she did not even try to get up. Even with me holding her, the calf inside her did not budge even an inch. Glyn asked me to give him some more hay twine; I did, and we hooked that on to its hoofs, too, so that I could pull. We pulled till we sweated through our shirts. Both of us placed our feet up against the pitiful cow's rear end for leverage and gave a pull that was all we possibly could.

At first nothing moved, nothing slipped farther out into the outside and life. Then there was a slurping, squishing sound and out came the solid black calf's head. Its tongue lolled out of its pale pink gums and white tiny teeth, its head flopped lifelessly. Unfortunately, I stopped to look. If we'd both kept heaving, the whole calf probably would have come once we got it moving, but instead, its chest and shoulders, even bigger around than its head, were stuck.

Glyn looked at the pale, almost purple color of the tongue and said that based on the time the calf had been in the birth canal, he thought the baby was unfortunately dead. I did not want to believe that. I could not, until we got the calf all the way out. We pulled and pulled for a half hour till we were both "give-out." The cow had contraction after grunting contraction—nothing.

Finally Glyn asked if I had any chain. I told him I did, that it was up at the house, chain I used to hold Grr sometimes when he was above and beyond his farm-dog calling. Glyn told me to go get it. We hooked the chain around the cold little hooves and pulled some more—still nothing. Now everyone was drained of strength, of ingenuity.

Glyn said, "Peter, we've got to use your truck to pull that calf out."

I looped the chain around the back bumper; Glyn sat on top of the cow and I pulled, ever so easy. Glyn said if we didn't get the calf out, it would soon be dark and the cow would probably die, too.

I pulled gently, if that's possible with a truck, and in a few minutes, with Glyn pushing his hand inside the cow to shift the stuck calf's body, the calf plopped out onto the grass. I instantly jumped out of the truck. The calf did look large compared to its mama, especially in the neck and shoulders. It also had a wide head. The hair was black and slick, coated with the fluids from the birth canal.

I didn't know, maybe it was alive, maybe I could massage its heart. I tried. Maybe I could clear out any fluids or tissue it might have swallowed. I opened its mouth and saw nothing impairing its breathing; its tongue was a grayish pale pink. Neither had it swallowed its tongue. I massaged its heart again. I tried to lift it up; it dropped back to the ground with a dull thump. The sound of lifelessness. No, please, not my first calf. This isn't fair. I was so consumed I'd forgotten about my fine neighbor Glyn Smith. He was standing a few feet away, respectfully knowing what I was experiencing. He'd probably experienced this more times than he'd care to remember in his fifty-plus years of farming. I stared a hole in the side of that calf, hoping beyond hope that maybe, just possibly, it would start moving, breathing. It never did.

Beside the dead calf—it would have been a baby bull— the black, white-faced mama cow was trying to get up, making a pathetic sound, kind of a cross between a moo and a crying sound. It was definitely no straight moo; it was the sound of a mother who'd just discovered her baby was dead. She tried to get up, lifted herself up normally, if shakily, on her front legs, but she could not get all the way up. Her whole back end, her legs and all, appeared like floppy rubber. She made that sound again, as she dragged herself around the front hooves toward her dead, chilling calf.

"Peter," Glyn said. Obviously, as a pastor he'd dealt with people facing death a lot. "We did what we could. We saved the cow's life."

"Yes, we did," I responded. "What's wrong with her?"

"Well, I'd say she might be paralyzed in her hips."

"Paralyzed. How did that happen?" I asked. I felt low, knowing I might have caused her paralysis by pulling the calf out of her with the pickup.

"This kind of thing just happens," Glyn said. "So much pressure has been put on her pelvic bones and her birth canal by that long birth attempt, that sometimes the cow loses the use of her back legs. . . . Usually she'll get her strength back; it might take a few days. You might need to bring her some food and water." Glyn said he'd have to get home, and I told him I appreciated his help. He said anytime I needed him, give him a call.

The cow, whom Rebekah named Nancy, did recover three or four days later so she could walk, no matter how unsteadily. I called the dead wagon for the calf. Her first calf, and mine. I was sad for us both.

20

I Thought She
Was Beautiful

The sermon was from the Book of Revelation. The pastor
quoted, "I watched as the Lamb opened the first of seven
seals. Then I heard one of the four living creatures say
in a voice like thunder, 'Come!' I looked and there before me was a white horse! Its rider was given a bow,
and he was given a crown and he rode out as a conqueror
bent on conquest. . . . Then another horse came out, a
fiery red one. . . . I looked and there before me was a
black horse!"

When he mentioned a horse for the third time, I remembered what I had almost forgotten. I'd told Betty
Sain over in Bell Buckle that I would come to her farm
to test-drive a horse she had located for me. Betty was
an amazing woman. She'd been consumed by horses
when she was nine or ten and since then she'd dedicated
her life to them. In 1966 she was the first woman to win
the World Grand Championship at the Annual Tennessee
Walking Horse Celebration and Show.

The ground floor of Betty's barn contained saddles,
bridles, and the stallions, as well as her office and a couple of German shepherds who were locked in a stall and
let out at night to guard the place. Betty lived on the
second floor of the barn in a loftlike apartment with a

kitchen, living room, bedroom, and bath. The living-room walls were covered with pictures of Betty's magnificent black stallion, Shakers Shocker.

Shocker came into Betty's life like an angel unaware. One day Betty's mother was driving down the slim, green-sided roads of Tennessee horse country when she spotted an exceptional black colt lying near its grazing mother. Horse people pride themselves on being able to recognize top-flight animals from a goodly distance. She told Betty about it. Betty called the owners and bought the leggy black baby champion. Shakers Shocker and Betty made riding history, but the stallion died young, killed by a mysterious virus. The first thing you see when you drive up to Betty's barn is the gray marble gravestone of Betty's beloved stallion.

Barbara, Rebekah, and I arrived at the barn. Two peacocks on the fence sounded an alarm with their bizarre screams. Betty came out wearing faded jeans and a blue-plaid cotton shirt. She was direct, her hands were strong, she could handle ready-to-breed stallions, and she was only about five feet six and 125 pounds. Her blue eyes sparkled and her blond hair shone in the sunlight as we exchanged greetings.

I asked about the horse she had for me. "I rode her yesterday," said Betty. "She's a real horse, Peter. You *have* ridden a real horse? This is no deadhead."

"Yes, sure," I answered.

Of course I had: I'd ridden farm horses in Alabama at M. C. Jenkins's farm. What about those horses I'd ridden in the midst of the Sawtooth Mountains in Idaho? Those were real, living, moneymaking cowboy horses. They couldn't have been called deadheads. I rode those Idaho horses for hours and hours, herded a whole large group of cattle up a long, cliff-sided draw.

No problem. I'd seen pictures of these Tennessee horses, where the riders wore tweed coats and nice

creased pants. They were probably so easy to ride that
you could cruise on top of one in a tuxedo.

Betty led us over to a stall, motioning for us to stand
back. The mare emerged. She was exquisite; her features
were chiseled and she was not so muscle-bound as some
stallions I'd seen. But I'd never even held the reins of a
stallion, much less ridden one. A mare would be better,
much better.

She had a look unlike any horse I'd even been close
to. Her hoofs didn't stand weighty on the ground; they
seemed to lightly skim the surface as though she were
about to dance. She was keen, bright-eyed, narrow in the
face, black and slick and perk-eared. Her size didn't scare
me, nor did anything about her. I thought she was beautiful.

Betty, who would ride with me, saddled up the mare
and her horse with English saddles. I'd never ridden English saddle and it looked awfully slippery. On second
thought I probably should have changed out of my church
clothes.

We mounted the mares. Since I was used to horses
who needed a lot of encouragement, I gave the mare a
small kick with my heel. She responded as though I'd
plunged a harpoon in her side.

We pranced out of the barn and headed toward the
back gate. A peacock ran out of the tall grass and the
movement made the mare sidestep. That made *me* kind
of nervous but only a little. We rode through the gate
and headed up a hill toward what Betty called her "wilderness" piece of farm. Betty wanted to show me that a
Walking Horse could do anything, even pick its way
through rugged, rocky footing. Betty wore black-leather
riding gloves, and holding the reins firmly, sitting straight
and easy, her blond hair glowing like a halo, she made
me think of Joan of Arc leading the armies of France.
Betty and her mount were a powerful couple. As for
me, I was feeling less in command of my mare every minute.

We arrived at a trail made by Betty's goats, which curved like a worm around exposed limestone. Some of the rocks protruded out of the ground a foot or more. We began our ascent up the steep hill. We got to a bend in the narrow trail that went left, then swerved right before straightening out. My mare stopped. Was she confused, was she born to be wild? She was jittering in place, not stopped and stubborn as though she wanted to head back to the barn. What was she doing?

Was there something down in the grass that frightened her? A copperhead, a rattlesnake? There were plenty of those in these parts of middle Tennessee. I saw nothing. I tightened my easy grip on the reins, pulling in the inch or so of slack. She seemed to tense up. I squeezed tighter with my legs, hoping to give her a subtle message to go on. Betty was getting quite a ways ahead. I nudged the mare with my right heel and suddenly she felt like a NASA rocket ten seconds before blast-off. She was going to do *something*. But she would not move forward. I slapped on the reins a bit and bore in with my heels some more. The mare reared her front hoofs up above my head and threw me right down on the rocks. I listened for breaking body parts when I hit.

I picked myself up off the ground. Rebekah was watching her daddy. I had to set an example. And if this was to be my mare I could not allow her to think she could throw me and get away with it. I crawled back on. Nothing was broken, nothing was numb, there was no bleeding, but something inside of me felt oddly dull.

It would be best to sit still once I was remounted, to collect myself and calm the horse. My nerves were not now in a daring mood. I should be very deliberate with all my movements on top of her, I told myself. I felt scared, as if I were at the edge of a cliff with a five-hundred-foot vertical drop-off. The next command I would give this mare would be one so exceedingly gentle there would be no way she could misinterpret it.

Betty had stopped and was watching. This was a test ride to see if a Walking Horse would be suitable for life on the Jenkins farm, around the cattle and dogs. I thought I would rein the mare around to the left away from the rock, and head up to Betty. When I pulled her about, she reared again. I felt like I was straddled to a 200-mph Indy car and I only knew how to drive a Chevy Biscayne with automatic transmission and power brakes. Again I could not hold on, and again I was thrown onto the rock. This time I hit wrong. I knew it, but I did not know yet that I was hurt. I led the mare around and pointed her back to the barn, her head shaking, her ears agitated. I didn't want to climb back on that horse. My rear end and some part of my back felt like it had been banged on by a sledgehammer. But I had to ride back so I mounted Miss Malicious again.

Betty rode up quickly. There was the silence of concern in the fine Sunday air. I could tell she felt real bad.

She said, "Maybe this isn't quite the right horse for you, Peter." When Betty was near, that mare was a different horse.

"Maybe not," I breathed heavily.

Barbara drove home. All I remember of the drive is a slowly developing panic that I did not want to confront. My legs were getting numb. This was nothing like when one foot went to sleep. Both of my feet were asleep. I said nothing. I rested my hand on my thigh. My thigh did not feel normal. It felt as though it was going numb, just like my mouth felt when I got a shot of Novocain at the dentist. I denied the feeling. I put my right arm out the window. Rebekah fell asleep on my lap. I could not feel her there. I put my hand down and tried to pinch my thigh. There was a slight bit of feeling, no more than a pinprick. This was not happening. I'd been hit hard before, I'd fallen hard before, but never before had I felt like this.

When we got home to Blue Springs, I lifted Rebekah

over me and then I tried to get out. There was no, No, NO FEELING in my legs! Some way, I limped into the house and half collapsed into my reclining chair. I asked Barbara to get me the phone. I called my friend Bill Fuqua, who, besides being someone I looked up to, was also a local cardiologist. He had checked me out to see if I was healthy enough to go to Mount Everest. And whenever anything happened to me I called Bill.

"Can you move your feet? Your legs?" he asked me. He talked faster than most Tennesseans I knew but then I guess that came natural for Bill. As a young medical student at Vanderbilt, right after World War Two, Bill was one of the world's fastest humans. He had run the one-hundred-yard dash in 9.6 seconds, when the world record was 9.3 seconds.

"Yes, I can move them, I just can't feel them. They're just numb. Totally numb," I answered, getting increasingly petrified. I was sure I was going to be paralyzed.

"Good. Good. That means you've not severed your spinal cord." (WHAT! WHAT!! WHAT !!!!!!)

"When that happens," Bill continued, "which it could have easily done, then you lose all ability to move below the break. You know how many football players break their necks from a blunt strike. That fall you took from that height *could* have been much worse than any hit you could take in football." Bill should know for he was a second team All–Southeastern Conference wide receiver and still held the Vanderbilt U. record for longest pass and run play, eighty-seven yards. (Of course, Bill had never told me that; someone else did). His mind was going at its usual quickened pace, thinking through all the information he knew about spinal cord injury, numbness, and so on.

"I'll tell you, Bill, I'm scared. My body is numb from the waist down." What a terrible thing, I thought, when I heard myself say it.

"What's happened, Peter, is that you've shocked your

21

My Shocker

There came a time a few months later when Betty wanted
to introduce me to another horse, a black stallion sired
by Shakers Shocker. I was anxious, afraid. I wondered
if it was worth trying again. If I did test-drive this stallion at Betty's place I would not ride near rock, only on
soft, level land. There wasn't much level ground at Betty
Sain's but there was enough. This time I went by myself
to Bell Buckle. Betty was there, as always, and so were
all her animals.

Before she showed me the stallion, she told me a story.
A snake had been coming to her lower barn lately, the
one where the geese and peacocks nested in the corners.
It was also where the mama goats sometimes shaded
themselves or hid their tiny kids from the night-killing
bands of coyotes. One afternoon Betty was down at the
barn watering stock when one of the gray geese began
making crazy noises. She went inside to see a huge corn
snake attempting to swallow one of the goose eggs. She
picked up an old sliver of barn siding and slapped at that
snake and told it, out loud, to never come back.

The next day the setting goose began making the same
kind of racket and Betty went down to find the snake had
returned. This time she hit that snake on the body with

157

a stinging switch, and again warned it that if it came back
she was going to have to hurt it. Most farm folks would
have killed the snake the second they'd first seen it. But
Betty loved all living things, even snakes. However, all
living things had to "behave themselves." The next day,
that old hungry snake was back at the geese's nests. Betty
gave it a lecture, but first she got its attention. She took
a pitchfork and she purposefully stuck one tong in the
snake's loose skin to pin it down.

"Now, old snake. This is springtime and there's plenty
of food out there on this farm for you to catch. There's
baby mice and rats and rabbits and quail and frogs and
all kinds of living things. You cannot have my geese.
Now, I'm a-tellin' you, if you come back here ever again,
I'm gonna have to kill ya, ya hear me?" She released
the six-foot-long snake and it slithered away. It never
returned even though that barn was filled with peacock
and goose nests, which were a lot easier than hunting for
wilder prey.

I believed that Betty could talk to animals and get them
to do almost anything. Perhaps they knew she would
never hurt them. But I'd never heard of anybody con-
vincing a snake "to mind." But, then again, they say
that's why Betty won the Walking Horse World Championship. She got her stallion, the biggest love of her
life, to do what she wanted. She wanted to win. She
wanted to show them it could be done.

I got the feeling Betty was telling me the snake story
to check me out, see how I was feeling, see if I was
appropriately relaxed and ready to ride. It would be a
mistake for me to try again if I was terrified. The horse
would know my fear, just like the snake knew Betty was
serious.

Shockers Black Magic and I got along from the start.
He had a thicker neck and bulkier muscle than the bronco
mare. He did not act like a rocket ready to erupt into
G-forces and blurring speed. It seemed as though he could

be a friend to humans. Right away I did not like the Black Magic part of his name, so I decided that if he became mine I would change it to Buck. His full name would be Shockers Buck. The Buck came from the main character in Jack London's book *Call of the Wild*. Betty explained that Shocker was not a big stallion like his father had been. His mother, named Hillcrest Sugarfoot, had some of Merry Go Boy's blood in her—one of the famous Walking Horse sires. Shakers Shocker, my stallion's sire, had Midnight Sun in his bloodline. Midnight Sun died when he was twenty-five and is considered one of the greatest sires ever.

I rode my Shocker. He was a joy. I told Betty he was the kind of horse I needed. She said fine, that he'd always been a people horse and exceedingly gentle for a stallion. She told me that many stallions could not be allowed to run free with other horses or cattle for they would try to kill them. Betty said that there were some stallions who would even try to kill people. She said you should never turn your back on them. Betty said that some good horse-loving people raised my Shocker and that was one reason he was so easy to get along with. She would bring Shocker over to my farm next week. I was going to have my own horse, finally.

My first ride on Shocker in my own pastures, through my own gates, around my own cattle, was invigorating. Perhaps *invigorating* was not the right word—maybe *challenging* was more like it. But it was at times more than challenging, it was on the verge of being terrifying. But at least on my farm there was little exposed rock and a lot of spongy pasture.

I did not really know how to get Shocker's bridle on, and the same went for his saddle. I stood there trying to figure it out. The bridle I got on after a few tries. The saddle I also got on after a few tries. More than a few. I'd watched so many other people put this leather strap

in that metal loop and tighten this and that. And Betty
and M.C. and Rodney Hopwood, they all did it like it
was the easiest thing in the world to do with one's hands
and fingers. But it's not at first. I mounted the wide-
backed black stallion, but not before I'd led him out into
the big middle pasture where there was no rock. We ambled off while I remembered what Betty said to me: "Now
ya'all are just going to have to get to know each other. Every
horse and person have to get to know each other if they're
going to work together. The only way to do that is by just
being and doing together."

I would ride over to Jess and Mary Lou's through the
new gate between our farms. They knew horses. Jess
rode a horse to school, like most of the country kids did
then. They knew a good horse and so I'd show them my
Shocker. If I made it. It was a bit more than half a mile
through the back of our farms. If I took the road in front
it would be about a mile and a half. No way would I take
this stallion out on the road, not yet.

Getting through the pasture was ridiculously relaxed
and easy. There were no cattle around, for they had ambled down by the creek. I dismounted to open the gate
between the Jenkins land and the Morton land. No problem. We entered a tractor "road," which was two grass-
less ruts winding around a small grove of elms and thorn
trees. The pigpen was to our right, on two or three acres
of land that had been scratched and rooted down to the
bare earth by the incessantly food-seeking hogs. The pen
was enclosed by a fence that had seen its best days. Jess
had told me that there were few fences that could hold
hogs long. Hogs can root through anything.

I really liked the idea of riding my Walking Horse
stallion over to visit the neighbors late on a Sunday afternoon. Shocker's even, non–up and down, non-banging
stride was what these horses were bred for. Jess and Mary
Lou had always ridden Walking Horses when they were
younger.

When they were dating, when Mary Lou was still Mary Louise Alexander, Mary Lou used to come over to the Morton place just about every weekend. Jess and Mary Lou had been seeing a lot of each other, you might say. Dashing Jess had caught Mary Lou's eye in school because Jess looked so fine on his horse. Mary Lou says the first thing she ever noticed about young Jess Morton was the "fine, snazzy horse he was ridin'."

Mary Louise and Jess usually went riding, both on their favorite horses. But one day Mary Louise asked if she could ride Jess's horse. Jess said that would be fine, yes, ma'am. Mary Lou had a distinct reason for wanting to ride Jess's horse. She'd gotten wind that maybe Jess had been courtin' and sparkin' another certain young lady. Mary Lou of course did not approve of this, so she devised a test. When Jess and Mary Lou rode to the end of Jess's long drive, they always turned right, they never went left. THAT certain other girl lived to the left. Right before Jess and she came to the fork, Mary Louise pretended to lose her grip on the reins and that ol' horse of Jess's started walking in the direction that had become habitual. It went LEFT and kept on going straight till it reached that other girl's house. Mary Louise was pretty upset. Jess quit seein' that girl, the one that his horse knew about. You could say the old horse played a big part in Jess and Mary Lou's romance.

My Shocker did not seem at ease as we passed the eroded hog pen. A hog squealed and he jerked to the side, kind of lunged. Fortunately my balance was firm. As we went up a knob to a place called the loafing shed, where the cattle waited to be milked, he got snorty. His breathing was strained and he stopped and began pawing the dry ground. There were some gate-sized chunks of flat exposed rock right before us. Why was he stopping? Did these horses of Betty's have a thing about rocks?

He refused to go forward. So, gently, I turned him around and tried to head to the left past the old granary.

Shocker would have none of it. He stopped again. He acted as though he were afraid of something. But what? No snake was in the grass. There were none of Jess's cattle around, no loose hogs. I turned him around again and this time we rode all the way to the left and paced in a circle around all the buildings. Shocker breathed loudly. He was nervous about something.

Finally we got up to the Mortons' front yard. I dismounted but Shocker was still riled. Jess and Mary Lou came out of the side door and Mary Lou said, "Ooh, that's sure enough a pretty horse, Pe-ta."

I was having to hold on to Shocker's bridle with all the strength in my right arm. He was jerking his neck around, trying to turn circles, paw the ground. He didn't act like this at Betty's, I thought. If I weren't so easy with Jess and Mary Lou, I'd be embarrassed now.

Jess spoke the truth as usual. "That stallion's been raised in a stall, he ain't been raised on a farm. He needs to get used to everything round here before he settles on down. You sure a stallion's what you really need, son? Those thangs can be right hard to handle." No sooner did Jess say that than Shocker saw the Mortons' old pony a few yards down the hill. He almost jerked my arm out of the socket. "See what I mean?" Jess said.

"He'll settle down, Jess," I answered. "You know this horse was sired by Shakers Shocker?"

"He looks just like him in the face," Jess replied.

I rode on home and this time Shocker was a bit more at ease. I let him loose in a pasture and he started grazing right away. My Shocker had a lot to pass on to his foals and maybe someday he would have the chance to do that. First he needed to get used to life on the Jenkins place.

22
Night Moves

When a black-and-blue, calf-killer norther reaches us in winter, Canada is on my old outhouse list. When the winds blast down from the frigid north, they send me inside by the wood stove, and the cows and horses to sheltering by the south side of the barn. It's actually warmer *outside* of the barn, away from the wind, than inside where no sun can reach their cold bodies. The landscape is very still during a winter norther, because it's too cold for man or animals to move.

Sometimes in deep summer, cool air comes to us from Canada. Everyone's glad to feel it. When Canada sends down its delightful air in the summer, I have fond thoughts of places like Manitoba and Saskatchewan. When it's been above 95 for a few weeks and the slimy air is crawling all over your body, a relatively cool, dry day of benign sun is excellent. What happens when a Canadian cooler rolls in at night is that the sensually delightful northern air touches the sultry, slow waters of the creek and creates fog. Lots of fog. The dense gray fog rises up from the low-lying creeks, like the one in front of the farm, and the grayish white fog fills the low places in our valley.

This happened the morning after Wally and I returned

from our cattle-buying expedition in Texas. It was also on this fog-softened morning that some of my neighbors driving to work past my farm thought they saw a monster in my front field. If it was not a monster, had some strangely shaped spaceship landed? If not a UFO, could it be some extraterrestrial four-legged creature? If not that, was this hump-backed thing a mutant from a nuclear reactor meltdown? If not, was the moose-sized thing a diseased life with odd body parts in funny places?

It was none of the above; it was something few of my neighbors had ever seen. It was my new herd sire, born of champion bloodlines, raised on the outskirts of Alto, Texas, at the Hicks Red Brahman Ranch. Wally and I had picked him up on the way back from La Campana Ranch. Alto's East of Dallas, East of Rural Shade, Texas (a town), East of Buffalo, Texas (another town), in what's called East Texas. It's a land of rust-colored dirt, mounds upon mounds of fire ants, straight-tall pine trees, and the Hicks place on undulating Highway 69. The Hickses have a fence-post mill on one side of the road and their Red Brahman stock on the other. I met Leo Hicks, the Hicks brother with the crew cut, while walking across America. I had promised myself if I ever had cattle, I'd have one of his bulls. I did, now, except my neighbors on this fog-hung morning didn't see him quite that way.

For the rest of the week, well beyond the time the creek fog cleared, Jess Morton and Mr. George, among others, asked me:

"What happens when you breed a moose to a camel?" (My new bull had longer legs than cattle around here, almost as long as a moose's, and a hump almost as big as a camel's.)

"What happens when you breed a mule to an elephant?" (My new Brahman bull had a longer than usual snout, and long ears like a mule, except they flopped down about a foot, like an elephant's. I thought of calling him Dumbo, but Rebekah, who was watching that Walt

Disney video said, no Dumbo was cute and my bull was . . . well, he wasn't cute. Even at four Rebekah was smooth and diplomatic.

Jess Morton wondered out loud if the "thang" was part human. Others asked if it was really a bull or was it part outer-space being. No doubt he looked otherworldly. Someone asked me at Luther's Grocery Store, "Ain't that thang some kinda holy animal to them Indian people? You reckon it can breed your cows, it being holy and all? You know some holy thangs ain't allowed to mate, ain't that right?"

There was no dignified name for this new Red Brahman bull from East Texas. Some bulls go by such tags as Intimidator, Conquistador, Tan Thunder, Rambo, Macho Man. Some bulls' numbers become famous: F-243 . . . XT-98. I couldn't name this bull Potent Power or Perfection so I called him UFO. Actually, I'm not sure a real UFO landing would have stimulated much more smalltown "tawk."

So UFO became the herd sire of my herd, which was about one half pure Hereford cows and one half Beefmaster cows with the sprinkling of Santa Gertrudis I had just brought back from our South Texas swing. Since my first calving deaths with the black heifers, J.B. had helped me locate thirty mature cows. Herefords, I believed, would do much better if they were crossbred to a breed like Brahman. Brahmans liked hot weather, and were more tolerant of the stresses of bloodsucking flies and strength-robbing worms. We had as many hot months here as cold. The Hereford is definitely a cold-weather-loving cow—the opposite of the Brahman. In the summer, the Hereford stays in the most saturated shade it can find, not eating, not gaining weight, a sitting lump of closed-eyed beef just waiting for the monster flies that don't like the sunshine either. The Brahman cattle graze all day, except for possibly the hottest two hours of the afternoons in July. They also don't get pinkeye, an infection that can blind Herefords, turning their eyes opaque white.

It is true that Herefords are normally much easier to handle, and when an animal weighs close to a ton, like some bulls do, or well over one thousand pounds, like a good-sized cow can, ease in handling is real important. A leash does not work. Mr. George taught me early on you don't force cattle to do things, you lead them to do things, like when you want to move them out of one pasture to the other. Leading them with a bucket of sweet feed is an easy way to teach. The first time all 75,000 pounds, plus or minus, of the Jenkins herd came trotting behind me was exhilarating. But you have to be quite cautious with this much living muscle and bone; they're easy to stampede when you're in front of them and they all want what you're carrying in a little bucket.

Mr. George wondered one afternoon, as he was working on rebuilding the springhouse, putting on a new tin roof, if UFO was so ugly that these pretty shapely cows would not have him. I'd found out a few weeks earlier from Leo Hicks, when I'd not seen UFO breeding *any-thing*, that Brahman bulls are sometimes shy and usually breed only at night. If Leo told me that, then it had to be right, no matter how ridiculous it might sound. He'd been raising Brahmans for years. When that absurd-sounding bit of info got around Blue Springs, there was a whole new group of UFO/book-man jokes.

"I wonder if that UFO-thang passes out bags to the cows he breeds at night so they won't see him."

"You reckon that book-man been hoodwinked by some slick-lyin' Texan who sold that boy a high-dollar bull that's sterile?"

A bull that would only breed at night? A shy *bull*? Leo did say, when I called him, that one way you could tell if a Brahman bull was going to breed was if a cow was in heat and UFO stayed right by her side all day long, following her around, instead of sitting like a statue overlooking his herd. That was a good sign. Of course, Leo said, the best way to find out what UFO can do is to wait about nine months. The minute one of his calves hits the ground, you'll see those long, floppy ears and you'll know it's his.

There was no doubt UFO was not your normal bull. Maybe it was because Brahman cattle had some sense that they were holy animals in India. There they could not be eaten, they could go anywhere they liked. They could lie in the middle of the road, even go inside the temples. UFO was one of those animals that did not act like an animal. Being around him in the field, you got the impression he knew what humans thought. He seemed sort of psychic.

UFO was also as tall as a decent-sized horse, and although he was a purebred Red Brahman bull, he was not predominantly red in color, he was mostly gray. UFO had iron-red spots, and some iron-red blotches the size of a small rock. His two horns were not dagger-sharp like some Santa Gertrudis bulls I'd seen, they were a polished-ebony color and rounded and gently curved at the ends. His tail was short and he had the Hicks brand on his rump and the number 537. Leo said that when he was a calf, they made a pet out of him and that he was so gentle the kids would sit on his back. You spend a lot of time with this ol' bull, Leo said, and you may be able to ride him. I doubted I'd ever ride him, I just hoped he was feeling plenty uninhibited when night came.

It was nine months since UFO came to the farm, and there were no calves. A neighboring farmer cornered me one afternoon in Luther's store.

"Your crazy-lookin' bull done any good yet?" he asked.

"Well, not yet. Should be any time now," I said. I wasn't in the mood for any more of this bull-jive.

"You sure that bull got all his god-given parts, boy?"

"I don't know, bud," I answered. "From what I can see he seems to have everything he needs."

"Well, if he's got everything he needs, how come I ain't never seen him a-usin' it, anyhow? I drive by your farm early every morning and late every afternoon. Uh, boy, you sure them people that sold you that ugly thing ain't sold you a steer?"

I wanted to ask him if he was sure he had all *his* god-given parts, but then he acted as if he might have showed me right there in Luther's so I didn't say anything.

I just said, "You keep watching my bull and you might be surprised, bud." He left with his beer and got into his four-wheel-drive pickup. I hoped UFO's first calves were triplets, and the finest calves seen around these-here parts in years. That might shut him up.

The big day didn't happen until late December right after Jed, my son, turned one year old. I knew one of the Hereford cows was due any day. Her udder had filled up with milk, her four teats had become full like they do right before the calf begins its trip down the mother's birth canal. She was seven or eight years old, so she was not very nervous as she'd already had four or five calves. She had been standing off by herself a bit the last few days, which meant she was ready to calve.

It was not a bad day to be born: a yellow sun, a blue winter sky, and soft winds. I had my tractor warming up and was about to spear a round bale from the barn when I saw the sign of a birth. A mother cow was bending down over a blob of something on the ground, licking it. That probably meant a calf was just born. The licking by the mother not only cleaned off the afterbirth, her rough, coarse tongue stimulated the newborn's circulation.

I went over closer. The calf had been born by the new pond, the one that I'd dug recently to supply the middle of the farm with water. I could see the calf was trying to lift its head; it was flopping up and down like a fish out of water. It was brown-and-white, a pure Hereford. It couldn't have been sired by UFO. It had now been ten months.

I went up to see if the newborn was a bull or heifer calf. When I was five feet from the calf, it wobbled to a standing position. Its ears seemed to drag the ground. If those ears could have flapped, the calf would have been airborne. Its legs were as long as a baby deer's, and its knees were bigger and bonier than usual. UFO was a *bull*, not a steer! UFO had produced a son! My relief was enormous.

The progeny of UFO's night-moves was almost killed off a few weeks later when in mid-January the temperature went to 16 below zero. Already eight inches of snow had fallen, deep enough to cover dead tree stumps, exposed rocks, and baby calves. The night the thermometer crashed I barely slept, I was so concerned about the animals. What would the cows do tonight? Would they know enough to get into the cedar woods above the pond on the back of the farm? Cedars created a wind-and-snow-stopping shield, and when we had our rare snows, there was a snow-free patch of earth around them.

There was no way the whole herd could fit in the hall of the barn, nor could they all get into the primitive milking parlor on the side. I worried that the cattle might try to squeeze in too tight and crush the new little UFO calf.

I worried about what would happen if the new calves lay down, or lost their mamas. Could UFO take this kind of lung-freezing, bone-snapping cold? What about the Santa Gertrudis heifers, now fully muscled out and pregnant? Guaranteed it never got this cold in South Texas! The frustrating thing was that there was nothing I could do for any of them. What if they wandered out to find better shelter and stumbled into the creek? It was the only water on the farm that would not be frozen solid enough to hold them. The thought of sleeping out in this kind of weather seemed impossible, even though, come to think of it, I had done that. Crossing the Cascades of Oregon, I'd slept out in way-below-zero weather, but I had a mountaineering tent and down sleeping bag rated at 10 below zero.

At 2:00 A.M. Jed rumbled and cried a bit, wanting a bottle. I scooped up Jed, who rested his curly-haired head on my shoulder. My experienced right forearm felt dampness, so in the same body bend I grabbed up a Pamper. I walked out by the wood stove on my way to the microwave. I felt no warmth pulling me toward our big black Buckstove. It was cooler than usual for this time of night because the wailing north winds were sucking the heat out of the chimney. I could hear the brittle limbs of the guardian-rock trees slapping the tin roof. Jed nestled deeper into my chest.

I touched the top of the wood stove. It was cool, so I stoked it with some dry oak logs. There should be enough red glowing embers to create a new fire. I laid Jed down and got his wet diaper off. By the time I had warmed up his bottle, Jed had gone back to sleep.

Out the kitchen window, I saw headlights in a near field. It was Jess gathering up his herd, getting ready to milk. I was glad I was not a dairy farmer. They had to milk twice a day, seven days a week, 365 days a year, no matter what. I remember when that oppressive schedule of milking slammed home to me. I had asked Mary Lou if they ever took a vacation. She said they'd only taken one their entire married life, in 1956. Jess, like most dairy farmers, always had trouble finding help milking, so he usually hired paroled convicted murderers to work for him. Jess said he'd have nothing but murderers; they could be trusted, unlike thieves. The best one he'd ever had was an ol' boy who'd shot and killed a deputy sheriff because that deputy "smart-mouthed" him after he'd pulled him over for driving drunk. When Jess and Mary Lou took their only vacation, they lived in an antebellum home, a beautiful one-story, sprawling mansion with fourteen-foot ceilings. They went to Florida, to a Gulf Coast beach. While they were gone, Jess's beloved family home burned to the ground.

I put baby Jed back in his crib, the same one Rebekah had used, and covered him with a baby quilt. He took about three swigs from his bottle and was back in baby-sleep land. Jed slept on his back, his arms and legs going in all the directions of the earth, like he was the most secure baby on the planet. What if there were calves born tonight? Mr. George and Jess, both, had warned me that a calf born on a night like this could be easily frozen before dawn, especially if the mother did not know how to protect her baby. I was grateful little Jed and Rebekah were warm and protected.

Dawn was close and just before it breaks is often the coldest part of a winter day. I put on my parka and jeans and heavy-soled boots and went out to see if anything had lived through the night. I walked through powdery snow well above my ankles, heading toward the barn. UFO was standing there stiff as an icicle. About eight or ten cows were inside the barn, but none of the cows who were due to have calves. By now I knew them all.

I glanced down to the spring, which was covered by deep snow. Otherworldly fog rose over the creek. I could see nothing anywhere that looked like an animal. Where did they all go? I would have to walk to the back of the farm. Maybe they went into the woods for shelter.

They heavy winds had obscured all tracks so I moved through the open field toward the line of cedars that topped the ridge. That would give me a good view, but I saw nothing living in any direction. As I headed down the hill, toward the east, without warning a red-orange light split through the tree trunks. The sun was here, though its heating rays would be awhile coming. The cedar woods were in front of me. I was about halfway there.

In a low place below the sinkhole I found the rest of

the herd. They were standing together, their rears toward
the coldest winds. In this place the air was always still;
not good in summer but fine now. I saw no calves. I
scanned the rest of the herd and saw, out by three old
stumps, a lone cow. She'd either had a calf or was about
to. I went over to her; she mooed menacingly.

There, curled up in the snow, was a dried-off, licked-
clean, extremely healthy-looking calf. I could see its
frosty breath. The mother had picked this sheltered place,
behind a pile of dead trees and tree stumps directly blocking the north wind. When I talked to Jess later on, he
told me that an experienced mother cow will sometimes,
in weather this cold, stand over a just-born calf and
breathe on it. I could see the cow's footprints all around
the calf, circling it closely. She must have been breathing
her baby warm.

I headed back feeling better. They'd all done great;
my whole herd was alive and well. I could walk back
now, load the pickup with hay, and feed them all. Halfway up to the ridge, I looked up to see a cedar touched
beautifully with a partial icing of powdery snow. The
wind would catch some of it in mini-clouds and swirl it
gently around the tree in the wind's patterns. The cold
and snow had looked cruel on the way here.

I looked down because I almost stepped on something.
It was too big to be a fresh-frozen cow patty. I looked
again. It was a calf; it seemed to be frozen dead. I was
just going to walk by, until I thought I saw an eyelid
move. But it was just a bit of snow falling from the lid.
The calf was not laid out on its side as I imagined a
frozen calf would be. It was curled up, its small head
lying on it snow-covered front legs. Where was its
mother? She must have left it when it died.

I walked by, but I couldn't keep on. I turned back and
reached down to see how stiff it was. Had rigor mortis
set in? When I pushed on its chest, one eye opened. It
was alive, at least it seemed to be! I reached under its

body, like I did to see if a calf was male or female. I felt live warmth. But the living portion of this new life was not going to win out over the freezing death much longer if I didn't do something soon.

I would have to pick it up and carry it to the barn. A big calf could weigh eighty-five to ninety pounds and this was a big calf. As I reached under it, I scanned all around the twenty-acre pasture. Messing with a newborn calf with a mother around was dangerous; many of them would attack you. But still no mother was in sight. As I got the calf situated in both arms, I saw that it had floppy, UFO-type ears. Mr. George told me that if a calf is born in really cold weather, sometimes its ears or tail will freeze and eventually fall off, because the blood flow is weakest in its extremities. I carried the calf to the barn, a good half mile, broke open a bale of finest-leaved grass hay I could find, and laid her on a little blanket of sweet-smelling hay.

The sun came out, it warmed up to about zero, and a few hours later the calf's mother was walking all over, bawling like mother cows do when they've lost their calves. I went out and herded her over to her baby. As she nursed her newly found heifer calf, I thought that this was one birth date I'd remember! January 16, 1984, the night it was 16 below zero. The saved calf was easy to pick out in the herd because, sure enough, her frozen ears did fall off. We named her No Ears and she turned out to be one of the best cows I ever had.

23

Radar, The Macho One

I admit that for a long time I had a prejudice against small dogs. I thought I only liked and wanted big ones. Small dogs to me were yappy, rabbit-sized animals whose eyes bugged out and who darted to and fro looking for some bigger dog or gas-meter reader to attack. I'm not sure where I came by this bad attitude.

There was absolutely nothing in my background that influenced me in my lack of affection toward small dogs. I could think of many small dogs I'd met working at the vet's whom I liked, a Welsh corgi, two rugged beagles, a whippet, fox terriers, a white Scotty, and an aggressive schnauzer. But then they were all sporting dogs. I'd never personally had any dogs other than massive and muscular Cooper and now, the fast-growing Alaskan huskies.

Everything changed after I got to know Radar. He belonged to Barbara's parents, Ernie and Betty, who lived in southeastern Missouri. Radar was a bossy half–fox terrier, half-Chihuahua, and he strutted, barked, and was a fine little dog until someone stole him when Betty and Ernie were out in Phoenix visiting relatives. Radar was black and Betty named him after a character in her favorite TV show, *M*A*S*H*. Betty wanted a small dog because she and Ernie traveled a lot and Radar was easy to take with them. And Betty loved a dog that would sit in her lap. Radar was lion-hearted. If Betty was out gardening, plucking tomatoes off the vine, or picking green beans and a snake or mouse showed itself, then Radar would jump to her defense. Radar would not only attack a snake or mouse; he would very probably attempt to tear to pieces (little bloody pieces) a charging bull elephant.

I'm quite sure of that. One time while Betty and Ernie were visiting, Ernie and I were standing in the side yard talking about sharpening my chain saw. Betty as usual was in the kitchen, taking over, making the homemade doughnuts the kids loved. Redheaded and mostly fearless as she was, Betty's personality matched Radar's. Neither one would take anything from anyone, and if they were bored they might stir something up just for grins. When Betty was a barefoot country girl in the Ozarks, she'd dare any boy to throw a rock farther than she could—and few would win. I suppose if challenged she would have bareknuckle boxed 'em. Radar was just as hot-tempered and high-strung.

As Ernie and I talked, we watched Radar try to attack PJ. PJ, being a bit bigger than Radar, did not act overly concerned. He was my Polled Hereford bull and weighed about sixteen hundred pounds. Black Radar weighed ten pounds, max. The bull was grazing right next to the yard fence line and I suppose Radar assumed he was a threat to us. After all, he'd never seen a bull before. As far as Radar knew, this brown-and-white behemoth was the biggest dog he'd ever seen.

Instead of hiding behind our legs, he ran right through the holes in the wire fence and began his attack on PJ. It is true that Radar was bigger than a biting fly and so there was no way for PJ to swat this frantically charging dog with his tail. The pasture grass was eight to ten inches high, compared to about two inches in the yard, so Radar was nowhere to be seen. Some grass moved around PJ as Radar circled him, but the grass was taller than the tiny attacker. We could only hear his yapping, yipping bark.

What could PJ do? He was not fast-footed enough to try to squash Radar with his splayed hoof. Radar certainly couldn't do the big boy any harm. So far this attacking half-Chihuahua had not sunk his teeth into PJ. But then, I'm not sure his teeth would have reached above PJ's hoof, and if he bit into PJ's hoof he might break off a few of his own sharp, vicious teeth. Radar barked and lunged and attacked until PJ ambled off, down the hill toward a solitary hackberry tree with twin trunks. The bulls liked to rub on the trunks because the bark had hard, rigid bumps.

Grr and Lacy were still afraid of the cattle and stayed inside the fence. Radar quickly reappeared from his hunting foray. When he got back in the yard and through the fence he strutted his stuff like a leader of the pack. Ernie just shook his head.

Radar didn't sit down in the sunny yard to take his deserved rest. His oversized male hormones were enraged. He enlarged his already expanded chest and trotted proudly to where Grr was lying down. Grr was now four months old and weighed thirty-six pounds, over three times what Radar did. It was unfortunate for Grr, the still goofy pup, that it was a luscious day, because if it had been cold or a little wet, Radar would not have come outside. But here Radar was and innocent Grr would not be spared the terrible, brutal, vicious attack Radar would now try to inflict on him.

Gangly Grr stood up before macho Radar got to him. Ten feet away now, Radar charged Grr. Radar was snapping his tiny teeth together. Before Radar could make contact with Grr, Grr fell over like a too-warm marshmallow. Radar snapped his teeth like a starving piranha and dove for Grr's throat. To Grr it was a fun-in-the-sunshine game; he was about as afraid of Radar as he would have been of an attack-trained mouse. But Radar, the short, chest-protruding little mutt, was deadly serious.

Lacy reacted differently. She exhibited a portion of her personality that I'd never seen before. Grr lay on his back wanting to play with Radar. Radar wanted to inflict damage on Grr, whom he perceived as a bigger, more virile dog. Lacy, who had been lying on her side in order to soak up sunshine warmth, leaped to Grr's side in the time it took the little black hornet of a dog to growl again. Radar made a wrong assumption based on Lacy's actions and figured she was there to help whip up on Grr. He went for the throat again.

Lacy slapped Radar with her front paw. She slapped Radar hard enough to knock him back on his little butt. Then she bared her teeth, in a truly vicious-looking pose. Her double line of white teeth and the daring quiver in her upper side lip were wolfish, no doubt. Radar became deeply embarrassed and then began shivering with the appropriate measure of fear. He may have been imagining what Lacy could do to him, even at her young age. A young Alaskan husky with a lot of Indian-dog blood is not what any half-Chihuahua should mess with. Grr stretched out on his back and was actually rocking back and forth scratching his ever-growing backbone. Radar ran off and stood next to Ernie's shoe.

24

A Few Thousand
Acres to Explore

I couldn't help comparing Grr to Cooper. Having Grr was like having another son. It had been almost ten years since Coops died and the puppyish things Grr did—chasing butterflies, falling over and lying on his back to be scratched, discovering movement in the grass and biting down to find a field mouse—all reminded me of the things Cooper had done. I'm not sure Coops was so quickly coordinated but there was little chance of wolf blood flowing inside Cooper.

Also, Cooper didn't have Lacy to grow up with. The competition between them spurred them both on. And I didn't have the long solitary hours to spend with Grr and Lacy that I did with Coops. Cooper grew up in a college town of the early seventies, a far different place from a farm in Tennessee. Ten years had passed. Now there was daughter Rebekah and baby Jed and wife Barbara and the farm and the business and ever-increasing types of insurance and a pickup truck and a mortgage and electric bills and barn roofs needing repair and so on and so on. Cooper and I were an inseparable team, living a simple life free from commitments.

Grr's hunting abilities would very likely be much more developed than Cooper's. He would be surrounded on all sides by farms. On these farms lived plenty of cows, chickens, horses, hogs, barn cats, and farm dogs. And there were many wild animals, too. There were deer in the backwoods. Recently I'd seen a doe and her twin fawns. I saw many tracks by the deer's favorite watering place at the last pond. The deer had cut a narrow path through the most fertile part of the woods, where the large pignut tree was surrounded by leafy walnut trees. They used this trail to come from my neighbor's farm, leap the back line fence, and make their way into the back hayfield.

A great horned owl lived in the third biggest cedar. There was a den of red foxes in the hardwoods behind the twenty-acre hayfield. Recently I'd seen two young foxes, their orange-red fur almost floating through the high grass. Their mother must have been calling them from the fringe of the forest. There were rabbit nests everywhere, under thistles, in old groundhog holes, in brush piles, in fencerows. Quail placed their camouflaged nests under the blackberry thickets in grown-over fencerows. There were at least three families of skunks, one in the red barn, one under loose rocks where the cactus grew, and one near the silo. A great blue heron hunted all the ponds and flew across the easy-weaving pastures like he owned the place. I figured Grr and Lacy would be believing they owned this place soon.

A pack of shadow-living coyotes howled up on the ridge behind the house, especially in summer and fall. When they had their "singings" it sounded as if there were fifty of them. There was much for Grr and Lacy to get into around here. Right now they hunted only a few field mice. I couldn't help but wonder how long it would take them to come into contact with the skunks, the deer, the game birds. Just so long as they stayed away from the coyotes. The coyotes would lure them and slice their throats and eat them before they ever knew what happened.

Never would I forget the time Cooper chased some kind of wild thing into a drainage pipe. We were in the mountainous regions of Pennsylvania then, the eighth day of the walk. It started in a flash, like Cooper's first contact with animals usually did. As we walked along, Cooper burst down into a grassy area by a stream. We were on a dirt road. I had no idea what the animal was, but it streaked into a drainage pipe that went under the road. It made a terrible, shrieking, squealing noise that intensified because of the pipe. I walked on, figuring Cooper would be along right away as usual. No animal was about to come out and fight Cooper. But Cooper was whining, a high-pitched whine associated with the agitation and excitement of the hunt. I called for him. He would not come; he stuck his head in the long pipe and growled. Could it be a fox, a coyote, a bobcat, what? It moved much too fast for a woodchuck.

So I went over to my traveling partner, bent down, and looked inside the pipe. I saw nothing. I decided I'd cross the road and look into the other end. I was hopeful the animal had already split, left the territory. The way Coops barked though, I doubted it. I could see something. Something, a silhouette, a long, slim animal, the shape of an otter, mink, weasel. I thought, "OK, Cooper, let's go. You can't mess with one of those, they are too fast."

I walked up onto the road and called him. The hunting lust was rising in him. He would not come along. I sat there on my pack and waited, figuring the animal, probably a mink, was smart enough to stay inside the pipe. But, unbelievably, the animal, a long blur of brown fur, darted out of the pipe at Coops's end. And attacked him! I have never seen anything move so fast on the ground. It was all over Cooper's body like a small devil wind. It didn't seem possible anything could move so rapidly. Somehow Cooper got hold of it in the middle of its body and bit down till it was dead. But the mink got in a number of vicious bites. Minks, relatives of skunks, have potent musk glands and this one emitted a repulsive smell. Cooper would not eat it.

I couldn't help but imagine what Grr would be like a year from now, a fully filled-out, mature Alaskan husky. Would he graduate from chasing butterflies and playfully crunching field mice to other things round these parts? Surely. I just knew there was no way I could keep him chained to a tree like they have to do in Alaska. I hoped I could train him to stick to woodchucks and that would be it. Maybe it was fortunate that I had the rest of the fall and all winter to train Grr and Lacy about farm-living etiquette. The winter would be good because there would be the least possible temptation for them. In winter, the baby animals of last spring who survived the foxes, owls, coyotes, barn cats, bobcats, and minks were now experienced enough to resist Grr and Lacy's amateur hunting attempts. The calves had long since been born. They were vulnerable only for a few hours before they were licked clean and stimulated to stand, however wobbly, and get that first milk.

Jess Morton's hogs did not have many piglets in winter. The chickens that Jess and Mary Lou had, plus the guinea fowl, and the herd of chickens Mrs. Hardison had across the street would be able to see the dogs more easily in winter, since the deep pasture grass of summer and early fall would be gone. I was silently hopeful that the dogs would not roam across the street, but stick to this side of the road, where they had a few thousand acres to explore.

25
Blue-eyed Omi

The other puppies I'd brought back for my friends were doing well, except Lacy's brother that went to West Texas. He, the most magnificently marked and built of all the pups, died of some virus not long after arriving. Skip's and Murray's pups were getting along well in the Pacific Northwest and Wally's white, blue-eyed Indian pup was as amazing as ever. Omi was her name and she climbed fences, ate policemen's hats, jumped all over everyone, and generally acted like she had five times the adrenaline output of an Alaskan husky and ten times that of a normal dog.

This puppy, Wally's family's first, was named by their elder daughter, Andrea, after she read a story about an Eskimo dog in a *Ranger Rick* magazine. It was December 5, 1982, and Wally, Brenda, Andrea, and Julia were living in a stately and lavish two-story Victorian home surrounded by pecan trees on one of Bud Mitchum's farms. Omi was a dog that could not be contained. If they put her in a back room she got out by climbing out a window, tearing out the screen in the screen door, whatever it took. If they put her in a fenced-in yard, with quite a high fence, she'd climb out. This dog climbed fences better than an eight-year-old kid.

Never had I seen a dog, or known of a dog, that could climb fences. Even chain-link fences. I'd seen a dog or two jump over a split-rail fence, à la Lassie, but climb a fence with all four paws earnestly reaching for the next opening in the wire?! Pure-white Omi just had to be wherever the people were. If Andrea and Julia were getting on the yellow school bus, driven by Richard Jenkins, one of two Spring Hill policemen, then Omi would ride the bus, too. She'd climb a fence, leap to the ground, and sprint toward the squeaking sounds of the stopping bus. Richard, a black man, who was our town's policeman at night, attempted to shield his hat from the attacking Omi but she got it, ran away from the bus, and ate it. Every new person Omi met was a warm body to jump all over. Omi loved Andrea and Julia's yellow and white kittens almost to death, holding them ever so tenderly in her mouth, sometimes about as tenderly as a moose's leg bone. Thankfully, Grr and Lacy were nothing like Omi. Omi did not show even a sliver of this kind of personality trait when I chose her in Alaska, but maybe this was an illustration of why Indians don't like white dogs. "Many times white dog with white eyes crazy," Jerry said. "Only good as white man's picture dog, that's all."

The first few days of December 1982 were some of the busiest and fullest the Heberts ever had. They'd bought a new car, a small Chevy station wagon, in Lewisburg, and Andrea had had a Christian conversation experience at a church slumber party. After they'd bought the car, they came home and called for Omi. For twenty minutes they called, but she never answered. Wally thought he heard movement out beyond the pecan trees but it was only fluttering leaves being wind-rustled in the dark. He heard something across the narrow, curved country road. It was Bud's sheep. Wally walked every inch of that property, calling, whistling for the white, blue-eyed dog from Alaska.

Wally walked east, all the way to the Derryberrys',

their neighbors. Then he went west. He had his flashlight. The wind was strong enough to make the fences
creak and bang a loose tin sheet on the barn.

Maybe someone stole Omi, Wally thought. Omi stolen
would be better than what Wally was visualizing. If Omi
had been around and alive, she'd have jumped on Wally
long ago. Wally began walking up the pecan-tree-lined
gravel driveway, then turned around. Maybe he'd not
gone far enough west on the road. He moved the beam
of the flashlight back and forth. He saw a piece of something white. Maybe it was the girls' homework papers,
in the ditch. He came closer. It was not a paper, it was
Omi.

What he'd feared had happened. Omi had been run
over and she was already cool and dead. Wally, Brenda,
Andrea, and Julia had her funeral the following Sunday
morning, the morning Andrea was baptized. Omi had
been almost too thrilled by life. Julia, then seven, asked
Rebekah and me to go to Omi's funeral but I couldn't.
Even today, when I see a dog lunge into the road, or just
walking close to the road, I get tense, as if a thousand
acupuncture needles have been stabbed into me by someone trying to inflict psychic pain. Every time I see a run-
over dog or cat I remember the details of Cooper's death,
his burial, our life together. It makes me dread the next
burial. Why do things have to die?

26
Gray Nose

I had never seen dogs in love before. Grr and Lacy were in love with each other. Often they'd lie together, before they were a year old, next to the woodpile behind the smokehouse, all afternoon and bite each other softly. I assumed they were kissing. They definitely weren't fighting.

If Grr made Lacy mad, she would lift her wolf-mean upper lip, let it quiver, and growl in such a way as to put the fear of fangs in Grr's heart. After hearing Lacy angry there was no confusing her love-bite and her mad-bite. But mostly Grr and Lacy would both lie on their sides in the lush green of the grass rejuvenated by cooler fall air and more frequent autumn rain, with their noses touching. Their tails wagged excitedly, pointing in opposite directions.

When they tired of lying around, one would get hold of an orange broom handle that Rebekah used to "sweep" the yard. If Lacy got it first, she'd sprint for the pasture, turning her head to the side to get the broom handle through the dog opening in the fence. Then she'd run as fast as she could. She was still faster than Grr, so she toyed with him. Her gait was like a greyhound's, as her front feet and back feet almost touched in midair. She was fluid and so swift. Grr had more muscle, and less fluidity in his skeletal system, so he could not move with the ease of Lacy. His gait was more like the stiffer gait of the long-distance sled dog.

Lacy would get out ahead of Grr and, at her whim, let him catch up to her. Lacy would slow down till Grr was at her right side, about a foot behind her, then she'd turn her head just enough for him to get hold of the broom-stick.

Then the astounding exhibits of coordination began. Both of them running at close to full speed, both holding on to the broom handle. Without warning one would trip and they'd both roll over and over. The first time one fell, I thought it might be an accident, but they did it every time. Grr had the stronger neck and jaws and usually ended up with the handle in his mouth. One time they weren't really watching where they were going, they were looking at each other, jostling, each trying to throw the other off balance but neither one could, until unbeknownst to them they were at the creek bank. That section of creek bank had about a five-foot dropoff, right into a deep pool about six, seven feet deep. Black Jess said there were big carp and soft-shell turtles in there. Both Grr and Lacy went zooming through the air and splashed, crashed into the cold water. Grr came up and out of the creek with the orange broom handle in his mouth. From then on they loved to swim together and generally lie around in the water. Here in middle Tennessee it never got cold enough for them to stay out of the creeks, and only the ice kept them out of the ponds.

Grr thought up another way to play after the mop-handle game grew boring. He would grab Lacy's tail while running full out. Somehow he did not bite down hard enough to hurt her, but he coordinated his movements so that he just spun her around in a circle. Then they came face to face and Lacy would spread her front legs for increased turning ability and run by him. They were off again. One winter afternoon they were running after each other near the middle pond. It was covered with a rare one inch of ice. Lacy could see it coming but enticed Grr to keep looking back by yelping, whining as they ran, and the millisecond before Grr hit the edge of the ice she grabbed his tail and he went pirouetting at full speed into the center of the pond. They were amazingly creative in their play, maybe an indication of the depth of survival instinct in their blood, now transformed to passing their time. Survival was not their concern.

I would have thought survival should have been a concern for Gray Nose, but he was awfully daring. Gray Nose was a fox squirrel. Fox squirrels are gray and orange-brown in color and about twice the size of gray squirrels. Gray Nose was over two feet long. He was either a rabid squirrel or a manic daredevil. He would come down the trunk of the biggest maple tree right by the root cellar within about four feet of the ground.

Gray Nose saw Grr and Lacy lying there, but he'd come to taunt them anyway. He'd get a few feet off the ground and when Grr, then Lacy, tried to attack, he'd run at that same height off the ground in a circle, around and around that rough-barked maple. The tree was at least three feet thick. Grr and Lacy would first get confused, as if there were more than one squirrel. Then, as they'd rush around the tree, they'd get dizzy and then aggravated with themselves. After Gray Nose got them dizzy enough, they'd knock into each other as their world spun around them. A few times they got so dizzy they fell over.

After the wise fox squirrel got the fast-growing pups sufficiently disoriented, he would actually come to the ground. He chattered loudly, till they saw him, a melting, spinning image of gray fur. They were in disbelief that a squirrel had this much nerve to challenge them. All their instinct told them this should not be happening. When they began their weaving, dazed run at Gray Nose, he sprang to the top of a fence post where they could not reach him.

When Grr and Lacy got to him, the squirrel leaped and ran toward the hickory tree in the southwestern corner of the farm. Gray Nose had about fifty yards to go, and amazingly he seemed to have calculated how far Grr and Lacy would have to run back up the hill to get through their hole in the fence and then back to him. They never caught up, but Lacy was so aggravated she left Grr behind. Gray Nose yelled at them in squirrel language until they came home.

From that day forward, the Gray Nose, Grr, and Lacy challenge continued. Gray Nose became more belligerent, more daring, and Grr and Lacy learned more of his ways. They were also growing up and becoming more coordinated, faster, quicker, able to jump higher, and were capable of working more as a team. This fox squirrel had to be the wisest rodent in this county. I'd never thought of squirrels as intelligent before, certainly not daring, and definitely not death-defying. But Gray Nose was. And he was a great teacher.

A week or so later Gray Nose called out to Grr and Lacy. He would actually alert them that he was again in their midst and available for their lessons. This time he was away from the yard in a walnut tree. When Grr and Lacy showed up, that nutty squirrel dropped walnuts on them, hitting them more than once. The dogs were humiliated. No small animal with dull gray fur who lived in a tree should be so capable of bothering them and teasing them. It wasn't right. These were Alaskan huskies, of Indian-dog bloodlines. No moose, no caribou gave a husky much trouble. But a squirrel! This sheer bout of squirrel humiliation was beginning to affect their self-esteem.

It was when March came, when the pups were not very puppylike anymore, that Gray Nose paid for teasing Grr and Lacy. They could all have lived together if Gray

Nose had only gone in for the occasional chase, but these dogs' pride had been wounded. If they caught Gray Nose they would show him no forgiveness.

The March morning was crisp but Grr and Lacy were not on the front porch in the usual warm spots. I looked down the driveway to see them lying in the frost-covered grass near a telephone pole. Why were they lying there, I wondered, when it wasn't even in the sun? Then I looked at the telephone pole and on top of it was Gray Nose. He was in a perilous position. The stupid dogs had almost caught him. His tail was shaking and jerking and slapping the pole. There was no clean-cut plan of harassment now. He was trapped. It was a good forty yards to the nearest tree.

I went in, drank coffee, and ate two pieces of well-done whole-wheat toast with chunky peanut butter and strawberry jam. The dogs would get bored and leave soon, I was sure. They weren't the waiting types. But they were there at the end of breakfast and there still when I came back for lunch. So was Gray Nose. After lunch, on my way back to my office, I saw the dogs had moved at last. They had caught the squirrel, after he had harassed them for six months. They were chewing on him in unison. I was not in the mood to see Gray Nose up close, covered with damp teeth marks.

Although I understood why Grr and Lacy had become so determined to get that pesky, arrogant fox squirrel, I was saddened that the peculiar and interesting Gray Nose was now gone from the farm. I didn't think too much more about it until about a week later when Grr and Lacy went streaking across the front field and through the pasture after another squirrel. The squirrel got on top of a fence post, leaped to the next one, jumped down, lazed along on the inside of the fence while the dogs were on the outside unable to get in, chattered at them belligerently, and then leisurely climbed up into its favorite maple and waited till Grr and Lacy got under him. It was Gray Nose!

They had not caught Gray Nose but some other squirrel! Old flirtatious Gray Nose continued to stay one leap in front of those two still-determined Alaskan huskies for a long time. They would never catch him; the closest they ever got was when Grr got hold of an inch or two of his tail, but Gray Nose whirled around and bit a small slice off the end of Grr's nose. At that Grr let go and from then on Gray Nose and the dogs pretty much left each other alone. Grr and Lacy graduated to bigger, easier prey to catch. But Gray Nose certainly trained them well for what was to come.

27

A Very Particular Lady

Some people like to be dirty and some people don't. I love to be dirty. It doesn't really matter whether I'm covered with pieces of hay, dripping with sweat, or coated with sawdust. I like it. Part of being dirty is getting clean again. A shower after sweating through all my clothes in August feels as good as anything the universe has to offer.

Mary Lou Morton, my neighbor and friend, is exactly the opposite of me. She can't stand being sweaty and dirty and that's tough when you've married a farmer. It's even tougher if that farmer is a dairy farmer, who also raises hogs. To see Mary Lou Morton shopping at Grace's, one of Nashville's finest women's shops, in a forest-green suede suit and a beautifully tailored silk blouse, no one would think this elegant southern lady lived on a 273-acre farm in Blue Springs, Tennessee. Observing Mary Lou stepping out of her color-coordinated Cadillac (always chosen so the interior complimented the colors she most loved to wear), one might think she was a member of the rich old southern gentry, born to stone mansions, winding driveways, and Georgian architecture. Mary Louise Alexander Morton never, on first impression or on hundredth impression, seemed like a Tennessee farmer's wife.

It's not that Mary Lou didn't love the Morton place she came to live on after she married Jess Morton. It's not that she didn't like other farm people, she did; many were her intimate friends and bridge-playing partners. Miss Mary Louise was just born particular about things. And she was raised to be discriminating, too. Her family had the finer things: crystal, old English china, European antiques. And there was a family of light-skinned black people to help do the work. They were part of the same black family who had worked for Mary Lou's grand-daddy. The Alexanders had gone through some bad times, but they had old money, beautiful things, and fertile land to help them make it. When a lot of people think of farmers, maybe especially Tennessee farmers, they think of faded overalls, sun-crinkled skin, and strong-stout hands. A fashion statement for a farmer might be a new baseball cap from Du Pont. But there are also many farm wives just like Mary Louise Alexander Morton.

Mary Lou's daddy told her as a little girl, "Darling, I don't want you going in the barn." Mary Lou took that to mean that "ladies don't go into barns," especially cow or hog barns. Mary Lou was sure that her daddy wanted her to be a lady. She'd do as she assumed her daddy wanted, and keep out of those old, dirty, breezy barns and hog pens. Mary Lou was determined that she'd not ever *begin* to do things like milking and shoveling. The only barn Mary Lou would enter, and do so gladly, was the one that housed her favorite Tennessee Walking Horse, Polly.

When Mary Louise Alexander was ten years old she caught scarlet fever. Some thought the young beauty with the magnolia-white skin might die. She was the kind of girl who never made mud pies, nor did she climb oak trees, catch mushy-sided tadpoles nor explore haylofts like other little farm girls. Although little Miss Mary

Louise preferred the pretty Victorian-appointed parlor to the hay-carpeted milking parlor, that didn't mean she wasn't tough. Scarlet fever could be a killer back then, but Mary Lou survived it just fine.

Miss Mary Louise was a choosy little girl. She didn't like those big, ol' rough farm dogs either. She preferred petite, pretty inside dogs, and while she was ill her daddy, Mr. George Alexander, put a precious, tiny, curly-haired black puppy on her pillow. The pup was a perky half-toy poodle and Mary Lou named her Tootles.

Mary Lou loved cuddly little Tootles; she was a best friend for a little farm girl who didn't like the hot sun. But the Alexander farm dogs one day lured spunky black Tootles out of the yard and got her to chase and kill a neighbor's sheep with them.

When Tootles was caught with the killing party she was not allowed to come into the big house anymore. Old Jimmy, a black man who had lived on the Alexander farm all his life, built little Tootles a doghouse. From then on, Tootles had to be chained to her doghouse. It wasn't long after that Jimmy's daughter, Ida Lou, discovered poor Tootles hung by the neck. Tootles had jumped up on the roof of her doghouse, watching for Miss Mary Louise to come home from school. Her prancy little paws slipped and somehow got twisted up. Tootles was hung at the end of that cruel chain. Right then Miss Mary Louise decided she'd never again have a dog who would go outside into the big tall-grass pastures, tick-filled woods, or barns with claw-happy barn cats and attack rats.

That hanging influenced Mary Lou's decisions about what kind of dogs she would have for the rest of her life. Still, it was over twenty years before Mary Lou got another dog. She was in her mid-thirties, had two daughters, and had been married to Jess Morton for a good long time. The dog was named Tootles II and there would be no way this Tootles would ever chase any sheep, for it was a Pekingese. Her ancestors were traceable to China and the Tang dynasty of the eighth century. Only the imperial family could own a Pekingese dog, and to steal one of the sacred dogs was punishable by death. Three distinct characteristics of the Pekingese gave it its various names. It was called the "sun dog" because of its luxurious reddish-gold coat. It was named the "Liondog" because it looked like a tiny male lion. And the Chinese royal family called it a "sleeve" dog because it would fit into the sleeves of their flowing silk robes.

Mary Lou didn't carry Tootles II in her sleeve, but she saw to it that Tootles would rarely leave her sight. Tootles lived for seventeen years; then came mighty Muffin, another Pekingese. Muffin went everywhere Mary Lou went except to church. If the local Methodist preachers had preached to dogs, those royally created, royally treated Pekingese would have been at every sermon. Methodist ministers had long since stopped preaching hellfire and brimstone, so the dogs would probably have snoozed through the Sunday service. No telling what Sunday-go-to-meetin' clothes Mary Lou would have had for them.

Jess never bought Mary Lou a car without Mary Lou's dogs having a major impact on the kind of car she got. Not only must the upholstery complement Mary Lou's stylish clothing, it also *had* to have split front seats, the kind that had padded armrests that folded down. This was because Tootles II, and later Muffin, owned the backseat. On hot days they would be able to feel the cooled air blowing at them through the space in the front seats, created by their very own fan, which was plugged in to the lighter. This way Jess and Mary could leave Muffin in the car on a warm day while they were at Stan's Restaurant in Blue Springs, with the windows down, the engine off, but the fan running.

When it was cold Mary Lou dressed Muffin in a green wool coat with a white rabbit-fur collar. Muffin's fur was an attractive shade of brown and the green wool coat was "quite becomin' to Muffin's color," Mary Lou said. If it rained, Muffin wore a yellow plastic raincoat with a special hood. It was well made, Mary Lou said, and it fit over Muffin's head very nicely.

When Jess and Mary Lou went to a movie in the big town, Muffin would go, too. They'd always sit in the back row by the door in case Muffin got bored and wanted to leave. Usually Muffin enjoyed the picture show just as much as Mary Lou and Jess. Muffin most of all enjoyed the weekly trip to the beauty shop. Muffin always sat on Mary Lou's lap, even when she was under the dryer. Mary Lou herself did all of Muffin's beautifying. "I brushed her hair real nice," Mary Lou remembered. "She liked to have a bath. I kept her so clean and pretty. After all, she slept on my pillow."

Muffin loved going places in her car seat, which was just like a baby car seat. It hung on the backseat, and though it had no seat belt it allowed Muffin to see out the windows as they drove down the beautiful roads of middle Tennessee. When Mary Lou went clothes shopping, Muffin went right in the mirrored dressing room with her and stood on the seat and observed all that went on.

"That Muffin nearly never set foot on the flo-ah," Mary Lou said in her sweet, almost girlish voice, "except when she was at home. When Jess and I went to the horse show, Muffin had a special seat in ah box and we'd open her little carrier, put it on the seat, and let her watch those beautiful Walking Horses step out on the track." Jess often half-joked, "That dawg's treated better than I am."

"Jess has his outside dogs," Mary Lou drawled, "and I've got my inside dog." One of Jess's outside dogs was Queenie, a rugged, brutally handsome, fearless German shepherd who would take on any of the animals on the farm no matter how bad or wicked or belligerent. When Jess sent his other dog, Old Lady, a true heeler, to go

herd this cow or that bull, Queenie wanted to help. So
she would do the only thing she could think of; she'd
grab hold of the bull's tail. When she bit down on the
bull's tail, the bull jumped up, but the end of its tail
would stay clamped in Queenie's sharp white teeth. Jess
said he had a big bunch of "bob-tailed" cows and bulls.

Since the horrible fire in 1956 that took their historic
and regal antebellum home, they'd lived in a smallish,
white clapboard, ranch-style home. Around Jess and
Mary Lou's white ranch house, with its green roof and
dark-green shutters, was a beautifully kept yard. The yard
was shaded by a magnolia tree, two mimosa trees, a
snowball bush, six or seven rock maples, two water maples, a monstrous red oak, a few white lilacs, two bridal
wreath bushes, and a couple of young hackberry trees.
Boxwood bushes stood in a well-shaped line across the
front of the house. The yard was bordered by long lines
of daffodils and a white plank fence.

Outside the gates of the white wooden yard fence was
the domain of the wilder animals of the Mortons' place,
plus the place where Mary Lou's car and Jess's pickup
were parked. Out there lived the hogs, the cows, the
bulls, the mules, the Walking Horses. Out there were the
pigeons, the outside dogs, and the barn cats, but usually
not Mary Lou and almost never little Muffin. Out there
was where the cows gave birth to their calves. Life and
death took place there constantly. Once a black-and-white
milk cow had made the mistake of having her calf near
the yard gate that Muffin used to enter her inside domain.

"Muffin was just trotting around mindin' her own
business when suddenly that cow turned and attacked her.
It was just harrable," Mary Lou said.

The cow lowered its head and began butting innocent
little Muffin. Muffin had no idea how dangerous a cow
can be when she's just had a calf. And the cow didn't
realize Muffin couldn't hurt the calf. Mary Lou, not a
cow person, did not stand idly by to watch her precious

Muffin be injured and maybe killed. She drew back her purse and began beating the poor cow about the body with it. Mary Lou had just returned from her beauty shop, so every hair was in place and her makeup was freshly applied. But for once Mary Lou didn't care if she got mussed. She just hauled off and began beating that huge holstein cow with her leather purse, all the while "squealing" for Jess. Jess came to the rescue and Muffin scampered off, "her tiny heart just a-beatin'," breathed Mary Lou.

Once they got inside the yard and inside the sanctuary of their house they soon settled down and were fine. The inside of the house was where they both felt most secure. Mary Lou loved the color green so much that all the floors were covered with green carpeting of various shades. This was because Muffin used to slip on the oakwood floors, and Mary Lou was afraid she'd break her tiny legs.

The devastating day came when mighty little Muffin had to die. It was 1:15 A.M. on January 9, 1985, ten years and two days after she was born. Mary Lou was saddened to the depths of her soul. Even today when she speaks of Muffin, tears come to her eyes. A few days after Muffin died, Mary Lou had an elaborate graveside service and burial at Cedar Hills Pet Cemetery. Their motto: "For Those Who Really Care." When Tootles died in 1973 and Mary Lou purchased the beautiful plot for her casket, she also purchased another plot, knowing someday she'd have to bury another dog there, even if it was ten, fifteen years later. Mary Lou wanted the plot right next to Tootles, in the corner of the pet cemetery near some attractive flowering shrubs and solitary cedars. Mary Lou wanted her dogs off to themselves, not next to other people's animals, except for those of her sister, Miss Peggy. Miss Peggy had the three plots just below Mary Lou's, where she buried two cats and one dog.

Muffin was laid to rest in a plushly lined metal casket

and covered in her own blanket. The pet mortician laid Muffin's head on a silk pillow. There was a big bouquet of red carnations by her tombstone. Attending her funeral were Jess and Mary Lou and a few members of the family, as well as a representative from Cedar Hills. Mary Lou has never gotten another dog since Muffin was laid to rest. And Jess has never forgotten the night Muffin died. She was lying on Mary Lou's bed, barely able to breathe or move. Mary Lou could tell she wanted to get down, even though it was past midnight. Since Muffin didn't have enough strength to jump down, Mary Lou, frantic by now with worry, placed Muffin's fragile body on the green carpet, thinking maybe she needed some water.

Muffin, barely able to walk, struggled into sleeping Jess's room, looked up at him, walked back into Mary Lou's room, lay down and died. Mary Lou has always believed little Muffin wanted to tell Jess good-bye. Since that devastating day in 1985 when Muffin was buried, Mary Lou keeps pretty silk flowers on Muffin's and Tootles II's graves. Christmas and Easter are extra-special times for Mary Lou to remember the loves of her life, both living and gone, so she always puts special flowers by her dearly departed Pekingeses' gravesides. There are red-silk poinsettias in winter and Easter lilies in spring.

28
Lie Down Beside Me

As the dogs grew, and Lacy seemed to be maturing significantly faster than Grr, it became obvious I could not treat both of them the same. One late afternoon I was rushing around outside gathering Rebekah's toys when I saw Lacy cleaning herself the way a cat does. Lacy's Siberian husky blood shows itself often, such as the way she manicured herself.

She had spent the last several hours in the creek. She was on the porch to pick off all the dirt and deposit it right there. The front porch was not the best place for bits of dried algae slime mixed with mud, and the smell was grotesque at best. There was more in those globs than just mud and algae. Maybe they'd lain in something dead, like a rotten carp. If Lacy was in this bad location, there was no telling where Grr might be that could be even worse. Tonight some good friends were coming over for dinner, to see our place for the first time.

I was rushing around getting ready, and when I saw Lacy I got aggravated the way a redhead can.

"Lacy"—I raised my voice—"get, GET off there, NOW!"

She wouldn't look at me; instead she cowered down, exactly the way I'd seen wolves move, and slunk off the porch. I hosed off the slime and forgot about it. Much later, when I came out to feed the dogs their evening meal, Grr was doing his usual body wag. Food time for Grr was a wondrous occasion. Lacy lay about thirty yards away, regal in silhouette, dignified in the angle at which she held her graceful profile. However, when I called, she did not come, she did not even look in my direction. She did not move.

Grr ate his dinner as if his mouth was a vacuum cleaner on high power. Then he went toward Lacy's bowl. She made no move toward stopping him, although normally she would have pounced on him, showing him no mercy for taking one step in the direction of her food. Usually she ate in a slow, deliberate fashion, almost always leaving a few bites, which she allowed Grr to have but only after she slowly stepped back a distance from her plate.

Was she upset with me or was she sick? No. She was sitting in too powerful a posture to be sick. Her feelings must be hurt. I picked up her dish and brought it over to her, then I knelt down and spoke in a soft, apologizing tone.

"Come here, Lacy." She would not move toward me at all.

"I'm sorry I raised my voice at you. I didn't mean it. Now come here, sweetie, and eat your food."

She would not look at me, even after that. Usually if I knelt down anywhere within sight of them, they'd both be all over me, jumping, with wagging tails, licking tongues, and affectionate noses. They were getting so strong I'd even stopped kneeling down because they'd knock me over if they hit me together.

Grr, for whatever reason, stayed away from this tense moment. Maybe Lacy communicated some message to him silently. Grr was afraid of Lacy's anger and precise fang placement.

"Come on, Lacy. Come and eat. You're going to be hungry soon. Come here, honey," I pleaded ever so nicely. She would not, even yet, look at me with even one eye, or turn her ear toward me. She held her stoic head straight ahead.

The moment reminded me of when my dad used to spank us when we were young and then come into our bedroom and tell us he loved us very much, we just could not do such and such: like talk back to Mother, throw water bombs on neighbors we didn't like, or have rock fights. A rock fight was the way my youngest brother, Freddy, lost the sight in one of his eyes, and rock fights were guaranteed spankings.

I went back into the house and even then Lacy would not go near her food. After I'd been inside a few minutes and had stepped away from the window and the door, only then did Lacy slowly, stiffly, stand up and casually, as if she wasn't really hungry, step over and eat her Alpo Liver Chunks. Lacy never set foot on that porch again.

Trying to teach Grr something was a completely different situation. I could attempt a lesson a hundred times, beginning with a low voice and ending at a decibel level comparable with a dynamite blast, and it was still like trying to communicate with a rock.

During my adjustment period, while I tried to learn how to communicate with Lacy, I called Jerry in Alaska. Lacy was not one of his dogs but he knew Alaskan dogs better than anyone. I asked him why Lacy was so different from Grr.

"It has nothing to do with male, female; has to do with blood. Some dogs you lift your hand to put hat on, they hunch down, afraid you hit them. Grr's mother, Unanza, like that, yet never has this dog been hit, even when she kill pups. Grr is not like that, right?" Jerry wanted to know although he seemed to already know the answer.

"No, if anything he's the opposite. You could lift a sledgehammer over his head and he'd think you wanted to play," I said.

"I know, he take after his father, Friendly. You cannot upset that dog no matter what you do. No way to break spirit in those kind of dog but kill them. Some dogs you break spirit real easy. Lacy seem that kind of dog. Must be her Indian-dog mother like that," Jerry responded.

I thought back and remembered that Lacy's mother was a thin, slinky, black Indian dog, not tall in the shoulder but long in the body. Lacy's father was a magnificent Siberian husky brought to Alaska by a blond, tan former surfer from Southern California. She thought it would be romantic to meet an Indian man and live in the wilderness with him, in a trapline cabin. She lasted only through one winter but she gave her Siberian husky to the Ketzlers, Athabaskans who owned Lacy's mother and sold her to me.

"Some dogs," Jerry volunteered, "you don't know what they do. You walk near, they shrink away, look at ground. Then some dog, you lift hand to scratch your face they act ready to jump for your throat. My people usually never keep dog like that."

He went on to explain that he had all kinds of dogs and he was not partial to any type. He liked the rockheaded, always friendly Grr type as much as the hypersensitive, more moody Lacy type.

"Every dog has to be understood first," he said, "and treated according to its 'way.'"

Siberian huskies did not originate in Alaska, but nearby in northeastern Asia, in Siberia. The Chukchi people had to do something when climatic conditions altered their life-styles and their game became scarce as it moved to areas of better grass and tundra. The nomadic Chukchis had to expand their hunting grounds. To do so they created a special breed of sled dog that could move over expansive distances, have phenomenal endurance, and carry light loads in low-temperature cold. Not only that, but these dogs would have to do this work utilizing little energy. Game was scarce and the Chukchi people were not able to feed their dogs big quantities of meat. The Chukchi people were notably proud of their breed and kept its genetic purity throughout the nineteenth century. From this tribe and their dogs came the sole ancestors of the breed now known as the Siberian husky.

Shortly after 1900, Americans living in Alaska began to hear stories, spreading from one trapper's cabin to the next fire in a moose-hunting cabin, of an incredible strain of sled dog from Siberia. In 1909, the first team of Siberian huskies was entered into the All Alaska Sweepstakes Race. The next year, a team of Siberians, driven by John "Ironman" Johnson, won that tough and rugged four-hundred-mile race. Leonhard Seppala also became known for breeding high-quality Siberian huskies. His famous dash to Nome to bring the diphtheria serum that saved many lives became the basis for the now famous Iditarod Race. Seppala had been winning most of the races in Alaska with his teams of Siberian huskies during the decade following 1910.

Siberians are known to be very friendly and gentle, and although observant, they do not possess the qualities of a watchdog. Also, Siberians are free of the body odors that so many dogs have. Their usual height at the winter is about twenty-two inches for a male and about twenty-one for a female. Lacy was already eighteen inches. They normally averaged about fifty pounds, and Lacy was already forty-two pounds; she appeared to be nearing her mature height and weight.

Lacy didn't seem to be much of a watchdog; she wouldn't bark when anyone came up to the house. UPS man, lost cattle hauler, real-estate agent, surveyor, the man from the dead wagon, she barked only when about to kill something or if Grr aggravated her, or when Gray Nose drove her to it. When she and Grr were almost full grown, all they had to do was stand next to a stranger's car and those people wouldn't get out.

But if little Rebekah started to cry, they were at her side in seconds. They would lick her thin, soft arms and peer from side to side as if they were looking to tear anything to pieces that messed with their baby. One time Rebekah tried to open a metal gate that led into a smallish pasture where I kept two bulls. Lacy perceived danger and I saw her step in front of Rebekah and gently ease her away from the gate.

Although Rebekah was tiny compared to these fast-growing huskies, it certainly did not keep her from trying to take care of her dogs. Late one morning I was out in the backyard, stripping one of the original poplar mantels from the house, when the little princess of my heart stepped surefootedly off the back porch to see what her daddy was working on. Grr and Lacy recognized her footsteps and were on both sides of her before she reached me. They formed her own moving, four-legged bodyguards.

She knew they'd be there so Rebekah, who always had some goal on her mind, told them to sit. Grr fell to the ground and even Lacy sat. I couldn't get Lacy to sit! Rebekah's hand went inside a bag and out came a plastic bottle of Johnson's baby powder. I assumed she was going to powder herself, one of her favorite new things. But she wasn't. She began powdering the dogs. Lacy sat there and allowed Rebekah to sprinkle powder on her till her black head turned white. Grr let Rebekah cover his whole body with it. She rubbed it on his head, his neck, his tail, his back, his paws, his nose, and his stomach. She powdered him all over till he looked like a ghost. Grr lay down and enjoyed it all.

I would soon have my first son—just three days from now it would happen, on December 19, 1982. I had plans for that boy, and watching Rebekah and her determination

not to be left out of anything, I could see we'd be doing
most everything together. I had high hopes for the relationship I'd have with Grr and Lacy, too, but on this
particular Tennessee winter day Lacy was almost killed.
Even worse, she seemed surely paralyzed for life.

Even with the window shut I heard the shriek of fear,
of obvious pain. I listened for more. There was none. It
was as if something had been killed quickly and then
crumpled on the ground. I got up, yanked my jeans on
backwards, slung on a jacket and hurled out the front
door.

Grr was at the bottom of the steps. I saw no cows in
the yard; finally they'd been cured of that. But Lacy was
not around. Usually she was the first to hear me coming
and meet me. I called her. I heard a rustle, a whoosh of
dried grass being stepped on. I looked toward the direction it was coming from, and saw the two quarter horses
owned by a neighbor who was renting my land.

I called for Lacy again, and heard a dog shrieking from
behind the house. Again she howled, a short burst of
painful sound, and no, it came from under the house. I
got the flashlight and looked underneath to see two glowing red-orange eyes. She yelped again. I slithered to her,
and reached to rub her. When I touched her back a cry,
then a growl came from her. I had to straighten out her
front legs and drag her from under the house. She acted
as if she would not come out, or could not.

When I got her out, she lay on her side in the grass
whimpering. Grr lay next to her, trying to lick her face.
She growled at him to get back. I felt her body to see if
I could find any protruding bones, any kind of compound
fractures. At first I felt none. Every time I touched her
left back leg she let out a cry and a growl. I got a little
ways away from her and called her to me. Grr came and
fell into my lap, which usually made Lacy jealous, but
she could not even stand and when she tried she fell over.

When I lifted her up she fell over. She could not support any weight on her back legs.

One of the horses snorted, and I shone my flashlight over in their direction to see the mean white one hanging its head over the yard fence, holding its ears back. Normally when horses hold both ears back, it means they want to fight or bite or kick. Could that horse have hurt Lacy? Could Lacy's back be broken, could her hips be shattered, her legs fractured? I carried her up onto the back porch. She hated being inside a house so I laid her down. If I slept that night, it was only in half-hour intervals because I'd get up and look out onto the porch to check on her. I hated to look because I expected to find her dead, but each time her chest was moving, she was breathing.

Three times I could not tell if she was still breathing so I turned on the back-porch light and stomped on the floor. At those times Lacy would weakly lift her head and glance at me. Grr lay next to her and stayed awake the whole night, his glacier-blue eyes glowing with concern.

The next morning, Dr. Porter, the closest vet, said there was something abnormal in her X rays, but there were no broken bones. *Something ABNORMAL!* What's *that*? He said she *should* recover fully. What do you mean *SHOULD*? He didn't really say. The doctor said to give her some aspirin and feed her as much as she'd eat. Even when she felt good she never ate much and that first week she ate little. I boiled fresh liver for her. She would eat only a few bites. Even Grr would not eat it after Lacy turned her nose up at it.

Would Lacy be crippled for life? After one week she could not stand up for long. Two weeks later, she still limped, usually on three legs. Three weeks later she could run almost as quickly as Grr, but on three legs. She stayed close to home, as Grr roamed. After a full month, Lacy was running on all four legs again, her shiny black-and-

white fur moving as a cadenced blur through the fields
as she and Grr ran and chased, dodged and darted, swam
and hunted. She never went within one hundred yards of
those two horses again. The only remaining fear I had
was wondering if any damage could have been done to
her internal organs. She should soon be coming into her
first heat.

Normally when I came home in the afternoon, Grr and
Lacy came running to meet me from wherever they happened to be. When I turned off the blacktop road and
crossed the cattle gap, it made a loud metallic clanging
noise. A cattle gap is a must for anyone living on a farm
or ranch with cattle and horses. Without it you would
have to open a gate every time you went to and from
your property. To put in a cattle gap, first you dig a two-
foot hole as wide as your driveway and about five feet
across. Then you build concrete walls with grooves on
the sides to hold old railroad ties, cut to fit. You can
drive over the hole supported by the railroad ties but cows
and horses are afraid to step in a hole, so they will not
cross it.

Grr and Lacy would hear the clang of the cattle gap
and begin running. If they were in the creek, they'd race
me back to the house, running right alongside me. Grr
was rapidly becoming as fast as Lacy, but still was not
able to cut to the right or left as quickly.

All winter I'd walked with them to every corner of the
farm, every sinkhole, all the blackberry thickets, each
pond, and through all the woods. They accidentally
scared up some mature rabbits but the tricky hares lost
them in moments. They saw a couple of newborn calves
lying in the grass covered with membranes and blood.
They instinctively knew enough to leave the helpless
calves alone. I hoped they'd do the same with other animals on the place.

If they messed with a baby calf and if they survived

the parent, then they'd have me to tangle with. I had a few extra-protective cows that would gladly kill these dogs, and a few of them had horns long enough to impale both of them on one horn.

They did come across some wild game that winter. Most of which lived past the middle ridge, where four old cedar trees grew.

Just after going through the gate on the mid-ridge, I saw three foxes far off in the pasture. Grr and Lacy did not see them as they were lower than I.

I eased over to the fence line with Grr and Lacy and somehow impressed them with the need to stay quiet. With some stealth we moved toward the foxes, our movements camouflaged by the pine, oak, thorn trees, and cedars. The worst and most visible thing for us to do would have been to keep moving in the open field. Was I teaching the dogs stalking technique?

We got to the next ridge, where the largest and healthiest red-oak tree on the place grew. Oftentimes the red-tailed hawk hunted out of this tree. I lay down and crawled to where I could peek out. Maybe Grr and Lacy thought something was wrong, maybe they thought I was their mother teaching them to hunt, but whatever the reason, they stayed behind me, semi-crouched, although on all four paws.

The foxes were still there. Grr and Lacy saw them and they were off. The dogs were halfway to the foxes before the mother fox saw them. She moved smoothly into the woods; her young followed her, their absolutely beautiful long red-fur tails a temptation to give chase. I sat up and waited, hoping Grr and Lacy would circle them back around and into the field again, but they did not. Cooper would sometimes do this when he was chasing buck deer.

While they were gone I lay on my back, feeling the damp winter firmness of the ridge and the slow penetrating warmth of the late winter sunlight. I loved to lie on the quiet ground and be calmed by the vast silence. I also liked to lie in bed at night, now that I was not so anxious about all the living and growing plants and animals outside, and watch and listen for nightlife. Last evening, past the porch swing, swaying a few inches back and forth from erratic northerly gusts, I could see patches of light in the yard. Blue light. Silver light. The light of the moon flickered and danced among the trees. While I dreamed of moonlight the setting sun turned red. Grr and Lacy came back and lay down beside me, well satisfied with their first lesson in hunting.

29

Hunting Machines

Barbara had a 3:00 P.M. appointment to get her curly hair cut. Jed was almost three months old, and so far it was tricky to tell much about his little personality. He did seem more even-tempered than his high-revved sister had been at this age. He was clicking, clicking in his windup chair while Rebekah played with her babies, one named Amy after a former babysitter, and the other Melissa. Melissa was Rebekah's imaginary friend. Both Melissa and Amy were asleep on the sofa covered with four baby blankets, three quilts, and two afghans, precisely arranged.

"Honey, do you think your babies are warm enough?" I asked her.

"Oh yes, Daddy. They don't kick their covers off like you, Daddy. How come you don't wear a nightgown, Daddy?"

"Well, uh, I don't like nightgowns." I tried to look serious.

"Daddy, why do you always joke me?"

"Because you're my sweetheart, honey. Can I borrow one of your baby quilts, Rebekah?"

"Why, you tired, Daddy?"

"No, I want to take you and Jed out on the porch swing."

So we bundled the little chunk up and put Rebekah's coat on her and we went out for the first porch-swing ride of Jed's life, and the all-important first one of the year. Jed loved the whole thing, so did I and so did Rebekah.

It was that fantastic time when my winter-white skin, which had been drawn to the magnetic seduction of the big, black wood stove, gave way to the warming of the earliest spring sun. Also the too-perfect daffodils were blooming, dazzling against the gray of the weathered barns and the tan grasses of winter.

There would be more assaults from winter, I was learning. There were at least four more winters to come, Dogwood Winter, Blackberry Winter, Redbud Winter, and Tumblebug Winter, among others. Tumblebug Winter was when the tumblebug rolled into a ball and began crossing the road. Now we went for Jed's first "walk" on the farm. Rebekah thought we should go on down to the creek.

We didn't look into the creek water long and we were headed back. I heard a shotgun blast. I saw two dogs running like greyhounds across the fence on Jess and Mary Lou's property. It was Grr and Lacy. A white slab of something was in Grr's mouth. They ran like they would never stop. That blast was probably the first gunshot they'd ever heard. No. No. No. No. No. Let it not be so. They didn't kill one of the Mortons' chickens! But that white thing in Grr's mouth wasn't my newspaper they were bringing home.

They had caught a chicken; they were terrified by the shotgun blast. I was sure Jess had shot above their heads. Unlike police who fire a warning shot, then shoot to stop or kill, Jess was just firing a shot to get their attention. Many farmers witnessing a dog or fox or coyote killing a chicken or any livestock shoot to kill the first time. If it was a neighbor's dog they just never said anything

about it. There were so many temptations over at the
Mortons' farm for these wild-blood dogs. Especially now
that spring was erupting. There were moist, just-born,
black-and-white holstein calves. There were wriggling
bunches of pink and spotted piglets, easy to pick off if
the mother happened to be wallowing in cool mud. There
were wandering, none-too-smart chickens; a flash of alert
guinea fowl, rabbits' nests, and Mary Lou's tamed fox
squirrels. It might be too much temptation.

They obviously had been tempted today. They'd killed
their first chicken and tasted the blood of something bigger than a field mouse. I called them as I neared the
hanging tree by the spring in an all-out run. They came
over in a high-output trot and Grr leaped over a low place
in the fence, with the chicken in his mouth. I didn't know
he could jump that high. They were proud of what they'd
caught and they wanted to show it to me. I thought all
dogs had a genetic bit of info bred into them on the age-
old danger of killing chickens, but there are no chickens
in Alaska.

I grabbed hold of the dead mass of white feathers and
tried to get it out of Grr's crunching teeth. These were
jaws that could crack moose bones. The chicken did not
come loose.

"Grr, give it to me," I growled. He would do no such
thing. That chicken was his reward for conquest and he
would keep it. They ran up to the backyard and lay on
either side of the place where the top of the root cellar
came out of the ground. The limp chicken lay there with
them.

It was time to teach them an important lesson, especially since they appeared to have no idea that what they'd
done was bad. I'd call Mr. George. He knew everything,
it seemed, about farming, animals, weather, people,
whatever.

"All right," Mrs. George answered. They always answered this way. I didn't know if that meant they were

"all right" (in good health) or what. At least I'd called early enough. One evening I'd called three different local folks, including Mr. George, at a few minutes before 9:00 P.M. I woke them all. These people woke up in the dark and often went to sleep when it got dark, which in winter meant they could be in bed early. Mrs. George put on Robert, as she called him.

"Mr. George, how are you doing?" I asked.

"All right," he said.

"Listen, my dogs just killed a neighbor's chicken," I said, listening for the tone in his response. "What should I do?"

"Well, sometimes you get a chicken-killing dog. What I've seen done is they tie the dead chicken around the dog's neck and leave it there till it rots off. That'll usually cure 'em."

"Rots off?"

"That's the idea," Mr. George said in his usual slow, deliberate style of delivery. There was no need for Mr. George ever to be hyper; life on the farm and around here took place at an energy-rationed, ordered pace. "That dog will think of that horrible smell when he sees chickens and maybe he might not kill any more."

"Can you think of anything else I could do other than letting the chicken rot off Grr's neck?" I wondered, imagining the rotting stench, the green and blackened flesh falling off the bones, possibly loaded with maggots. I couldn't do that.

"Well, son, you can chain them dogs. You be careful with them. They'll get you in trouble with your neighbor faster than your bull would if he jumped over ya'all's fence and took up breedin' with someone's cows. It's a good thing to have good relations with your neighbor, son."

"Yes sir, you're right. Thanks, I'll talk to you later."

"All right," he answered.

I called Jess and Mary Lou. Mary Lou answered and

when I asked her what kind of chickens they had she said they had game chickens. I asked her what color they were. Brown, mostly, she said. At least that white chicken was not theirs.

"Here, let me put Jess on," Mary Lou said.

She said it would be a moment because Jess was looking out the window.

"Hello," Jess said, when he got on the phone. It took quite a while for him to leave his window.

"Jess, I hate that it's happened but it looks like Grr and Lacy have killed someone's chicken. At least I'm glad it's not yours."

"Well, that's what I've been looking out the window about. Seems like we did have a white one running with those game hens. That's all right, no problem," Jess said. I asked Jess a few questions about when was the best time to spread fertilizer and soil fertility. Also, I wondered if Jess knew of anyone who would come and cut my hay for me. We talked pleasantly for a while, the murdered chicken all but forgotten.

The next day, Grr and Lacy killed another chicken, a small brown game hen. The next day they crunched another, except this time they had figured out that they should not bring the chicken home to show it off to me. They understood that there was something about killing chickens that was wrong, something about it upset me. It was confusing to them, since they seemed very proud of their abilities. But they were smart enough to eat it elsewhere, although for chicken number three, elsewhere was behind the kids' sandbox. Chicken feathers blew across the lawn. I called Jess and asked him how much I owed him. He said don't worry about it. Mary Lou told me later not to worry, she never liked those chickens anyway. If it wasn't a dog killing them, it was a big barn cat, fox, coyote, weasel, mink, red-tailed hawk, owl, or some hungry human. So far we were up to chicken number three. How many chickens were presently alive in and around our little valley? Twenty, fifty, a hundred and fifty?

After chicken number three, I began to wonder if I'd have to start chaining Grr and Lacy like Jerry and all Alaskan mushers did with their huskies. Grr was certainly the instigator. I watched them one golden afternoon from the front yard as Grr crawled under the yard fence by the barn. Once on the Mortons' side he'd stop and look longingly at Lacy, who was still in the yard. Lacy appeared to be debating within herself, "Maybe he's not headed to Mortons' and the chickens, maybe he just wants to go down to the creek on a different trail." . . . "Surely he won't go after another chicken. He's my best friend and he's calling me. I need to go with him."

Grr would take five steps and look back, again, with those begging, pleading, big blue eyes. And Lacy couldn't resist the come-on looks. She went with him and about five minutes later I called Mary Lou.

"Hi, Mary Lou, how are you today?" A dismal tone crept through my worry about Grr and Lacy's escalating crime spree.

"Fine, Pe-ta. How are you?" She sounded her usually peppy self.

"Have you seen my dogs anywhere in your yard, like maybe, right now?" I figured she was standing in the kitchen by the windows that looked into the backyard.

"Why, yes, they're in my yard right now. They sure have grown since you brought them here," she exclaimed. "Oh my. That tan one with the blue eyes, he just leaped about five feet off the ground and caught one of our chickens in midair. Why, I wouldn't believe a dog could do that if I had not seen it with my own eyes!"

My whole being sank lower than it had been in years. Right then I wanted to beat Grr till he would never want to see another chicken. I knew what would have to happen. I'd have to chain them up, at least Grr, or send them back to Alaska. Since Lacy was Rebekah's dog, I didn't know what to do about her. I'd have to chain her, too. Right then I got in my truck and went straight to WalMart and bought two leather collars and some stout chain. To chain the dogs would take away their ability to run, to chase, to leap into the creek. They would not be able to lounge around on a water-cooled, flat creek rock. Maybe chaining them might teach them not to kill the neighbors' chickens. Did they have the intelligence to understand cause and effect?

Chaining the dogs was totally depressing. They'd whine, they'd cry, they'd beg to be set free. I chained them first to a fence post, and when I came back for lunch to check on them, they were completely tangled. Grr had tried to leap over the fence and almost hanged himself. He was twisting, turning, shaking his head violently. I had to get a stake I could drive into the ground so the couldn't get tangled, yet still have plenty of shade. They moaned for days. They howled practically all night and sounded so sorrowful, so pathetic. They made starving-wolf sounds as though they were babies lost from the pack.

It was Saturday night; Grr and Lacy had been chained for three or four days. They were howling again, loud enough that I could hear them even through the racket of the high March winds. I couldn't stand the howling anymore. I went outside and let them free. I hoped the chickens and guinea fowl would be roosting safely in a tree. Grr and Lacy could romp in the night and be back in the morning. They headed to the back of the farm, not toward Jess and Mary Lou's. Maybe they'd learned their lesson.

A cold spring rain soothed me to sleep, slapping down hard on the tin roof. I was worn down from the worries of regular life, plus Grr and Lacy and their dilemma. Would I have to keep them chained permanently? Would I have to give one of them away to someone farther out in the country than we were? A dog like Grr couldn't be sent far enough into the country. So far it seemed as if all wild and domestic life, other than humans, would end up being his prey. He and Lacy could not have a better life, or could they? Would one or both be better off back in Alaska, either chained or pulling their hearts out in Jerry's team as swing dog, wheel dog? *Maybe one would become a leader.* I couldn't deal with the permanent chaining of them nor could I think more about sending them back. It had taken me so long to reach the point where I was ready to get another dog after Cooper. I could not give up this easily. They needed more training.

By the next morning they'd caught all of Jess and Mary Lou's remaining chickens. There had been three left, all fast-running, fast-flying game hens known for their ability to survive outside. Jess said he'd never in his life seen dogs hunt like Grr and Lacy did. He was amazed the way they could leap into the air after the hens, shooting off the ground like small pheasants. He said they could do more in the air than a lot of dogs could do on the ground. If I could have brought myself to beat them senseless with one of the dead chickens, I would have. But I couldn't. I was angry enough to want to tear something up. If I'd had an overgrown thicket I would have attacked it with a machete.

What could I possibly do now? I chained them up again and every day I took one of them running or walking around the farm. Alone, with just me, Grr was a blue-eyed tan angel. He was a long-legged trotter, and he held his trot exactly at my pace. We always slowed down when we hit the hill leading to the cedars on the ridge where the owl perched in the daylight and the mourning doves found cover at night.

His expression was alert to anything we might flush or smell. Grr's movement was that of the wolf covering massive distances for one reason: meat, fresh meat. He was less a dog interested in my interests, my whims, my moves. He was more a hunting machine, a dog built to move and keep moving, till the eventual confrontation of life or death was played out. Grr was bred for this and I continued to wonder whether he'd ever adjust to living on this tiny spot of land. To some dogs this farm would be their whole universe. They'd be content to stay around the house, the yard, the barn, wander to the creek, maybe go check out Glyn and Toby Smith's garbage cans, catch an occasional rabbit (an inexperienced one). I got the feeling Grr would, if he could, roam over a couple of countries satisfying his need to search, to kill.

A week later I let Lacy loose. I wanted to see if she would get into trouble on her own. Grr and Lacy reminded me of my high-school friends, Al Manriquez, Craig McAllister, and Bob Elsaesser. Put us all together and we'd take things to the edge, maybe over the edge, but alone we were relatively harmless. Alone, Lacy lounged around the house, strolled down the driveway, acted about like she was ready for her pension and retirement, a perfect citizen of our little valley.

Then I chained Lacy and let Grr free. He seemed just fine. He, too, lay around feeling sad for Lacy's confinement. He gained a few pounds. He was becoming a powerfully sculpted shape of perfection. He was better put together than any of the dogs I'd seen in Jerry's dog yard. He now weighed over eighty pounds and when he leaped at me I had to brace my two hundred pounds of respectable power to keep from getting knocked off balance. We'd wrestle a lot; I taught him some good moves. He was impossible to pin down on his back.

Maybe they'd learned, finally. These animals were no doubt smart. They'd figure out weaknesses of their adversary so easily during the chase. Maybe they had finally understood what they could do and couldn't do, living on this farm, surrounded by these neighbors. They were alive so far because the neighbors were very understanding and real appreciators of dogs.

30
Chicken Wipeout

It was a spring day that makes you want to kiss someone you thought you hated. The maple leaves were so tiny and new and fresh and pure. They had not been attacked yet by life, by hot sun and insects and tent caterpillars and drought. Nor was there the threat of death by winter cold for seven long months. The day-old leaves reminded me of what a baby looks like when it's just born. On this spring morning I could stand the dogs chained no longer. I let them loose. I set them free. They didn't come home for two whole days.

I tried to think the best of them. They were running with the joy brought on by spring and its warming air. They were swimming in the realtor lady's little lake. Mostly I thought the worst. They were living off deer they ran down. They were huddled over the fresh-born, now-dead calves, sheep, pigs of my neighbors . . . they were shot by any number of farmers who would have the right to do so. There was worse, but I stopped imagining. It was horrible. I couldn't stand to see them chained up and yet I didn't think I could stand to lose them to a bullet, or a truck tire.

The next day they didn't come home either. The following day before lunch I got a phone call.

"Yes, sir," a soft southern female voice said, "are you Mr. Jenkins?"

"Yes, ma'am, I am," I said. I'd never spoken with this lady before, I knew that.

"Are you the man who lives on the old Boatright place?" she asked. It sounded as if she was not used to talking to strangers on the phone. She did not seem comfortable. The fact she knew the farm was the old Boatright place meant she probably was an old-time resident of the area.

"Yes, ma'am, I am."

"Do you own those two dogs, one's kind of a cream color, the other's black-and-white? They run real fast-like?"

"Yes, ma'am, I believe those are my dogs. May I ask whom I'm speaking with?"

"Yes, sir, my name's Mrs. Hardison. My husband and Mr. Clyde, he lives next to Glyn Smith, they did some fencing work for you one time." She still seemed powerfully shy and soft-spoken but she had something she still had to say.

"Them dogs of yours. I'm afraid to say they done killed all my chickens but five. I only got five left." There was silence. I expected her to erupt in some form of anger.

"I'm very sorry, Mrs. Hardison. If you'd let me know how much I owe you for your chickens, I'll gladly pay you whatever that is. I'm sorry, very sorry, ma'am. Those darn dogs have caused me a lot of grief," I said, sick of hearing myself say and think this.

"We know how some dogs can be," she said.

"Would you mind telling me," I asked, "which one of the dogs did most of the chicken killing?"

"I reckon it was that tan-colored one, but the black one killed some, too," she answered. She said bye. I told her I'd call her back tomorrow.

That evening they came slinking back, their shiny fur

glowing from the setting sun. I didn't have the energy to lecture them or yell at them. I just chained them up and filled their water bucket. The next morning I awoke to find Grr had slipped his collar and was gone. I called some but knew he wouldn't come back.

I called Mrs. Hardison. She sounded the same.

"Yes, Mrs. Hardison, how much do I owe you for those chickens my dogs killed, ma'am?"

"Well there was about twenty-five killed and they cost about six dollars apiece. I had five left yesterday, Mr. Jenkins, but that big male dog of yours, he's been back and I only got a rooster left"—she paused as if she saw a ghost or dropped something—"and, Mr. Jenkins, your dog, I see him outside now, he just caught my rooster." Mrs. Hardison's voice did not explode. She remained as calm as a saint.

"Mrs. Hardison, I chained him last night; he slipped his collar. I'm sorry, I really am. I'll be up there to get him right now and your check, I'll put that in the mail this afternoon. I'm very sorry."

"Yes, sir, Mr. Jenkins," she said and hung up. That as the last time I've ever talked to Mrs. Hardison. I could not find Grr.

After work, on the way up the driveway, I saw a couple of kingbirds and two bluejays flying erratically, circling, diving, and screaming at two dark, shadowy silhouettes shaped like hawks. Except any hawk that size in these skies this time of year would have to be a redtail. But these had not the copper-colored tails of redtails that capture the sun and shine like a burnished copper roof. Their wings were longer, and the movement in their wings was not like the soaring or short wing flaps of the hawks that lived on this place. It was a pair of owls. The kingbirds and angry bluejays must have flushed them from the oldest and most dignified cedar tree on the place that was in the tree line separating this farm from the Morton place. The owls nested there. They hated flying in this bright sun.

I noticed unusual movement across the fence line, past the owls' cedar tree. That cedar also doubled as the place Jess Morton's bull liked to lie under. Jess's herd of milk cows, their udders full of milk, appeared to be moving abnormally. Normally they stood quietly, their heads pointing in the same direction, grazing. Every couple of minutes they'd eat what was in front of them and move forward a few feet. Their bright black-and-white coloring was surrounded by the neon green of the fast-growing spring pastures.

Also among the black-and-white cow shapes was a smaller, lower shape moving behind them, moving faster than they. The shape was tan. It was Grr. He was chasing cows, A MONSTROUS BAD THING! Especially was it a death-wish to run dairy cows! Stress right before milking could throw their milk production off. Run too hard, they could abort. Dairy cattle were meant to be slow-moving creatures.

If Jess saw Grr he might be shot this time. The massacred chickens could be more or less overlooked, but the cows were the Mortons' living. I'd heard Jess talk of shooting one of his own dogs, a dog he really cared for, for chasing his cattle. It was as if Grr, now in his teenage years for a dog, could do nothing but wrong; every day he did something worse than the day before.

I climbed over the fence and ran up and dove on top of Grr. He was consumed by the chase and the fact that he could now flush a whole herd of holstein cows, averaging about fourteen hundred pounds each. Moving all this beef by himself had to be heady stuff compared to scattering a bunch of chickens and guinea fowl. I wondered if he expected to be able to make the cows fly like he did the birds. How far would he have taken this chase scene if I hadn't been here? Jess was standing by his barn and when he saw me tackle Grr he came down to where I was.

"This is some kind of dawg," Jess said in his deep voice.

"I'd like to send this thick-headed idiot back to Alaska," I said, angry.

"That dawg don't have a lot of sense, does he?" Jess commented. "That black-and-white female dawg, now she's a smart dog. She can learn. This male, I'm afraid he's going to be a lot of trouble."

"I'm afraid you're right, Jess. He's been gone for a few days, he slipped his collar. Sure doesn't look like he missed many meals," I said. Grr looked like he'd gained weight.

"I never said anything, but last week he and Lacy, they chased that old pony of ours we keep here for the grandchildren into deep mud, she couldn't get out. She was stuck. Old Dixie, she doesn't move real good since she got foundered, anyway. Me and Jess had to drag her out of that mud with a rope. Didn't think we'd get her out."

Could I take any more of their escapades? I wondered how my folks had stood the stress of going through the rule-stretching adventures of all six of us Jenkins kids. I wanted to disown these huskies. Give me a bottle of aspirin!

"I'm sorry about this, Jess. I'll take him home and chain him now. I'll see you later."

Since he had no collar I would have to carry Grr. He would be a year old on June 15. Grr was solid muscle, an incredible specimen of dog, and heavy. How would I get him over the barbed-wire fence and not lose him? There was no way I would drop him on the ground—he'd be gone. So I had to carry him over a hundred yards down to the creek, wade the creek where the water gap had washed away, and walk back up the fence row to behind the barn where I would have to chain him again.

My arms felt like they'd lose all their strength, he was
such a muscle-packed, squirming weight. The sunset was
beautiful but I didn't pay it any attention. What would I
do with this dog?

31
The Rival

Poor Grr. Things in his life were not going well and he acted as if he was genuinely confused about why he was getting in so much trouble. All the things he was doing came so naturally. What was wrong with killing chickens and chasing cows and ponies and deer and cats and everything that moved, other than humans? At least hunting humans had been bred out of him. When he looked at me he was so pathetic. "Come on, Peter. What's wrong with this? Why are you mad at me?"

First I took away his freedom. That was horrible, but what was to come next was the ultimate torture. The Hardisons' brown part–German sherpherd dog had discovered Lacy. That next week Lacy came into heat and the brown dog caught her scent. He trotted over thinking he'd live around our house till Lacy was his. His plan was to breed Lacy to himself. My plan was to breed Lacey to Grr. Grr's plan was to breed Lacy *soon*. Also, and equally important, he wanted to keep all the other male dogs away from his love.

Grr and Lacy had grown up together. Lacy was the only dog Grr ever really knew. Everything they'd done for the first time, they'd done together. They left Alaska together in the same shipping crate. They huddled to-

gether at Skip's condo in Washington and were almost
jailed for lonesome-howling all night and keeping a doctor awake. They learned how to run together, and invented the game of broom-handle grab-and-roll. They
caught their first mouse together, their first woodchuck.
They crunched and gagged on a sharp-toothed skunk, but
never did kill it. They shared every meal together and
Lacy always left a few bites for Grr. They both let Rebekah brush their hair with my brush and cover them with
baby powder. They ran to her if she ever cried or was
afraid. They lounged in the cool creek, in the clearest
spring-fed water or rolled and slid in the slimy strings of
algae. They would, I'm sure, fight any dog or animal to
the death if one tried to do the other bad harm.

They got into deep trouble together, too, beginning
with eradicating the neighbors' chickens, and lately chasing Jess and Mary Lou's cows. Grr and Lacy had shared
the fine and rough times together. They'd slept together
almost every night of their lives, except for the first puppy
days. Lacy spent her first few weeks on that river-rock-
and driftwood-strewn island in the middle of the Tanana
River in Alaska, and Grr spent his in a burrow dug deep
in the cool damp earth by his mother, Unanza, in Jerry
Riley's dog yard near the banks of the river.

Now a new time in their lives was beginning and Grr
was sure he and Lacy would experience this together,
too. It was the first time for mating, for new dog-life to
be made. Grr wasn't sure what this new time between
him and Lacy meant but he was ready to find out, to go
through it together, he and she.

Now in her time of great heat Lacy became a different
dog. She would turn away from Grr. She was not interested in him nor, for that matter, was she interested in
the old things they used to do together. Now she was not
always there to run off to the creek, or go hunt chickens
or harass Gray Nose. There were other more compelling
needs and urges rising within her. She would create new

life and she was uninterested in creating this new life with magnificent Grr.

She was now almost a year old and Grr was more than ten months old. He was more muscular than she, much stronger, seemed to have greater stamina, was more aggressive, and was now even faster than Lacy. He was so proud of his new speed.

First Lacy, whom I had not chained, disappeared. I could not bear to keep them both chained all the time. They howled. They howled and they cried. Sometimes almost all night. It was a howl like no dog's I'd heard; it was deep, more forlorn, more bluesy than the coyote pack up on the high eastern ridge.

When Lacy came home, she was trailed by four dogs, all males. Lacy even walked differently; her body moved with the awareness of her femininity. She'd been gone for a day and a half and Grr had howled for her, called for her. I'd never seen three of the dogs before. One was a shrimpy white dog with long hair, about the size of a cocker spaniel. There was an Australian shepherd, stocky, shorter than Lacy but quite masculine. Another nondescript dog trailed her. But the Hardisons' shepherd walked right next to Lacy. They acted as if they knew each other very well, the way they walked shoulder to shoulder. When one of the other male dogs came close to Lacy, both of them growled at him.

When Grr spotted them coming he went crazy. He lunged at the chain. He couldn't take seeing Lacy with these other male dogs. He acted insane with jealousy. I didn't like what I saw either. I did not like Lacy being with any male dog other than Grr. I threw a few rocks at them. They ran away; so did Lacy. I called her back; she came but so did the brown Hardison dog. I felt that I should like the brown dog, since Grr and Lacy had eaten the Hardisons' chickens and Mrs. Hardison was so nice about it, but I did not. He was too experienced, too sneaky. He was too old for Lacy. The brown dog seemed to have Lacy under some spell.

He could tell what I was doing as I stalked around the yard looking for a rock to throw at him, so he trotted far enough away so that I could not reach him. How did he know how far I could throw? I knew he had too much experience. He'd been through this before. He was a philanderer! He was after my Lacy! An angry owner had tried before to chase him away, throwing rocks at him, yelling at him to leave. Maybe even shooting over his head. Maybe I should do the same.

Jess told me to put Lacy up in the loft of the barn; then he told me he'd seen plenty of dogs climb ladders. I was sure Lacy would not stay in the loft of my barn. Jess recommended putting her in the smokehouse, but then he said plenty of dogs could dig down and get into it. Was there anything I could do to keep Lacy from getting bred? I'd need a fenced-in kennel with a roof on it to protect her. There was no way I'd get that built in time. Was she already bred?

I walked over to Grr. I slapped him affectionately on his power-packed shoulders, exploding with energy from being chained up, not able to run. He was definitely not mature yet. He had never been in a fight that I knew of other than wrestling/playing with Lacy. I knew if I let him loose, he'd attempt to chase the other male dogs away. I was sure he could handle the three smaller dogs; I'd seen him take on a woodchuck as big. But the brown dog now slinking back up the hill, trying to hide in the gold-brown dead grass in the pasture, was another matter. He seemed to think he could hug the far-south fence line, then come down the sparse tree line next to the middle pond, and make his entrance into the backyard. Surely he'd been in plenty of battles. He appeared to be four or five years old.

It was time to allow Grr to enter another phase of his young life. Surely he would attempt to keep Lacy—

beautiful, feminine, prissy, slender, flirtatious Lacy—to himself. Grr and Lacy were now entering the world of male/female, mating/mates, heat/all-consuming urges. Grr was lunging so hard against his chain I was afraid he would literally break his neck. He snapped the chain so strongly when he came to its end that it would throw him to the ground.

I stood next to him and knelt down. I put my right arm around him. I attempted to calm him. He could see only Lacy, now sitting far from him in the side yard, apparently so that the brown dog could see her. She sat in her usual statuesque position. She seemed aware of her attractiveness. Why was she being so cruel to Grr, hurting him so?

Lacy was obviously in the first phase of her cycle, the proestrus phase. It was to last nine days. Her vulva was swollen; there seemed to be a slight discharge from her vagina. In this portion of a female's cycle, the males are attracted to her but she allows no actual mating, not until the next phase, estrus, when ovulation occurs. Grr had fifteen or sixteen days to make sure only he fertilized Lacy's egg.

Grr never did stop howling and barking but he did sit down a moment and leaned his powerful body on mine. I unsnapped the chain. He leaped the back fence for the first time and went after the brown dog. The brown dog had a long stride and Grr did not catch him, although he came close at the creek. The dog went back up the other side of valley to the Hardisons' white-frame farmhouse, on the opposite hill, which was shielded by a powerfully large oak. Had Grr won this showdown with the farm dog so easily? I doubted it. Grr sank a few teeth in the other three as he ran at them, knocking them down, sending one rolling like a flipping car in a high-speed wreck. I was hoping Grr would stay around the house because I was going to chain Lacy to her doghouse. He did, for once. I guessed his urge to mate was stronger than his urge to kill.

He lay next to her in the grass that was turning a deep green and growing taller with the cool spring rains. He lay there for two weeks. When Lacy retreated into her doghouse, Grr lay across the front door. Nothing would slip in there, even if he did sleep a few moments a night. It was the time of year to begin sleeping with the windows open again and most nights there was a dreadful commotion around Lacy's house. Grr must have fought off two, three, four dogs a night. I had no idea if the same ones returned each night, but from the sounds of the fighting, the yelps, the howls, Grr fought them off, inflicting enough pain to keep them away for good.

All the males stayed away during the day except the brown farm dog. He was a bit taller than Grr, fully mature, but not as muscle-packed. He would sit under a grouping of two hackberrys and a dead, gray elm just watching, sniffing, waiting for Grr to leave, to lose concentration, to turn the wrong way. Sometimes he'd circle around the barn to the front of the house for a differnet look or scent. When it was cool or overcast he'd just sit and wait and watch. Lacy would see him and whimper, wanting to be with him. Grr would look confused, his blue eyes showing signs of a sense of helplessness. He did not know how to handle this rejection from his best friend. Lacy now seemed only to tolerate Grr, like an older sister would tolerate a younger brother. Lacy's period of estrus ended. It seemed a good chance that if anyone had bred her, Grr had. We would know something in about two months, sixty-three days to be exact, from the moment of fertilization.

The Hardisons' brown farm dog kept coming to see Lacy even after she was bred. This surprised me, but then Lacy was an exceptionally lovely dog.

When it became obvious Lacy and the brown dog were going to be together and that he would wait for her for a long time, I let her go with him. It seems that one trait country people and country dogs have in common is that they know how to wait for what they want. Maybe he would teach her some good farm-living habits, like leaving chickens alone (of course there were no chickens left anywhere near here) and staying away from pigs, cows, calves, and other farm animals. Lacy could probably teach the brown dog a few hunting techniques.

Grr even tried to go with them and the brown dog acted as if it would be okay with him, but it was not all right with Lacy. She continually turned on Grr and tried to slash him on his tan shoulder with her longest teeth. She'd chase him, but could no longer overtake him. Grr finally gave up and came back to where I was trimming off some low growth on some shade trees and cutting out some wild honeysuckle that was choking an apple tree. He fell on top of my right foot. That was his way of telling me he wanted my attention. I stopped what I was doing, put my pruning shears down, took off my leather work gloves and sat down on the ground. Grr laid his head and chest and front paws on my lap. I rubbed between his ears. His tan fur was such an unusual color, with guard hairs that were slate gray. His eyes were the color of a robin's egg. Why Lacy chose that other dog over Grr was a mystery. Maybe she just knew him too well.

We went walking, in the opposite direction to Lacy and the Hardisons' dog. We headed for the back ridge. Grr had no adventure in his steps, no mischief, no daring, no trouble to get into this day. When we walked near Jess's hog pen, I could hear the hogs' squalling. Grr didn't lift his head up to look, nor prick his ears in that direction. He was depressed. When I stopped on the ridge to look back down the hill toward the house and maples and barn and creek, which was a view I always took in, Grr fell on my shoe again. I sat down with him, put my arm around him and we both looked back. We were looking for Lacy and the brown dog. We did not see them, they'd disappeared. I had no idea where they went when they ran off together. Sometimes Lacy didn't come home till the next morning.

About sixty days later, Lacy, who now looked as though she'd swallowed a watermelon and waddled like a penguin, did not show up for the evening meal. I'd been feeding the dogs cooked pork liver, Alpo Beef Chunks, and high-protein dry dog food. She hadn't left the yard for three weeks, she was so pregnant. Jerry had said some Indian dogs could have fourteen, fifteen pups. I looked all over for her, but she was nowhere to be found. At midnight I heard an odd noise coming from Rebekah's room.

Lacy had had her puppies under the house, beneath Rebekah's room. Rebekah would be thrilled. I went outside with my flashlight and shone it in the direction of the sounds. There were Lacy's glowing eyes and baby puppy sounds. Grr was lying in the yard. He growled, started barking, and looked out into the dark pasture beyond the yard fence. I directed the light out into the field. It was the brown farm dog. Was he here every night, or did he know the pups were being born? Were they his puppies or Grr's, or could they be someone else's? Why had Lacy had her pups under the house? I'd filled the end of the dog house with the softest, sweetest-smelling hay I could find. I even sorted out the stalky, rigid stems of the grass so that they would not poke any of the tender pups in their blind eyes. I wondered if Lacy would let me crawl under there to get the pups in a day or two and put them in the doghouse where we could all see them.

Two days later, I crawled under the house. I saw old, discarded bones under there from dogs past, and found a couple of antique medicine bottles. Lacy had nine puppies. They were all squirming together in a mass of new and vulnerable life. When I reached over—I was already lying on my stomach stretched all the way out—my fingers got within six inches and Lacy growled. It was not a menacing growl but a nervous reaction to my touching them.

I sorted through them a bit but she was obviously nervous. I could see that there were a few black ones. They must have been throwbacks to her pure Indian-dog mother. There were a few cream-colored ones (could Grr be the father?) and one or two husky-looking pups. Their eyes were not open yet. If any of them had blue eyes it would be a definite guarantee that Grr had "done good," as they say in Tennessee.

When Lacy had her nine puppies she changed again. She had no room for any other full-grown dog in her life, especially Grr. She even growled at the brown farm dog. Each day for three days we (myself and my cousin Billy Weeks who was visiting from up north), would crawl under the house with Lacy's food. She ate like I did when I was sixteen, everything in sight, as many times a day as I'd feed her. I fed her three times a day and even then she lost weight. She didn't have much weight to lose, but soon her hipbones and ribs were showing. She gave everything she had to her puppies. They gained weight, the little blubber balls, right before our eyes.

Lacy was an excellent mother. The only problem was that she was overprotective. She'd growl when anyone's feet walked into her view from under the house. She knew all my shoes and boots and Billy's, too. So ours were the only feet she let come near. The fourth day I crawled under with her and just lay there, still and silent, and watched her till she finished nursing. Then I crawled closer and gently scooped up one of the pups, the second biggest one, with Grr's coloring. Lacy didn't seem to mind.

I backed out with the pup in my right hand as Lacy crawled next to me on all fours. I got the feeling if anything, including me, even slightly threatened her babies, they'd have body parts bitten off. One by one Billy and I crawled under the house and backed out with one of her puppies. We were transferring them to the doghouse, which was now in its own fenced-in little lot. We nailed a board across the front of the doghouse so none of the nine full or part huskies could crawl away, and set the doghouse under a hackberry tree. There were three pups who looked like Siberian huskies, and because their markings were perfectly symmetrical, Jerry would call them baby picture dogs. One had wolf-gray fur instead of black for its darkest color, and they all had the white mask.

The short-nosed husky pups were not the most active or most aggressive. Those were the black ones, with brown spots over their eyes and white tips on their tails. There were three of these. Their coloring and markings were exactly like those of Lacy's mother, a full Indian dog whom I'd seen at the Ketzlers' salmon camp on the Tanana River. But Lacy's mother did not have a white tip on her tail. I looked at Grr's tail closely; neither did he. There were two male puppies colored like Grr, cream with white masks, and one whose mix of colors was a whirlpool blend of browns and black. She was the runt.

When Grr trotted over to see the puppies, Lacy whirled around and leaped on top of his neck and bit him violently, as if she'd never known him. Lacy didn't know Grr's mother was a puppy killer. Grr did not look or act crazy like Unanza did. From the night the pair of owls hunted in the blue-moon light and Lacy had her first litter, she had nothing to do with Grr, ever again. She would not play with him, she would not lie near him, nor allow him to lie anywhere near her doghouse. Grr was a persistent ex-lover/friend but Lacy was out-and-out cruel to him.

Grr just couldn't take it anymore, the rejection, the abrupt reversal of Lacy's affection. Before she went into heat they both lived to be together. There was unrestrained joy in all they did, their young energy poured all over each other. Mysteriously, at least to pathetic Grr,

Lacy's attention, her affection, had turned away and now he lived on the dark side of a howling, blue moon. He acted as though he wanted to die. I had no idea a dog could be so affected in his whole being. A deep depression set in on Grr.

Added to his sadness was the fact that I had less time for him and Lacy. The puppies demanded my attention with constant feedings, and lifesaving episodes. Some lay in the sun but some crawled and wriggled into places they should not go (like fresh cow patties, snake holes). One day a couple of the black ones crawled underneath the nearest bull, the hateful red Santa Gertrudis bull that had broken down the fence when I'd first brought him home. He'd been on the farm now for quite a while and I'd never been able to catch him.

Grr began to stay gone for two, three days at a time. He must have been running the ridges alone, chasing deer, catching woodchucks, rabbits, wild things. He would run till he had no power left, come limping home, and lie under the house for a day recovering. It was sad the way he held his head down. Before his glowing, upright Alaskan husky head tilted up like a rakish hat. None of the pups had blue eyes, but about half of them favored Grr. Grr never got close enough to see any of his pups.

32
Wolf Blood

One afternoon right before the days turned hot, I was standing in the backyard looking at thunderclouds circling to the southeast. We'd had ten inches of rain this week, more than some western states get in an entire year. Sometimes the circling clouds were prayed to: "Please come to us on our land." Now they were like an enemy attack; we hoped they'd come to some other place. Some people round these parts had been saying lately that this bad rain was a warning from God that the world was coming to an end. There would be floods, they'd say, then droughts, and finally things in the world would become more and more abnormal. There would be no more growing of food. Anarchy would break out and violent rioting. Then the end of the world would come. Some said the Russians were controlling the weather with satellites. Some said it was the jet-stream movement. Odd things were happening, most agreed.

Something, even from a distance, looked wrong about Grr, who was headed my way. There was a color that didn't look right on his normally white-and-cream fur. He got within thirty, forty yards and I saw there was something wrong around his head. He came into the yard, sneaked in under a hole he and Lacy used when they'd

done something bad. I wondered if he had been shot. He
had been gone for two days. I saw that Grr was walking
normally, but his head was covered in blood. His blue
eyes shone from inside a blood mask. His paws were
covered with blood too, red, red blood.

He could not have killed something small and gotten
that bloody. Grr looked like something from a horror
movie: the pricked ears, the blood-red dog/wolf face, the
ice-blue eyes, the rows of gleaming fangs, and the curled-
up, wide pink tongue.

"Grr, damn you. WHAT have you done NOW!!!!" I
felt like the parent of a child who cannot stay out of
trouble, but is always getting in worse and worse. Grr
fell over on his side. I wiped his head, hoping beyond
hope that he was cut, that the blood was his. But there
would be no blood on his paws if that was the case.

"Grr, you get away from here, right now. Leave. Go.
Take me to what you've killed, you . . . You . . ." I
looked up to see Rebekah waiting to hear what I would
say next. He jumped over the back fence for the second
time in his life and began walking up the hill. He walked
slowly so I could follow. He was taking me somewhere.

We got to a couple of dips in the middle of the ridge,
where the land sank in a bit. There was a pinkish boulder
in the midst of the green pasture. Pinkish rock. That's
not right. A rock should be light gray. What was it? It
was no rock. I walked close enough to see it was a hog.
One of Jess's hogs. This hog was no baby; he or she had
been fattening all winter on corn and other expensive
feed, starting out as a small 60-pounder. It grew to 150
pounds of powerful pig. Grr had not only killed it himself, but dragged it through a barbed-wire fence, and over
fifty yards. I couldn't take it anymore. There was no
teaching Grr. He was going to have to go back to the
Alaskan interior, where he'd spend his life pulling a sled,
racing thousands of miles, eating sun-dried salmon, and

chained to a spruce tree. I took Grr back and chained him.

I dreaded telling Jess, but I went straight over to his place. He and black Jess were milking. He didn't get mad, he just told me it could not happen again and if it did he'd have to shoot the next time. He did say that if we had not been friends, he would have shot Grr a hundred times before this. He said Grr probably could not be broken of hog-killing now. I apologized. I was sick of apologizing for Grr. I told Jess it would never happen again. I told him I'd call the dead wagon and asked him how much I owed him. He just replied that it could not happen again.

That night I called Jerry Riley. He had just returned from a potlatch at his home village, New Minto, above the game-filled Minto Flats.

"Jerry, you kill another bear?" I asked.

"No, Pete. You should have been with me. When we are together we have good fortune. Have not seen bear since you came to get puppies."

A potlatch is an Athabaskan celebration, celebrating someone's death. All the deceased's family, his friends, the people from his village, meet in a home and talk about him. When I'd picked up the puppies, we had gone to a potlatch for one of Jerry's boyhood friends who died too young. We had ventured down progressively wilder roads northwest of Fairbanks and Jerry spoke of what the potlatch would be like.

"At potlatch, you're supposed to go to the family that's alive and present . . . you are supposed to make them happy . . . talk about how good a hunter the dead man was, or if it was a girl, how beautiful she was . . . how good she was at making moccasins and keeping her house clean . . . you know, you talk of good things about her and you say, 'Oh, she's got a good home now.' My people, they believe you go to a better place when you die. At potlatch it is custom people bring fresh game too for everyone to eat. Usually bring moose. People love to eat bear at potlatch. I had idea we might see bear, Pete, so I brought my .357 pistol.''

How could I possibly forget?''

Jerry remembered the whole thing for me again. "We were about twelve miles from New Minto. We were in the hills. On the way to Minto, any way you go in hills, there's a chance you'll see a moose or a bear or something . . . fox or something and in this case we saw a bear. He was coming right at us in middle of road and we were going right towards him. I would say it was a medium bear. It wasn't too big. Maybe one hundred fifty pounds, one seventy-five. It was in the road and I said, 'Go ahead, Pete, accelerate and get there real quick and I'll try to shoot it.' Well, I got excited and as it crossed in front of us I shot and missed . . . we had a broadside shot and then when it got off road in berry bushes I shot it again. I don't know why I did that . . . I still don't know what happened to me. It must have been the excitement of the hunt, stupid of me to shoot inside car. Should have gotten out. The noise darned near blew my eardrums. It was horrible,'' Jerry remembered.

"Potlatch is an Athabaskan religious ceremony so we are allowed to shoot game anytime of year, anywhere we see it, as long as it is used for a potlatch. Whatever game eaten at a potlatch is a sort of sacrifice to the departed person. This bear, if we could get it, would make the family of the one who died very happy, like a blessing came to them, maybe some kind of good sign.

"After we shot the bear we drove fast into the village. Only two hundred people live there. A few young men were sitting around. So far, this a boring potlatch. The man who died, he'd been duck hunting in the Flats and drinking and fell overboard, got tangled in the weeds and drowned.''

I remembered it so well; it all came back.

Jerry, somber in expression, but churning and burning

on the inside, thinking of that wounded bear getting
away, walked up to each of the young hunters and told
them what had happened. He said that we needed them
to help us track and kill the wounded bear. Every one of
them knew a bear was dangerous when wounded; there
was no sense in just two people tracking it. It would
possibly circle around and attack us from behind. That
was why one of the young bear hunters brought a dog.

When we got to the place where the bear had been
shot, there was a splash of blood as round as a canta-
loupe. Every one of the young Indians leaped from the
two pickup trucks. Jerry said that they would instantly
get into a hunting frenzy, that they would run from one
bit of spilled blood on a blueberry bush to the next one
like a pack of hunting dogs. He said these were a generation of young Indians who did not like to be with
Gussicks (whites), but they'd be in their blood frenzy and
wouldn't notice me. They ran, leaping over fallen trees,
rocks, and thick-growing bushes. Jerry pointed out one
young Athabaskan with a narrow flat face, dark skin, and
high cheekbones and said when he was in Vietnam the
Vietcong were afraid of him, he terrorized them. Jerry
said his lieutenant would send the young Indian alone
into terrible places and he would destroy many people.
He was the one leading the hunters, the first to locate
each spurt of blood. They were like a pack of black-and-
tan cougar hounds, sensing wounded prey, running with
tongues out and eyes wide open and unblinking.

As we ran, leaped, and dodged stunted spruce trees,
looking for the next bloodstain left by the wounded bear,
the young Indians, most in their twenties, started yelling
to Jerry. "Where's Bear Hunter? Where's Bear Hunter
. . . where's Bear Hunter?"

As we ran side by side, Jerry ready with his .357, the
other Athabaskans with their rifles, I asked him who Bear
Hunter was. I was not sure if this "Where's Bear
Hunter?" was some kind of spiritual chant, a part of the

ritual of capturing game for the potlatch. To miss the game might be looked on as some kind of curse, a frown by the gods.

"Oh, Bear Hunter, Peter, his real name is Matthew Titus. People call him Bear Hunter. Used to be, not long ago, when young Indian man wanted to prove he was a man and brave, he would locate bear den. Then men would go to den, with young man, take long poles, poke pole down in bear den till young man feel bear. Make bear very mad. Stick sharp, too. Bear making angry noise, begin to come out of den. Other men back away; young man, this time Matthew Titus, stand right at entrance to bear den wait for bear to come out. Young man have ax in hands."

We were breathing hard and sweating but Jerry kept talking. "When the bear first comes out of den, a brave young man must show other men how to behead bear with ax. But when bear come out, roaring mad, Matthew Titus afraid a moment, miss bear with ax, and Matthew Titus turn and run, full out. Right away someone shoot the bear and from then on, for his whole life, Matthew Titus called 'Bear Hunter.' "

The bear was losing a lot of blood. The dog they'd brought to make sure the bear did not double back and attack us from behind was staying in the midst of the running humans. Grr would have loved this kind of chase.

"One time," Jerry told me, "we're going through these big trees and big snow and we're winding . . . they can't seem to follow the old mail trial. All of a sudden, there's a moose. Well, the moose is scared. He knows he's had it. So he's cornered, so when you see them hackles come up on his back you better grab for your gun because he's going to run right at you and your dogs. Well, if he ran at Charr she'd just jump it, but I don't want Charr to get kicked by no moose, you know. He'd be all right, Charr, you couldn't hurt him. He'd move and bite the moose right now. [Grr's related to Charr.]

That Charr some tough dog. A moose's hackles come up. You can see it right over his head because his head is down and he's in the charge position . . . his head is down and he's looking right at you and hackles are up. You carry a gun on the Iditarod, or the trapline. You yank that that gun right out and you make sure it's clean and not full of snow because if the barrel is full of snow and you fire it, it's going to split your barrel and blow powder all over your face and probably blind you for a minute. So you keep your gun clean, you know, and you're ready.''

We never did get that bear, but as I thought back on the potlatch hunt and Jerry's stories, I knew Alaska was the place for Grr. He was an Alaskan dog. He could not handle the restricted life of the Outside. Alaska was the place where Grr's family had been bred for that kind of life. It's a place where someone shoots a bear in the middle of the road, where dogs corner killer moose and attack them, where they run with men who check traps for mink, marten, lynx, wolf, and wolverine.

As I talked to my friend Jerry, I told him how Grr had been acting. Up until now I had not wanted to; I did not want him to feel that I could not train Grr, nor did I want him to feel bad that he'd given me a dog who could not be trained to live down here.

"Pete, I wondered how he would be on your farm. He's made to pull sled, run through snow. He sounds much like his mother. You put him on plane, I will take him, train him to be part of my new team. His sister is one of my best new dogs. I will run Yukon Quest with him." (The Yukon Quest is a new long-distance race like the Iditarod, except it goes between Fairbanks and the Yukon Territory of Canada.)

I felt great relief. Grr would be where he belonged, Jerry wanted him and would teach him what he was bred for. Grr would run with Jerry's dogs, run his heart out, and sire outstanding pups. There would be no more killing of my neighbors' animals.

We took him to the Nashville airport late one Sunday night and put him on Northwest Airlines. When Jerry and Margie picked him up in Fairbanks, they stopped at the brand-new Dairy Queen and gave Grr a hamburger, no pickles, no mustard. They said he inhaled it in the suction-style eating technique that I knew so well.

Grr settled down and became a fine sled dog, fit right into Jerry's top-drawer team, until he broke his chain and went free. The last Jerry saw of him, he had joined three or four huskies gone wild, tracking moose. If he was after moose now, I suppose his hog killing had been only the beginning of his hunting bigger and more powerful prey.

33

Call Lane Thrasher

What do you do when you own a wild, hateful red bull? I had no idea what to do because every idea I'd had I'd already tried. This particular bull, the Santa Gertrudis bull calf I'd brought from the La Campana Ranch that had broken down the fence the first time I let him out of the trailer, was grown up now. He was a red, long-horned demonic monster. I had not been able to catch him for three years. I was defeated. I hated him so much I refused to give him a name. He came to be known around these parts as No-Name.

When I walked near him in the open field, the bull would lift his head in a startled, paranoid fashion, flare his nostrils and begin to breathe heavily. Then he would start to step, almost prance, in slow motion toward me. All the while he was weaving his horns, each over a foot long, like a drug addict ready to start a knife fight. His strongly insecure eyes made me feel ill at ease.

If I walked toward him, outbluffing his scare tactics, he would walk away in circles, retreating, always looking at me as if preparing to charge. He was retreating, I told myself, but I never took my eyes off him. And that was the paranoid way this bull acted in the open field where cattle are supposed to be peaceful and content!

They should be gently grazing, mooing softly, looking pastoral, like a painting of a seventeenth-century English countryside. If this high-tempered, flared-nostriled red bull was like this in a forty-acre pasture, he'd need a straightjacket once he was cornered in the working pens by the barn! There were no straightjackets for bulls, nor were there any insane asylums, only stockyards and slaughterhouses.

If No-Name could crash down a stout barbed-wire fence as a 450-pound bull calf, I didn't want to think about what he could do now that he weighed 1,500 pounds and had horns that could poke all the way through me. His horns should have been registered as lethal weapons. The other bulls on the farm had long scars to prove that. No-Name sharpened them all the time by rubbing his tips on the sides of thorn trees. He was an outlaw: a bad, angry, crazed potential killer. The problem with having an outlaw bull, as opposed to an outlaw human, is that you can't call the police and have an outlaw bull arrested or jailed if it gets that bloodlust.

There are no written lawbooks pertaining to cows and bulls and the correct and lawful behavior they should live by. But there are laws, nevertheless

Law Number 1: It is illegal to try to gore, physically attack, injure, charge, and/or trample your owner, your owner's spouse, your owner's children, your owner's relatives or in-laws. It is also illegal to do the same to surveyors allowed on the property by your owner, high-school students mowing the grass, fishermen with permission to wade your creek, visiting friends and/or friends that happen to be neighbors. If this happens refer to Law Number 6. Neighbors who happen to be enemies—well, there are no laws pertaining to what your rogue animals might decide to do to them, there's just liability insurance.

Law Number 2: It is illegal for cows or bulls to refuse to go into working pens. It is against the law for said cows or bulls to instead run into impregnable thorn thickets on opposite ends of the farm in order to escape capture. This unlawful behavior tends to corrupt other cattle's orderly and proper behavior and may turn the whole herd into an unruly, stampeding mob. If this happens, refer to Law Number 6.

Law Number 3: when your owner attempts to herd his cattle into working pens, usually located near a barn, in order to sort the owner's cattle, or spray the owner's cattle for lice or ticks, it is unlawful for certain cattle to jump over gates, run through barbed-wire fences, kick down portions of barns, or otherwise destroy owner's working pens. Further, it is unlawful, punishable by Law Number 6, for a certain bull or high-headed cow to trample down a fence, thereby allowing for rest of owner's herd to escape capture as well.

Law Number 4: It is illegal for a bull or cow once captured in working pens to chase owner until owner or human assisting owner is forced to climb up plank fence of working pens at a fast rate of speed causing humans to fear for their lives. See Law Number 6.

Law Number 5: It is unlawful and ill-advised for any cow or bull to attack owner's car, pickup truck, horse, or any other moving vehicle used for transportation, with the express intent to cause serious damage. See Law Number 6 and farm owner's insurance policy for deductible. To make contact with owner—or, especially, owner's children or wife or friends—with horn or head or kicking hoof is punishable by instant trip to stockyard or bullet from owner's rifle, depending on condition of injured human and mood of owner.

Law Number 6: CALL LANE THRASHER.

The wickedly long-horned, badly behaved red bull broke portions of all these laws and wanted to kill someone, it seemed. As time passed it became obvious he was essentially uncatchable by me by any method I could think of or find out about. Something had to be done. He was big, bad, and red and needed to be gone before he really did hurt someone. No matter how much over the last few years I'd hoped that he would become easier to get along with, he never did. He was a habitual criminal who so far had escaped having to pay for his crimes. The last thing I wanted was for his insane behavior to be passed on to any offspring he might create.

I seriously considered borrowing a tranquilizer gun from a vet and shooting No-Name with it but decided against that when someone asked me if I'd ever tried to move one thousand five hundred pounds of tranquilized bull-muscle, bull-bone, and bull-flesh.

What to do? Why did it always seem that just as I figured out one problem with my animals some other more complicated, anxiety-creating one came to take its place. I forgot about No-Name; right now there was nothing I could do. Then one late golden afternoon, about 5:30 P.M., I was out running. I usually ran through the middle field, the one with the new pond, up to the highest ridge and through the open gate. If it was closed I had to stop to open it. If it was a melting-hot summer day I hoped for a closed gate so I could stop as my lungs were always groaning for more air.

As I slowed I heard a mockingbird impersonating some other birds and I heard something else. A faint sound, growing more defined. I turned to see No-Name, head down, angled so that his left horn, polished more ebonylike than ever before, was headed right at my left side and my heart. Some way, instinctively, I high-jumped over the unopened gate. He even gored the lone thorn bush that grew by the corner post.

I cursed him. I looked for a boulder to brain him with. I reached for a dead limb. I promised him he'd no longer be living here when the weekend came. Later, I called Mr. George.

"Well"—he always spoke slowly—"I believe if it was

me, and that bull did that to me, I might of shot him. Yes, sir. There ain't nothin' much more dangerous than a bull with them kinda horns that will come at ya when ya have your back turned.''

Other than get No-Name in the working pens, Mr. George didn't know what else to do. I seriously thought of shooting the demonic bull and just calling the dead wagon. The dead wagon was too good for No-Name.

I called Jess Morton.

"It's about time, boy, you got rid of that crazy bull. I knew he was crazy the first time I saw him across the fence. Of course I've been around cattle my whole life. There's only one thing to do. Call Lane Thrasher.

"That Lane Thrasher, now, ain't no cow, bull, or nothin' else he cain't get. I've seen him go into a thicket and come out with a bull three cowboys, mind you, couldn't get. He can rope anything—and man, he's got a horse that'll run next to any rogue cattle. I don't care how crazy they are. Why, your bull, that crazy thing'll be like roping a stick of butter, compared to some cattle I heard tell he's got a hold to.''

"Where does this Lane Thrasher live?'' I asked. So far he sounded like someone from a different time, a time when men like him drove herds of Texas long-horn cattle from Texas to Montana.

"He lives in Culleoka," Jess said.

"Cully-what?'' I wondered.

"Cully-o-ka," Jess repeated, "is a place below here, in the south end of the county. Small place, but that's where this boy lives. He ain't no boy, no more. Fact I hear his son rope with 'em now. His boy's supposed to be real good like his daddy.''

The Thrashers lived on a farm on Brush Creek Road. In Culleoka a lot of the folks lived on roads with names like Valley Creek Road, Covey Hollow Road, Tanyard Hollow Road, and Sheepneck Road.

I called this Lane Thrasher. His voice was soft and his

words were spare, like most people around here. He told me for one hundred dollars he'd come to the farm Friday morning with his son. They'd be glad to get him. No hype, no hard sell, no jive, just plain and simple: "We'll be there, and we'll get 'im."

The Thrashers were supposed to come before Rebekah left for the bus stop. Jess said he'd come by. He said he liked to watch Lane Thrasher work. Charlie Trout, who lived up on a dirt road behind the Lochridge farm and hauled my cattle to market for me, came early to watch Lane. They acted like they'd rather be here than at a rodeo. In a rodeo the roping stock was confined to a small fenced-in ring: No-Name had nothing stopping him. He could go through creeks, barns, into thickets, and I already knew no fence on my farm could hold him. I also knew he could run like an elk or caribou. The Thrashers, father and son, better be good and rope him fast. Jess said both Lane and his son were needed, because they'd both rope the bull and hold him between them to keep him away from their horses with his flesh-puncturing horns. Their horses had been gored before.

Charlie, Jess, Rebekah, toddler Jed, and I stood on the hill looking down toward the creek, waiting for a pickup truck pulling a horse trailer. I had closed a gate on the ridge to at least attempt to limit No-Name to the two most open fields on the farm. I did not, however, want to spook him or give him the slightest hint it was roundup time. He had an uncanny ability to sense when I was planning a roundup. Was he psychic? Roundup was always on Thursday, the day they held the cattle auction at Southern Livestock. Mr. George always said that it was a lot easier to lead big animals than drive them; then he'd wink and say the same went for people.

Leading them meant getting them looking for sweet feed (which was grain pellets with molasses and whole kernels of corn), and if everything went right I could throw out handfuls on the ground in front of the lead cows in my herd, Mrs. White and Miss Carla. (Jed had named her after his attractive preschool teacher. She seemed a bit upset until she laughed and said, "At least ya'all don't raise hogs!") The most aggressive cows would get the whole herd moving and heading toward the cattle pens—as long as nothing spooked them. If Lacy barked at the wrong moment, they became more hesitant. If they stopped the flow into the pens, then usually there was no way to get them back again until the next week.

If I'd caught some before the rest of the herd turned back, say one cow's calf was on the outside, then the mama cow would begin looking for a way out and they'd start leaping the fence, or trying to. I especially never understood how a bull would risk jumping over a high fence that had a sharp, flesh-ripping strand of barbed wire on top of it. No-Name, in the three years he'd been here, had never been caught with the whole herd. He always stayed away, like a wild animal who's never lost his suspicion of man.

We heard tires go over the metal bars in the cattle gap. It was a pickup pulling a horse trailer. No-Name was grazing alone, as he often did. When he heard the sound he threw his head up and looked closely at the pickup and trailer coming toward us. Lane, forty-five, got out and smiled at Charlie and Jess. He'd known them a long time. He had a contagious, glistening-white smile, daring yet happy. Lane looked like he could do whatever it took, yet he was modest, too. He asked where the bull was. I pointed over toward No-Name. His son, Daryl, already had their two horses out of the trailer.

Lane would ride Murdock, a big bay quarter horse that weighed over thirteen hundred pounds. Murdock's weight and strength were welcome when it came to roping rank, nutty cattle. Lane said, "This here Murdock, we named 'im after that goofy guy in the TV show *The A-Team* 'cause this horse's goofy, just like that Murdock. He's just snorty, he don't like to be fooled with much. He ain't bad, he just don't like ya foolin' with trimmin' his mane, things such as that. He's big and strong, though, he's sixteen one. Now that's a nice size for this line of work.''

As muscled and dense and heavy as Murdock was, he was more hyper, more prancy than Gray. Gray was the horse Daryl would ride. Gray was the exact opposite of Murdock. He was named Gray because he was gray, a soft, elegant, dignified gray. And he was elegant, his neck arched with a high curve, and his eyes were round and gentle. Gray looked like he could be part Arabian. He stood still, like a carving on a pyramid. Father and son—the Thrasher boys, as Jess called them—went to putting on their horses' saddle blankets and saddles and bridles. They checked the ropes they would use to catch No-Name to make sure they were looped just so.

Daryl, twenty-one, was a silent one. I don't think he said one word the whole time he was here. He was the real thing, though. If you put a white western shirt and black stetson hat on him to go with his dusty boots and long jeans, he could be a young Clint Eastwood. Father and son rode off together. Lane asked Charlie if he would please drive their trailer over to 'em just as soon as they got the bull so they could load him up.

Charlie told me the bull was as good as caught now. He said this was a good time to sell him anyway. Bulls were bringing over fifty cents a pound. Charlie said he'd heard Lane tell of catching "a big yeller bull, part Hereford, Charolais, and Simmental. Now that bull was a bad cat. He gored both of Lane's horses that day. They'd roped him in the middle of a briar patch and the horse got in too close. That crazy yeller bull stuck one horn in one horse's ribs and the other in between its legs in its chest. When they finally did get it and haul it to the stockyard it tore up two or three gates. That boy of Lane's, now, he's good. I think he won his first rodeo when he was eleven, or something like that," said Charlie.

The Thrasher boys held their horses back, letting them prance slowly. There was no reason to startle this red bull till the last moment. Ideally they'd rope him before he broke from his position. What we were witnessing was true team roping. They'd both be aiming for No-Name's head.

It was a fine thing watching this father and son team working together, riding side by side, their ropes readied. Both held their right hands low so their ropes would be out of view. No-Name was psychic and Lane sensed it. When they got within twenty-five yards they began to separate, keeping the bull between them. The rogue red bull was not in a good position to make his escape. He was cornered unless he twirled around and destroyed the fence behind him and made a new pathway. Would he come out of that corner and run between Lane and Daryl? Had he ever been roped before? I doubted it. Both men were erect in the saddle, tensed for the explosive charge of No-Name.

Something alerted the bull and he bolted. He was going full speed in two or three strides. He was extremely fast for a bull. Both of the horses cut in at him and the Thrashers' ropes were twirling in the blue morning air. Lane threw first, missed, and then Daryl did, and got No-Name. When his rope went taut and Gray slowed and stopped, the rope slung the agitated bull full circle. Lane was there and had his rope on the bull's neck fast, before he could think of goring anything or escaping. The bull was stunned and caught in less than five minutes. All this seemed too easy, especially after all this bull had put me through. The way the Thrashers worked was an art.

They loaded up No-Name, then rode up to me. I pointed to a yearling bull that had turned out to be "squirrly," as Jess said. It was one half UFO and one half Bent Horn, one of my good cows. The yearling seemed like he would grow up to be trouble 'cause he was trouble already. This one had stripes like a zebra, except the stripes were black and brown. Right now he grazed in the long grass by the old hog-killing tree near the always-flowing spring. The grass was high, over knee-high on the horses, and Zebra Stripes had no idea what had just happened to No-Name. I asked Lane how much it would be to catch him; he said he'd do it for fifty dollars.

Gray and Murdock hadn't broken out in a sweat and appeared to love catching wild-brained, rank, rowdy mutant bulls and cows. It had taken them four times longer to drive here in Lane's trailer than to catch No-Name. "Give us more" was the look on their dancing heads. They prance-stepped through the yard. I opened another gate for them and they stayed close to the yard fence so they could get behind the grazing yearling bull in order to begin the chase that would lead to his capture.

This was a small pasture, only about four or five acres. I'd enclosed it with a cross-fence and gate by the spring-house, low down on the hill beside three huge elms. One potential problem here for the riders was that this pasture was cut through the middle by the runoff from three springs. The water had been eroding the underlying limestone way before Chickasaw hunters traveled these ridges and had created a little valley in the midst of the pasture. The Thrasher boys would not be riding over flat, easy-tilting pasture like the one where they'd just roped No-Name.

If Zebra Stripes ran in the direction he was now pointed, he'd go straight down the hill, leap the stream and be up the other side before having to decide whether to turn to the right and go uphill or turn left and go downhill. Running cattle usually preferred a downhill retreat, and of course Lane and Daryl and Murdock and Gray knew this. So Lane, who would be on the downhill side, would lead his horse ahead of Zebra Stripes to direct him up the hill.

Since this yearling was one half UFO, there was always a good chance that when he got to the four feet six inch fence, he'd either run through it, which meant breaking it down (snapping cedar fence posts or bending metal ones), or leap over it. Sometimes the escaping bull or cow did not hit the fence right and was knocked back and down on its knees. Unfortunately, this did not occur often with my cattle. When it did happen I always thought of what Mr. George said: "The kinda cows I want are the kind that would stop when they got to where a fence *used* to be." I had no such cattle. The few that might be inclined toward this behavior were pure Herefords, but they were perverted by the wild-nostriled, smoking-eyed ones like No-Name, Zebra Stripes, Miss Glenda, No Ears, and others.

I hoped they'd turn the precriminal yearling around, real easy like, and head it away from the stream and flat, partially algae-coated rocks that the snaking stream ran over. Lane and Daryl could not know what I knew, because the grass and the wild mint were growing so high they obscured the fact that there was treacherous footing down there. And they had taken off before I could say anything.

They rode very easy, pretending to be conversing, not looking at the yearling, for when you gazed at one it became anxious with the attention. I knew they planned to get into position, if they could, before he broke and ran, then whirl and sprint and rope him before Zebra Stripes knew what was around his neck. He broke before they would have liked and headed straight down to the stream and leaped it. These long-legged cattle were as fast as certain quarter horses and faster than some.

Lane's horse lunged through the green grass. In two seconds they came to the slick, flat gray rock that I worried about. If anyone could get over it, around it, or through it, Lane could. Lane was looking up and ahead at the fleeing yearling when his horse stumbled, then tripped. It looked like Murdock would recover his balance. The horse was going to right himself. He didn't. He slammed into the upslope, fell, and flipped. Lane held on, even when his horse was sideways and in the air. One of the horse's legs was still on the ground and the other three were sprawled out of control. If anyone could miraculously stay on top of the horse, Lane could. He didn't. He slammed into the uphill bank with a thud we heard from seventy-five feet away. Daryl kept after Zebra Stripes and got him. No way would his daddy hit the ground and that thing escape the Thrasher boys. "Nothin' gets away."

Murdock fell and rolled onto Lane, all thirteen hundred–plus pounds of quarter hose. In those few seconds I never took my eyes off Murdock and Lane, but I wasn't sure how it all happened. Where was Lane? He lay still on his back in the high grass. Oh, NO, he wasn't moving. Surely this man had fallen so many times he'd forgotten all but the falls where he almost died?

His horse was up and moving a little. That was not good; the horse should be moving more. Daryl had Zebra Stripes roped and was pulling the yearling over to the trailer. Jess and I were walking down toward Lane. He rolled over onto his side; his ruddy complexion should have been showing up against the pale-emerald-green grass. His face was gray. Was this his last movement? Jess said he hoped Lane just had the wind knocked out of him.

Lane stood up, wobbly and drained of all color. His face was paler than his faded Lee jeans and bluish in tint. Bad, I thought. Lane didn't look for a hand or help; he wobbled up the hill toward the protective shade of a mature maple tree that grew in the yard. He sat down on the ground. He was in the kind of pain that would have made many others black out. I asked if he wanted me to get him anything or do anything for him. He said no. Now Daryl had the yearling in the trailer, his horse unsaddled with its bridle off, and was driving toward us. He parked and got his dad's horse. He never said a word even now, like "You okay, Daddy?" I guess he knew nothing had hurt his daddy bad before, so it hadn't now. I wasn't convinced of that. Lane still sat, was gray-blue in the face and breathing lightly because of the pain.

Lane stood when all the horses plus No-Name and Zebra Stripes were stored and ready to go to the stockyard to be sold at auction in a few hours. Daryl was in the driver's seat of their Ford pickup. Lane meekly stood and easy-like walked over and got in. I told him and Daryl thanks and they smiled and were gone, kicking up white dust as they rode down the gravel driveway. Later, No-Name went for fifty-three cents a pound, a fine price for a grown bull, and Zebra Stripes sold for forty-nine cents a pound, not bad.

Someone told me a few weeks later that two days after Lane's fall he rode pickup for bareback and bronc riders in a rodeo in Huntsville, Alabama. A pickup rider is one who is on horseback in the ring during the cowboy's dangerous ride. When the ride is over the pickup rider goes over to pick up the bareback rider before he gets thrown to the ground. Good pickup riders keep a lot of cowboys from getting hurt. Lane's been back to my farm twice to rope rogue cattle. Now when I get mad at a bull or cow that breaks the laws of the farm, I always say, confidently, "You better quit or I'll call Lane Thrasher."

34

"It Should Not Be This Way"

It should not have been like this. It was black outside and inside. It was cold and chilling outside and inside. This was not right. It was supposed to be warm with comforting, homey smells. This was Christmas Eve, a guaranteed one night a year when everyone should feel that God's big, strong, glowing arm is around them. All is supposed to be right with the world. Lights of blue and white and red and green and orange cast their tiny reflections on the ceiling of my living room as they blinked. The tapered lights made the silver tinsel of the tree glow in multicolor. The more the lights flashed on and off, the more upsetting their blinking became.

Instead of using all the Christmas ornaments Barbara and I had collected and saved over the last ten years, including some ornaments my mother had given us that I'd made in kindergarten, I'd had to go to WalMart and buy new ones. The comforting aura of a Christmas tree decorated with old paper chains that I'd made in first grade, or baked ornaments of dough that Barbara and Rebekah had fashioned, was not here in this house. Instead, everything was new and store-bought. There were silver-ball ornaments, there were silver-blue balls, there were new strings of lights. The kids and I had bought

some wooden, hand-painted Santa Clauses and reindeer
to put on the tree—made in Taiwan. Five-year-old Jed
wanted to hang his big hard-rubber, blue-green dinosaur
on the tree. I told him Santa Claus would have to bring
one and put it under the tree.

It should not be this way. This moment, this evening,
the thought of the upcoming Christmas morning, sucked
all the strength from my body. I felt weak, close to wobbly. I felt like my face sagged, my eyes hung down, and
my cheeks were falling, pulled low by a deep sadness.
Rebekah and Jed and Luke had been here a week and
now it was 10:00 P.M. Christmas Eve and they were gone.
I would not see them again for a couple of weeks. They'd
gone back to Barbara's house.

In the living room stood the cedar tree and an antique
poplar wardrobe with walnut veneer on the front. The
wardrobe was the only piece of furniture in this long
living room, whose floor was now covered with ripped
wrapping paper, crumpled ribbons, and discarded name
tags that said: "To Luke, from Santa." "To Rebekah,
from Grandma and Pop." To Jed, Love, Dad." A few
hours earlier, whenever Rebekah opened one of her presents from "Santa," she'd winked at me. She already
knew who Santa was (for an eight-year-old she seemed
to know too much), and enjoyed it when we shared some
"adult" knowledge that her two younger brothers were
not aware of yet. I had never before in my life opened
Christmas presents on Christmas Eve, but the children
would not be here in the morning.

In amongst the unwanted wrapping paper and presents
were some empty red-and-white Kentucky Fried Chicken
boxes left over from our dinner. The kids had wanted it
this Christmas Eve and I'd said, "OK." Some of the
tinsel that we'd all thrown onto the lonely, minimally
decorated tree had either stayed in lumpy bunches on the
bottom branches since Luke couldn't throw too high or
had landed on the green carpeting. Its silvery shine was

now mixed in with the discarded boxes and other remains to create a sickening mess. I left the lights on even though I couldn't bear to look into the room any longer. There was no pretty snow on the ground either. Outside was just as bad.

If I had been one to get raging drunk, or any kind of blasted, using booze or drugs, I would be doing all I could to get my hands on some right now. The kids were gone, Christmas Eve was still here, I was alone. Barbara and I had been separated for a year and legally divorced for the past couple of months. I was living in the Morton house, three fields away from her house, the one that used to be ours. We'd bought this chunk of the Morton farm, along with their house, three years earlier when Jess and Mary Lou had decided to retire and auctioned off their farm in three pieces. I didn't know if I could bear it, being alone in this house. I went into the kitchen area. The double sink was filled with dirty dishes; a couple that had had avocado dip in them had now turned black. Avocado dip was one thing I could make.

I turned on the TV, only to see Christmas shows. Watching sweet-faced people like Andy Williams or the Osmonds made me want to puke. But Andy Williams wasn't so bad, I thought; he'd had a lot of family problems. He probably knew how horrible a Christmas alone was.

I just couldn't call anyone. I didn't want to bring them down, nor did I want to admit I was so depressed and alone. I could not go to bed. There was something about going to bed to escape, to get a break from my hated troubles, that I couldn't manage. I was having trouble getting to sleep. When life was good I usually didn't like to go to bed anyway, there was so much to do, to learn, to read. I usually loved the night, even damp winter nights like this one. But I was as close as I'd ever been to being unable to handle my feelings.

I could not rationalize away this overwhelming black

meltdown of my emotions. I didn't know if I could take
the sorrow. When it was not so strong and constant,
things could derail it or sidetrack it. But on this Christmas Eve I could not get it to go away. The kids now
were probably thinking of Christmas morning and another visit from Santa Claus. When they asked me why
Santa came to our house, Dad's house, earlier than to
everyone else, I'd explained to Jed and Luke that Santa
Claus was like God for he knew everything that was happening in the world. He even knew when people got divorced. For families like ours, he did a special thing. He
knew that it was hard for a family to go through a divorce, so Santa came twice to families like ours. He came
to Dad's house on Christmas Eve and Mom's on Christmas Day.

Jed wanted to know if Rudolph the Red Nosed Reindeer knew which families were divorced, too. I said I
wasn't sure but probably Santa knew and told the reindeer which house to stop at. Even though Rebekah
seemed to know who Santa really was, she was interested
in hearing why Santa stopped twice at divorced families'
homes. I loved these beautiful children so much. I would
be as strong as possible for them. In their hearts they
knew things would never be the way they used to be, but
they sensed how much I needed them, and I could see
how much they needed me. Their small hands touched
me more than they ever had before. I loved their funny
questions more, the kind I'd asked when I was their age.
I had to answer heart-crushing questions from them that
I'd never had to worry about when I was five or seven
years old. They were my own flesh and blood and that
fact slightly warmed my frostbitten feelings. We all slept
in the same bed the night before they left. First came
red-haired, blue-eyed Luke, then Rebekah, then Jed; they
all sleepwalked in and joined me. Jed was the last to
arrive. It was as if he sensed everyone was sleeping in
Daddy's bed and he needed to be there too. But now they

were gone, and Barbara would have their questions, and warmth, and energy. Thinking of them and how much I wanted to be with them only made everything worse. It should not be like this.

Certain ridiculous thoughts streaked through my inside storms. Why not just get into my car and go 120 mph on I-65 and turn into the concrete support of a bridge overpass? I thought of stories of people sticking guns in their mouths and pulling the trigger. I had a twenty-gauge shotgun in the house. I contemplated the different ways people kill themselves. I think I had the courage to do it. That was no big deal. But I thought of the people I loved, who loved me. Since the divorce I'd discovered who were the real, close friends, ready to love me when life went bad.

This was a black night, a gray-black Christmas, a time when the light in my life was close to going out. When I'd think of the kids the dimming light would glow brighter. I'd think of the breakdown of Barbara's and my marriage and the glow would die until there was almost no heat, no spark, nothing but ash. I'd think of my parents and the spark would surge faintly again. I'd think of people I loved. I'd think of my responsibility to those I loved. I couldn't kill myself. It was a stupid idea.

I had to get out of this empty house. There was little furniture except for four new beds, one for me, one for Rebekah, and bunk beds for the boys, along with a couple of sofas and a mangled-looking ancient harvest table that I was attempting to restore. I would go for a ride. No. I did not want to ride by houses covered with lights and windows, where I could see families inside. I would go for a walk across my land, amid the sleeping, resting cattle. The land had calmed me so many times before, ever since I'd lived on it. I'd lain down on it, cared for it, been stunned by its bright beauty or its tender softness. I knew where every tree was. The cows, I knew them all. Half of them I'd seen born, even helped some of them to come into their lives. I'd fed them and cared for them. I liked watching them, enjoyed knowing their individual traits and quirks. Although it was winter, it was not a frigid Christmas Eve; it was oddly warm. The air felt full of thunder. Maybe I could go outside and dare a bolt of lightning to strike me. My life was like a cell with a blown-apart nucleus.

I went out the side door. I saw a dark shadow move across the night-ground. Was it a bit of moonlight shining on a branch of one of the maple trees and making the ground move? It was Tigger. He was hungry. I went back in and rounded up all the half-bitten chicken nuggets and chicken skin and chicken bones and mixed in some milk and Alpo Beef Chunks. Tigger was famished, must not have caught a mouse today. He knew nothing of Christmas. I sat on a cold concrete step and watched him eat. He needed me this evening. I was closer to him than ever before. I wished I could lift him in my arms, stroke his fur, fur as luxurious as a lynx's. But I'd break out in an instant allergic reaction. Just sitting with him while he ate added some drops of light to my dark loneliness.

When Tigger finished, he rubbed on my leg for the first time ever, his tail high in the air. I decided to go for a walk. Tigger came with me. I didn't get fifty feet before I remembered. Damn. I was mad at my idiotic, forgetful self. There was a heifer out there in the night who was having her first calf. She was one half Hereford and one half Santa Gertrudis. Her daddy had been that little orphan calf Tom Martin had given me in South Texas, except he had grown up to be over fifteen hundred pounds and was the head bull of the whole farm. What a transition he'd made from the edge of a horrible death to slicked-off number-one herd sire. His name was Cinnamon.

Earlier this heifer had been in labor near the house and making good progress in her delivery. But after two hours she had stalled, even though her contractions had been coming faster. Her whole side heaved and lurched when she had her contractions. I'd thought then that I needed to be sure to watch her. She might have a problem. I'd forgotten about her till this very minute, so consumed had I been by my own troubles. Had she had her calf earlier this afternoon? Very probably she had, and they were both fine. She was a large-boned heifer with a wide pelvis. She had been fully mature before she became pregnant. She had not had the normal warning signs of a problem delivery.

She wasn't where I'd last seen her. I walked straight down the hill through a grouping of walnut trees and headed to the creek. There was no young brown and white-faced cow. I came back up the hill closer to the fence line that used to separate the Morton and Jenkins places. Now it separated the two Jenkins places.

I stumbled suddenly; I almost stepped on the cow. She was on her side, still in labor, so exhausted she did not even try to stand. She arched her neck in contraction and pain. I could see nothing coming out of her. Maybe she'd had the calf and was having a problem passing the after-birth.

I was surprised after I almost stepped on her that she didn't get up and walk off or at least lift her head. She didn't even move. Was she dead? This night the clouds moved through the low sky about 25 mph and the dim-blue light came in and out, timed to the passing clouds. During one blue-light moment I saw the cow arch her head back. Did she move in pain, or was she trying to see who was near? She did not have the strength to lift her young head. Tigger was looking closely at her but the heifer did not notice.

There was no calf near, which was not good. But there were no tiny calf hooves showing, no front legs, no noth-ing. There was no water bag either. But she'd been mov-ing all day, the water bag could be elsewhere. I'd not thought of her birthing for at least ten hours. Something was wrong. I tried to search through my calving experiences looking for something to give me hope. I was not thinking very clearly. I had disjointed thoughts. I'd been having lots of those lately. I was so distracted I barely understood what had happened to this weakened heifer, yesterday a solidly built, thickly muscled, fully grown animal.

I felt as if someone had stuck hypodermic needles in every one of my muscles and bones and drawn out all the energy. But I could not just walk away from the cow. She, like me, was so weakened by her struggle she could not even stand. Normally a cow, especially a jittery heifer, would not let anyone, even someone they were comfortable around, as my cows were around me, get close while they lay down. I'd seen them stand up with half a calf hanging out of them, the head and front legs almost dragging the ground as they walked away.

I knelt down behind her. She was fully dilated; the on-and-off moonlight made that obvious. Maybe she would let me reach inside her and I'd see what I could feel. Surprisingly she did. I doubted she allowed me to examine her because she sensed she needed help. No, for her to allow this meant she was weakened to the point of being impervious to any outside interference with her body. Why were the baby's little soft hooves not appearing yet? I reached in. I first felt what seemed to be a nose, nostril. This was not right. There should be hooves. My mind began to search, to think beyond its sense of sadness and deprivation.

I reached around the nose to the slope of the calf's head. There was some hope—the calf could still be alive because it was, after all, still inside the birth canal. I pulled my hand down to the nose and went under the jaw. I pushed so that my arm went inside her almost halfway up my forearm. Just as I expected, the calf's front legs were bent in half and wedged below the lower entrance of the heifer's birth canal. I would have to get hold of them and shift them to the side till I could straighten them out. Then they'd be in the proper position, straight out, in front of the nose.

Now when she pushed and had contractions, the bent-over front legs blocked the calf from even being born. There was no calling anyone. I'd have to get this calf out by myself or they'd both be dead. I wondered about my ability to do it, if I had the strength.

I would have to walk back up to the house, get my flashlight and some baling twine in the hay barn. I would tie the twine around the hooves and see if I could pull the calf out. Normally, walking up this incline toward the silo and cutting over into the yard was easy, crisp-moving, but I was so close to limp myself, the walk further drained me. The thought of leaving her would normally have been unthinkable, but I thought it. I couldn't do it.

The flashlight was lost. I thought I remembered the boys playing with it in their room. Finally I found it at the bottom of their toy box. I got the baling twine in the barn and went back down to the cow. She had not moved, but was still straining with an occasional contraction. She lay right next to the cedar tree the great horned owls nested in.

The flashlight worked but barely. I held it in my mouth, put my feet on her pelvic bones on either side of her dilated birth passage, and looped the twine around both hooves. I leaned back and pulled with my arms and pushed with all the power in my legs. I pulled and pushed. The twine cut into my hands. I should have brought my leather work gloves. There was no movement; the calf was not coming, it was stuck, badly. Now that I had its legs unbent, either it head or shoulders were too big to pass trough her pelvic opening without help. Out in the wilds of the brush lands of South Texas, they both would have died during the birth.

What could I do now? A chain, that's what I needed. I had Grr's old chain stored somewhere in the granary. I'd have to try pulling the calf with a chain the way I'd seen the vet do once. Halfway to the small barn, whose weathered wood had been buffeted for many decades, I wondered if I had the strength to make it. What was wrong with me? I felt like lying down and dying, but I had to get this calf out of her. If it lived, that would be even better. I found the chain instantly (amazing) and went back to her. The heifer was motionless, except for the occasional, involuntary contraction.

The chain wrapped around the top of the tiny hooves. Well, they weren't so tiny. This was a big calf. Again I put my feet against her rear end and pulled with all my strength. No movement. I pulled, I was sweating. My hands were gouged by the metal chain. I'd forgotten my gloves again. I took my boots off and wrapped my socks around the chain. I heaved, I pulled, she had a contraction. She had another. I pulled, using the power of her pushing, squeezing interior muscles. The calf was moving.

She jerked her head up, I kept pulling. This was an extra big calf, probably a bull calf. My body had little left to give. I kept pulling. The heifer kept contracting; the calf came all the way out and hit the ground. The heifer didn't have the strength to look up. She lay there, flattened on her side. That eighty-five- to ninety-five-pound calf was out of her. Her life was saved for now.

I looked up. I wanted to lie down on the ground there with her and not get up either. Above us on the other hill, two fields away, was Barbara's house, the house that used to be our house. The light in her bedroom, the one that used to be our bedroom, was out, but the light shone bright on the second floor, in Luke and Jed's room. Maybe Jed had sneaked the light back on. Maybe Rebekah had gotten scared in her room and gone in with her brothers. Up there was where my children were, but

I could not see them now, or when I wanted to. I could not know what was going on inside their rooms, the rooms where I'd put them to sleep so many times, where I'd knelt by their beds and prayed for them and us. It should not be like this, but it was.

Right now they were probably sleeping hard and fast for Santa. He'd be there in the morning. Santa visited divorced families twice, they now believed. At least they could think of something special coming to them, my beloved flesh and blood. I must quickly, now, find out if the calf was alive. Its tongue was swollen and hung out, not a good sign. Usually, even a calf weakened by a long, hard labor wriggled around a bit. There was no movement. Was there hope? Of course there was. I always thought the best. It needed a chest massage. I began massaging its chest as I'd seen people do. I cleared its throat. I lifted it up. Breathe, I begged it. Live, I asked it. Tears poured from my eyes. Please live. Please come back. It was dead.

I stood slowly. Even standing straight took effort. Tears dropped onto my cheeks. Tigger was still here. I saw the light go out in the boys' room. I looked to the living-room window of the Mortons' old house, where the Christmas tree lights blinked on and off. That was my house now.

A few days later the heifer was walking around, still weak from her ordeal. She lived, but it took her a long time to regain her strength.

35
Double Rainbow

It was late in 1984. The day before yesterday a double rainbow had brought many colors to the golden, dry grasslands of Mongolia.

Today, we were leaving Have-A-Pond, the little settlement of seven families. We'd lived here for a time but I would have liked to stay much longer, at least for a winter and spring. There had been a change in the weather since the day of the double rainbow. Now the winds from the north warned the Mongolians that a winter influenced by Siberia's Arctic cold was on its way. Ran Ying, my Chinese-born American interpreter, Mongo Mama (the mother of the family we'd stayed with here), and I huddled against the courtyard wall made of pinkish-yellow mud and straw. It was that wall which a wandering band of camels had rubbed against last night. The still nights of Inner Mongolia are so massively silent that even the softest sound carries far.

I felt a bond of surprising depth with this Mongolian family. They had taken us in and shared with us what they had. They'd fed us their barley and tea for breakfast and feasted us with their finest sheep. Were the nomadic souls of the Mongolian people kin to mine, someway? Even though we could not speak directly to one another, was their love and my love of fine horses and herds of cattle a common bond that sparked our newly discovered friendship? Was it our love of the wild winds and the ceaseless roll of the grasslands that made me feel I was among my own people? We were saying good-bye and it was a bit awkward because I didn't know what to do to express myself to Mongo Mama.

I really felt like giving her a big hug, but instead I reached for pictures of my kids. I grabbed my camera bag and pulled out a dozen or so photos. My Mongo Mama's wide face lit up like the sun lights up the plains when it reappears from behind storm clouds. I asked Ran Ying to tell her that I liked it here in Inner Mongolia very much, but that I must leave. We told her that I must travel halfway around the world to get back to Tennessee, for in a few weeks my third child would be born.

She beamed and nodded, then went inside and brought out a small pile of her own photographs. All of them were of her three sons before they'd become young men. In half of the photos the black-haired, strong-bodied boys were riding their horses. Sometimes they roped off of them. The boys looked as though they had been born on the back of a horse. Their father, she said, whispering as only a Mongolian can, was once one of the Mongolian people's greatest horsemen.

I asked her the age of one who was streaking across the plains. He appeared to be chasing an unruly spotted stallion. She replied, "Ten years." Mongols are known for their wondrous horsemanship, abilities that have been recorded throughout history. When Genghis Khan led his Golden Horde, they took over much of the world on horseback, the world as it existed in the thirteenth century. If they became famished, a common occurrence, they would dismount and suckle one of the warrior's mares. The Mongols would cross mountain ranges covered with many feet of snow, no matter how many of them died, to defeat their pitiable foes.

We still stood huddled together. The unrelenting chilled winds born in Russia made Ran Ying and me want to stay close to the family's cooking fire. Mongo Mama kept glancing at my right hand. I forgot that I had a couple more photos to show her. I showed her one of a group of my cattle. It so happened that they were mostly Hereford cows, with UFO in the middle of them. Mongo Mama pointed to a treeless ridge (Have-A-Pond was in a bowl circled by ridges) to a grazing herd of about fifty cattle. That much livestock in China, where to own a pig is a great thing, meant the family was well-off. We both raised cattle, so we had that in common too.

The only photo left was one of my Shocker. Compared to their squatty, unrefined, shaggy band of horses, black Shocker looked like a god. Mongo Mama's expression bore this out.

"OOOOOOOOh," she cooed, "most beautiful stallion. Never saw such a horse." She was saying it in Chinese, spoken in a Mongolian's soft, poetic cadence. Ran Ying interpreted. I imagined Shocker had the stature of the fabled horses that the Mongol princes used when they rode with the winds.

"This is stallion you have in America," Mongo Mama continued. She got excited and spoke in Mongolian until she realized Ran Ying didn't understand Mongolian.

"Yes, it is. He is called a Tennessee Walking Horse. His pace is a natural walk, not a gallop. His ride is very smooth, never bumpy, and he can travel many, many miles while the rider is very comfortable," I said.

"Ooooh. We have our own walking horse, used when our people must travel far. Sometimes my husband, he has traveled over one hundred miles riding one Mongol walking horse, bringing other along to rest, then switching," she said. "But we have nothing like this black stallion. Have never seen horse so like this." She looked close and pointed out Shocker's white spot between his eyes.

An ancient flat wooden cart passed in front of us on the only road through here, a mildly rutted dirt lane. It was piled high with hand-cut grass taken from a treeless filed fenced with rock: Few Mongolians needed roads, for roads were for things with motors and few of them had such things. Many Mongols still traveled on the backs of their *ma*'s. *Ma* is the Mongolian word for "horse."

"Ran Ying," I found myself inspired to say, "please say to Mongo Mama. 'Wouldn't it be beautiful to see a stallion like this running with your horses?' " Ran Ying said it in Mandarin Chinese, the widely accepted language throughout China.

Ran Ying said, "She says, 'Yes, would be most beautiful.' "

It was late in 1988, in the tenth month of the year. Half a day earlier we'd awakened in Beijing to green tea in the Summer Palace. It was a comfortable harvest day in rural China. Here, today, two stallions, one black and one chestnut, were coming out of an extremely rare quarantine. They were the first horses that had been in quarantine in China for almost forty years. For the past month they'd been housed in an old military compound, tethered in nice weather to two trees and cared for by a small, sinewy Mongolian who would be their caretaker for as long as he or the stallions lived. He slept on some hay next to them every night. The black stallion had almost chewed down his tree. Was that a sign of hunger or anxiety? I wondered.

These were the first horses of any kind to be imported into China since the Communists took over the country in 1949. That meant that no fresh horse blood had been allowed to mingle here for almost four decades. No new stallions had had the chance to leave their genes with the sturdy, short-legged mares. It would be a historic time if we could get these two stallions from Tennessee to the heart of Inner Mongolia. Already they'd come about twelve thousand miles but the most rugged, riskiest segment of this horse adventure still remained. We had to drive these stallions from Beijing to a farm in the middle of Inner Mongolia over roads that few, if any, foreigners had ever traversed.

I couldn't belive that the Chinese government was allowing us to take the horses there ourselves. They had assigned to us a man from the Foreign Service Office; he always wore a trench coat and his name was Da Zu Ping. At first we called him just Da, but as we came to know him better, and we spent every waking moment with him, we called him The Big Da, and toward the end, Da Baby.

The chestnut stallion's name was Clouds Independence. He was being donated to the people of China by Marvin Powers, M.D., a doctor/horseman from a smallish town in rural southern Illinois. The black stallion's name was Shockers Buck. He was being given by me. All this had started with an off-handed yet inspired comment four years ago and soon it would become stark, blazing reality.

At first I was going to send just my stallion but then someone wondered what would happen if he got sick or died. Betty Sain pointed out that two stallions could have much more of a breeding impact than one could. Two stallions could breed up to three hundred mares a year, each. Then the fillies from those breedings could be bred by the stallion that was not their sire. Also, young stallions from these Tennessee/Mongolian horses could be sent out to isolated Mongol settlements and breed their mares, producing foals that were one quarter Tennessee Walking Horse and three quarters Mongolian horse. By the time the breeding possibilities began to multiply, the genes of the two stallions from America could have a large impact.

I remembered how much it cost to send a postcard from China. How much would it cost to mail two stallions? It ended up costing over $11,000 for their airline ticket, alone. We raised the money to cover that from the

Tennessee Walking Horse Breeders and Exhibitors organization and from the State of Tennessee Department of Agriculture. The stallions flew on a CAAC 747 which was part passenger and part cargo. The passengers sat in front and the horses in back, separated by a door in the middle of the cabin. At least once, almost every passenger got up to open that door and peer at the horses. They were more popular than the movie the Chinese showed on the long flight between New York and Beijing.

So much had had to be done to pull together this "stallion thang," as it came to be known. It seemed that a thousand telexes were sent between the Tennessee Agriculture Department and the U.S. Embassy's Agriculture Office. The Tennessee Ag Department took care of the jillions of maddening details. China is still not used to wheeling and dealing the way much of the rest of the world does, and everything always takes longer. Everything is always confusing when dealing with China, even for an old China hand. Then, when you slam on top of that the first horse exchange since the Communist government took over, well, it appeared that it would *never* happen a lot more than it appeared it would.

Every time we were hopeful that the last few problems had been solved, there came another telex from the Chinese. Soon after the Chinese sprang on us the fact that the stallions would have to be quarantined in the United States and China, in each place for thirty days, we got the following telex.

Telex #126: EASYLINK MBX 16sep88 06:42/08:07 EST

ATTN: David Waddell, Tenn. Dept. of Agriculture

FROM: Jonathan P. Gressel/ATO/US EMBASSY/ Beijing

SUBJECT: Tennessee Walking Horses

DATE: September 16, 1988

CHINA ANIMAL PLANT QUARANTINE (CAPQ) REFUSES TO
APPROVE THE HORSES FOR IMPORTATION UNTIL THEY
HAVE SATISFIED THEMSELVES THAT THE SERUM NEU-
TRALIZATION TEST PERFORMED ON THE HORSES MEETS
INTERNATIONAL STANDARDS. THEY WILL STUDY THIS
QUESTION ON SATURDAY AND GIVE US A RESPONSE
MONDAY. THE TEST REQUIRED BY THE CHINESE FOR
EQUINE RHINNOPNEUMONITOSIS IS THE COMPLEMENT
FIXATION TEST.

CAPQ REFUSES, UNDER REPEATED QUESTIONING, TO SAY
WHETHER OR NOT THEY ARE SATISFIED WITH THE TEST
RESULTS. IF U.S. VETS CAN ASSURE YOU THAT THE
TESTS INDICATE THAT THE HORSES ARE HEALTHY,
THEN YOU SHOULD PROBABLY COME ON OVER, BUT YOU
SHOULD HAVE DEFINITE APPROVAL FROM CAPQ BEFORE
SHIPPING THE HORSES.

That's real reassuring. Ya'all come on over but don't
bring the horses. I was so mad I thought about sending
over some frozen semen, but then the Chinese would find
some way to quarantine frozen semen. Either that or
they'd probably let it thaw out and melt. The bottom line
when dealing with the Chinese is: Number 1. Be patient,
be patient, and be patient some more. Number 2. And
never, NEVER lose your temper.

At this point I was about to tell the Chinese to shove
it. Calmer heads explained that since there had been no
new horses into China for decades, there had been no
new diseases either. And if a new disease was brought
into the country it could do much more damage than a
couple of hot-to-breed stallions could do good. The new
quarantine threw off our departure another month. Now

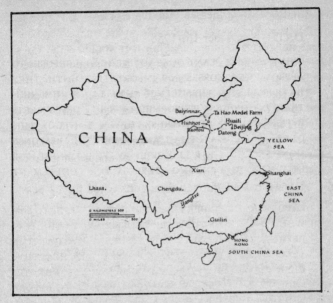

we were getting too close to winter. We had all agreed that if it did not happen in 1988, it would not happen at all.

We all were exceedingly patient and we all kept our cool, mostly. The Chinese, as they are also apt to do, worked out most of the details at the last minute and now, unbelievably, we were all in China. My Shocker and Dr. Power's Clouds Independence were ready to be loaded on a truck and driven for two or three days to their new home at the base of the Blue Mountains in Inner Mongolia. That is, IF the weather held and there were no blizzards swooping down from Outer Mongolia blocking our way or turning us back. It was October 27, 1988.

Our driver we called Panda. Panda was built like a panda bear. He had a very round body and it appeared that he had never washed his hair. We humans were told to ride in his van. The horses would ride in the truck. The Chinese must have assumed that our trip would be the van's last journey and if it held together, it would be exhibited in the Great Hall of the People.

The light-blue truck, a Tong Feng brand, which would transport the stallions, looked like a better ride. It was almost new. Did the fact that the horses had the better vehicle bear any symbolism? Before we went five miles the truck got in a wreck. A small rear-ender but a wreck just the same. Was this an omen?

First we passed through farmlands cared for by peasants. Every piece of ground was used. Every tree that lined the narrow roads was trimmed, there was nothing growing wild, every place looked like a Zen garden. Then the lands changed to arid mountain gorges of tan earth, brown rock, and an un-China-like quiet. We saw occasional herders of sheep and rock-hopping goats. We'd left the flatlands that held Beijing and would be in these mountains, the Greater Khingan Range, till we reached the valley on the other side. Only if we became badly lost would we end up in the Mu Us Desert.

I asked Da to ask Panda if he'd ever driven to Inner Mongolia before. He replied that he'd never been out of Beijing. He drove the mountain roads like they were the wide boulevards of his hometown. After having lived through Parnelli Yak on our way to Mount Everest last time I was in China, "Brylcreem Panda" was no problem. We added "Brylcreem" because it appeared that Panda used a bottle of it on his hair each day. Panda was a good driver, we all decided, after we survived the mountain passes and came out on the other side. We were getting close now to the Mongol people and the stallions' new home. Their truck stayed ahead of us. They didn't stop as much as we did.

We headed north, in the direction of the Gobi Desert.

Often we stopped at intersections that made the middle of nowhere look like downtown Dallas. Brylcreem Panda had no map. There were no lights anywhere. The Chinese have just, in the last year or two, begun driving with their headlights on at night. Crazed ideas the Chinese have sometimes!

The stallions could see out the top of the blue partitioned crate that kept them apart. I wondered what they thought when they gazed at their new homeland. To have had two stallions this close to each other for this long, during quarantine and now during our ride to Mongolia, without their trying to kick each other to death, was extreme good fortune. Shocker and Clouds Independence were unusually calm, good-natured studs.

Da and I got along very well. At times Da would put his arm around me and tell me that someday he would like to study in the United States. Da spoke of his upcoming marriage to his fiancée. He grinned and said he was more handsome than she was beautiful. Everyone booed the Big Da when he said that. Da Zu Ping was in his mid-twenties and the stallions were a powerfully important assignment for this young man who wished to be a career bureaucrat for the Chinese Foreign Service. His father was a retired railroad laborer. The Big Da was giddy with his responsibility, one that had come to pass principally because he spoke English. I, too, however, was an interpreter. Da would say something in English, and then I would translate that into southern English or at least into something the Americans could understand. I'd had plenty of experience with accents of all kinds.

The austere yet haunting views of oxen-plowed fields surrounded by arid cliffs continued. Were we the first North Americans, foreigners, to pass through these places? Asian history had blown through here for thousands of years. The stallions were surely the first ever to come through in an open truck, and certainly the first

Tennessee Walking Horses ever to see these Chinese villages.

Often we had to slow down to three or four miles an hour passing through a village. Just our truck and museum-quality van were enough to inspire local talk for the day. When black-haired young men climbed up on the truck to have a look at the stallions, they acted as though they had seen a vision. The sight of those magnificent stallions in the farming villages may spur stories that spin into bigger and more adventuresome tales when one day the village owns an offspring of Shocker or Clouds Independence.

We got to the capital city of Inner Mongolia, Huhehot (pronounced, Ho-Ho-Hot-a). Unbelievably the hotel where we stayed had a fax machine. We had emerged momentarily from the wilderness. But in the morning we'd return when we drove the stallions one more leg to their Ta Hao model farm. When we met the stallions' truck, I realized this would be the last morning I would see my Shocker. I climbed up on his truck and rubbed between his eyes the way he always liked me to do. He knew it was me. No one could scratch Shocker like I could. After the presentation ceremony at the farm, scheduled for 11:00 A.M., he would be their Shocker. His blood, sired by Betty's Shakers Shocker, would now mix with the descendants of the horses of Genghis Khan. His daddy was great, his breed was great, and his progeny would be great, here on the Mongolian grasslands.

We entered a dusty courtyard that held a slim line of trees and a few dull-tan adobe buildings. There was a table against one side and behind it a ten-foot-long red banner with white Chinese characters that said WELCOME TENNESSEE WALKING HORSES. There were many high Mongolian officials here to be seated with us and to make speeches. We Americans would say something, too. We brought a couple of handmade leather bridles, one decorated in green because that looked good on the chestnut stallion and one splashed with red. It would look magnificent on Shocker. I about had to slap myself—we were here! The stallions were here, brought in trucks and planes to this dusty spot on the other side of the globe.

A Chinese official with smiling eyes made a speech about how these stallions were a symbol of peace. They would breed with Mongolian horses, and their offspring would be the product of two great nations, two great peoples. A Mongolian official spoke of memories of his people when the grass was so deep on the plains that the only way one could see the sheep was when the wind blew the grass down. Dr. Marvin Powers spoke about a vision he had of the day when the colts and fillies from these stallions would be running free over the grasslands. Dr. Powers was a poet at heart. Steve Beech, a famed breeder of great Walking Horse studs and president of the Breeders Association, made a talk. After the speeches a Mongolian man and three Mongolian women came before us and draped white silk scarfs around our necks and sang us a Mongolian song, ''My Beautiful Mongolian Horse.'' It was about how brave a horse can be. How cunning. How lovely. So strong and brave.

All during the elaborate ceremony two young Mongolian men held the stallions in their places, flanking the red banner. Now the speeches were over, and it was time for Dr. Powers and me to take our last rides on our stallions. Dr. Powers had raised this young stallion on his farm in Illinois and I would be safe in saying that he loved it. Shocker was the first horse I'd ever had. He'd taught me much about the nature of horses. They are astounding animals. Shocker was my friend, his warm, wide back had always been ready to let me ride. Once he got used to the farm he acted as though he knew no other way to live.

We'd swum across the creek together, harassed the cattle on late summer afternoons, and just stood still next to each other. Often I just walked up to him in his pasture and put my arm around him and laid my red-bearded cheek against his black cheek. He liked that touch. I did, too. I had been watching the way the young Mongolian man handled Shocker and Clouds Independence. He was firm and gentle. He loved horses and he would spend the rest of these stallions' lives with them, unless something happened to him. They would be cared for well, by a people whose love of horses was in their history and in their blood. It was good. I told myself, that we were giving these stallions to these people. Giving was such an important thing to do.

I lifted myself onto Shocker's back for the last time. He acted a bit exhausted, understandably, considering what he had come through. Still, as all the people watched Dr. Powers and me, both stallions jazzed up to show them what a fantastic gait the Tennessee-bred-and-created Walking Horse has.

Dr. Powers dismounted to tighten his saddle. He had won World Championships in the category of riders fifty and over. He was a stylish rider and he surely had more knowledge of horses in his little finger than I probably would ever have, although he was modest about it. He was handsome, with snow-white hair that glowed among the dark-haired Chinese and Mongolians gathering around him. I got off Shocker, thinking it was time to let the Mongols take a spin on the stallions. The handler took Shocker from me and led him over toward Dr. Powers.

I had turned my back momentarily to put a new roll of film in my camera, when I heard a stallion whinny. It seemed odd, because I hadn't heard the stallions make a sound since we'd been with them in China. I turned around to see the stallions close to each other. They had done fine in their crate but there had been a partition wall between them then. BIG RULE NUMBER 1, when handling stallions, KEEP THEM APART. There was another whinny, this time a more passionate one, and I looked up to see one of the stallions kick out its back legs with all its might. It was Dr. Powers's stallion and mine was behind it. At the most powerful point in the stallions' kick, I saw Dr. Powers. His stallions' hooves hit him so hard they lifted him off the ground, maybe a foot in the air. He landed on the dry, grayish earth, looking limp and lifeless.

Someone grabbed the agitated stallions and separated them. Steve Beech, who'd been around horses all his life, especially stallions, had seen many people kicked. I didn't know at this point if he'd ever seen anyone killed, but from the way Dr. Powers lay facedown and motionless, that was a definite possibility. No one said a thing until Steve and Rick Ondrick, a representative of the shippers, turned Marvin Powers over. Blood already drenched half his head. His left leg twitched, his eyelids twitched. This moment was a nightmare in bright daylight.

I couldn't help but think about Dr. Powers's fine wife, whom I'd met. Who would call her? Oh, God, let Dr. Powers live! I bent down and undid his tie. Da and his boss, the top official in charge, seemed unsteady on their feet. Marvin opened his eyes. He appeared to have no idea where he was, who he was, or what had happened. He opened his eyes again, after blinking; he must have had a hard time gazing up at all the Chinese faces gazing back at him. Dr. Powers ran an emergency room back in Illinois but out here there were no ambulances and the nearest "hospital" was two or three hours' drive away.

When he came to, they led him into a dreary room to clean off the blood and revive him further. As we left the place of the presentation, after I'd said my last farewell to Shocker, Dr. Powers, his eyes somewhat glassy, leaned on me and asked me where we were. I told him China. I knew that did not register. In a day or two Dr. Powers regained his sense of clarity and realized, as he diagnosed his own injury, that he had not caught the full force of the blow but a glancing smash to his head. He recovered and wasn't in the States more than a few days before he was back in his practice as a country doctor as well as working all-night shifts in the local hospital's emergency room.

Before we left Inner Mongolia, two men came to my hotel-room door in Huhehot and knocked softly. One was short and round and one was slim, with high cheekbones. He looked like a Comanche. I cracked open the door. I had certainly not been expecting anyone this late at night. The two men pushed their way inside. One had on a trench coat. Then I recognized the smaller one; I had seen him downstairs in the lobby.

"Please don't be alarmed," the tall one with the high cheekbones said. "We must talk." This man spoke much better English than Da did.

They sat down on one of the beds. For some reason I did not feel any fear.

"You are the man who has brought the stallions from Tennessee, is not this right?" the tall one asked. He did all the talking.

"Yes, that is right," I answered.

The short, round one said something to the tall one in a foreign language. They were not speaking Chinese. It had to be Mongolian. Chinese sounded harsh and choppy, while Mongolian was pleasing and gentle, songlike and quiet.

"Are you the one who wrote the book called *Across China*?"

"Yes, I am." I had brought a few copies in paperback, hoping that I would see Mongo Mama at the stallion presentation, as I'd requested. The strange men were holding one of them now.

"May we look at it?" the tall one asked. I had no idea what was going on, yet still I felt absolutely no alarm.

"Yes, please do," I said.

They opened it up and began looking through the pictures. They stopped when they got to the pictures I'd taken around Have-A-Pond. "Did you stay with these people?" they wanted to know.

"Yes, I did," I answered, not wanting to say much before I knew exactly what they were getting at.

The tall one whispered, almost covering his mouth. "We know these people very, very well. This lady and man, those Mongolian people that took you in. The family name they gave you and the village name they gave you—there is no such name and no such village."

"What, why . . . ?" I was silenced by this information.

"We will tell you this. Your Mongolian family, as you called them, are honored that you have brought these great stallions from America. They know of this. But they were fearful to give their real names and the place they lived. They worried in case of a recurrence of what happened during Cultural Revolution. They feared potential reprisals someday."

Now it was beginning to make sense. The two men had a conversation in Mongolian. "Your Mongolian mother sent a message with us for you." The tall one smiled as if he enjoyed saying the words "Your Mongolian mother." "Do you still have that special medallion she gave you four years ago? She is most anxious to know."

"Please tell her I have it." They nodded with a controlled sense of pride, as if they knew what the special medallion was.

Mongo Mama had given it to me secretly, right before I'd left her home, tucked into a small yellow-silk pouch. She asked me not to show it to anyone until after I left China. Inside was an oval-shaped, silverish-metal medallion hung on a ceremonial-looking golden-yellow ribbon. The man's face on the metal was Ghenghis Khan, the hero of all Mongol people, the man who gave them a swelling pride and hope. A hope that someday, maybe, another Mongolian would rise up to lead them to greatness once again. That medal sits on the old oak mantel in my office in Tennessee and when I see it, as I do often, I always think of Mongo Mama.

The short man and the tall one stood up. I motioned for them to pause, and I gave them the paperback copy of my book and asked them to see to it that Mongo Mama got it. I had brought it especially for her. They said they would be happy to carry out the errand.

Then I said one more thing. I was somewhat sad that my Mongolian family had not been at the stallion presentation even though I'd requested it many times. All my requests fell on deaf ears, which is the Chinese way of saying no.

"Would you please tell them that I have brought the stallions here with the help of many American friends because of them. Because of our friendship. I want them someday to see the stallions, especially my black stallion. I hope that their village will have one of his sons and his son will breed their mares."

"Yes, you can be sure that we will proudly tell them. They will indeed be happy. Thank you, Mr. Jenkins, for your gift." I shook hands with the two Mongolians and they were gone. They never told me their names and I never asked.

Epilogue:
A New Nest

The old cedar poles aren't straight anymore but they still hold the old barn up. Many times I've thought of calling Raymond Johnson, the man who's so good with a bulldozer, and having him knock it down. But I can't bring myself to pick up the phone. I've thought about repairing it but it leans too far to the south because part of it was built on top of a wet-weather spring. A couple of the cedar-pole supports have sunk into the wet ground.

Pressure from the barn's lean made some of the rough-oak vertical siding pop off. Also, over the yeas the rain has rotted away some of the structural supports of the hayloft. It leans, too. Most everything about this old barn tilts. But that's all right because it still stores enough hay for half a winter's feed for the horses and cow herd. It still makes a good hunting ground for Tigger. Barn swallows nest in the loft as has a barn owl. It houses a family of skunks and a thick-backed woodchuck and often shelters many other living things from the occasional frigid ravages of a Tennessee winter. It even gives me a place to store two old claw-foot bathtubs till I figure out a place to use them. And it's still got room to do one more very important thing.

That leaning, two-story barn is where I go to be alone.

I think up in the loft. I especially go to the hay-blanketed loft in the fall, in the winter, and in the spring, before it gets hot. There are other places I could be alone (the shower, my office, the backwoods, my car) but no place I'd rather be, no place I can see so clearly.

I usually sit in the southeastern corner of the barn, where over the past few years I've thrown square bales that have broken apart. The baling twine that held them together broke as I carried them from where they'd been stacked to where I throw them to the ground to feed the animals. In that corner I can sit down and squirm around till my body makes an indentation to its liking in the hay. The smells up there are like companions—the delicious scents of cedar and fresh hay mingle with the scents of year-old and two-year-old hay and swirl around me.

This particular late spring day I was looking out into the backyard, where last fall Raymond Johnson, the maestro with a bulldozer, had pushed out the old three-plank fence. It had half rotted down and grown into a tangled orgy of dominating honeysuckle vines, saplings, and weeds.

I had meant for Raymond to take out the backyard fence last summer, during the horrible drought season of '88, but Jed and I had found a quail's nest hidden masterfully in that fence. No, actually, Jed found it. Jed is about he only person I know who can spot bird's nests, zooming nighthawks, camouflaged moths, and anything of nature before I do. There were many white eggs. We watched that nest and listened to the quail's penetrating call till one day the calls stopped. We looked and the eggs were all gone, hatched.

Now the place where the decrepit fence had been was clean and the grass and red clover seed I'd planted in its place was a dark, spring green. I looked and wondered where the quail had found a place to nest this year. From up here I could look out and see much of the farm and the animals that lived on it.

When I'm up here I often think back to the falcon. Sometimes a small falcon just like the one I had flies in front of my eyes. Many live in this area and nest in the dead trees. For that reason I have left some dead trees standing on the farm.

I often think ahead, wondering when I'll get another dog. Grr had been the first dog to replace Cooper, but blue-eyed Grr is back in the interior of Alaska, where he belongs. My next dog—which will not be mine, but ours—will have to be a better farm dog. Something between Mary Lou Morton's favorite dog, a Pekingese, and a part-wolf Alaskan husky would be good.

The kids ask me constantly, like a skipping record, when we will get another dog for here at "Dad's house." I keep telling them it is their house, too, and that we'll get another dog soon. I'm thinking about getting a whippet. They think that is a bizarre name for a dog. Lacy and CoCo, the Welsh corgi, live at both my house and Barbara's house.

I proudly gazed at the ten-acre field behind my house that I'd just last fall reseeded (no-till drilled) with grass and clover. A few weeks before I'd spread a couple of tons of fertilizer over it and now it was as lush and brilliant as a giant emerald. I was struck this day that I, who grew up in Greenwich, Connecticut, was now admiring and proud of my hayfield! How my life had changed.

Some of the changes are fine, real fine. Some have been wrenching. I can take the wrenching changes of life now a bit easier: the endings, the deaths, the lean times, the misunderstandings—maybe because I've had enough to expect them. It was good for me to have this barn loft to come to, to think things over, and this farm and the life on it to give me strength and energy too.

There are always things dying around here. But there are always things being born, too. Nothing stays the same for long.

It is ironic that I've settled in Tennessee not far from

where Cooper lies. I've thought many times of going to the place near here, in Summertown, Tennessee, where I buried him when I was walking across America. That was fifteen years ago and I always decide not to. His memory is strong enough for me.

Up here my mind goes traveling far. I yearn to be back in Alaska around Jerry Riley's home village among his dogs, with the salmon and mountains, rivers and lynx. I wonder how my Shocker, now the Mongols' Shocker, is adjusting to his new home in Inner Mongolia. It feels good knowing we'd worked so hard to get him and Clouds Independence to China while the fickle red-silk wall that had kept out foreigners for so long was open. It isn't easy having him live half a world away, especially since the wall seems to be closing again.

Often, the cow herd would be grazing around the barn, usually in the latest afternoon light. I'd see UFO's calves now nursing their own calves. Almost every cow and bull here had been born on this place. Much had changed on the old Morton farm, now the Jenkins farm. Thinking about all the changes made me feel old, but what I mostly felt was a rootedness, a connection to those rolling pastures and the life that lived on it. I've loved it here, when it was good and when it was not good.

The distinctive sound of a bird call made me look up. It came from past the backyard, past the three apple trees, the peach tree and the dogwood tree. It was the characteristic two-note call of the bobwhite. I hoped it had found a suitable spot to make a new nest. The quail's last nest had been bulldozed away. I'd purposely left two fallen trees in a wild, green-growing gulley. I hope it will make a secure place for the quail's new home.

About the Author

When he's not having an adventure in some faraway corner of the world, Peter Jenkins lives and works on a 150-acre horse and cattle farm in Tennessee. He is the author of four best sellers: *A Walk Across America*, *The Walk West*, *The Road Unseen*, and *Across China*. Peter Jenkins was awarded an Emmy for his on-camera work in a continuing news broadcast based on his book *The Tennessee Sampler*.

If you would like to write Peter, address your letter to: P.O. Box 20, Franklin, TN 37064.

The sights, sounds and feel of AMERICA

from FAWCETT BOOKS